PRAISE FOR
YOU CAN'T BE
SERIOUS

"It's crazy to me that a groundbreaking actor like Kal Penn is also so funny, humble, and down-to-earth. His life is fascinating and his book is wonderful."

—**Mindy Kaling,** #1 *New York Times* bestselling author of
Why Not Me?, *Is Everyone Hanging Out Without Me? (And Other
Concerns)*, and *Nothing Like I Imagined (Except for Sometimes)*

"Kal Penn's journey is insightful, funny, and instructive for anyone who's ever grappled with how they fit into the American dream."

—**Ronan Farrow,** *New York Times* bestselling
author of *Catch and Kill* and *War on Peace*

"Kal Penn is an American treasure. Which means that this book is essentially a treasure map. And the words inside the book are gems. And probably some of the words are also a skeleton with a bejeweled crown and an eye patch that has cobwebs all in between the skeleton fingers that are clutching all the gems because the treasure was so shiny and valuable that the skeleton happily perished while being buried with them. THAT'S how good this book is!"

—**Andy Samberg**

"Kal is one of the most intriguing human beings I've ever met. His stories are magical and inspiring, and the way he tells them provides a ton of lessons to be learned. All his stories are must-reads."

—**Rob Gronkowski,** *New York Times* bestselling
author of *It's Good to Be Gronk*

"An incredibly joyful and insightful experience for the reader . . . Kal Penn's journey is unique and special and demands respect. He delivers his story with a kind of compassion and humor we simply do not usually see. I recommend this read to anyone and everyone."

—**Kiefer Sutherland**

"This is such an enjoyable read—fearless, yet respectful on every page! The self-deprecation and other missteps had me rolling with laughter, and the candor with which Kal talks about some of his struggles made me emotional. An inspiring book!"

—**Tony Shalhoub**

"By turns hilarious, poignant, and inspiring, Kal Penn's memoir is a gem. A great read!"

—**David Axelrod,** *New York Times* bestselling
author of *Believer: My Forty Years in Politics* and
former senior strategist for President Barack Obama

"Kal Penn's new memoir is a must-read for brown kids in America."

—**Zofeen Maqsood,** *The American Bazaar*

"Looking for a book that'll make you laugh out loud? Look no further."

—*Daily Hive*

"A gift for anyone in need of a laugh or pep talk, *You Can't Be Serious* is loaded with a perfect blend of 'you can't make this stuff up' and 'don't stop believing' fun."

—**Roxanne Baker,** *SRQ Daily*

YOU CAN'T BE
SERIOUS

KAL PENN

G

GALLERY BOOKS

New York   London   Toronto   Sydney   New Delhi

Whether or not so noted in the text, some names have been changed, as have some identifying details. A few characters are composites and some events have been combined or reordered (these adjustments mostly just protect various aunties' identities so that they don't call my mom and complain that I spilled too much tea).

G

Gallery Books
An Imprint of Simon & Schuster, Inc.
1230 Avenue of the Americas
New York, NY 10020

First Gallery Books trade paperback edition August 2022

GALLERY BOOKS and colophon are registered trademarks of Simon & Schuster, Inc.

For information about special discounts for bulk purchases, please contact Simon & Schuster Special Sales at 1-866-506-1949 or business@simonandschuster.com.

The Simon & Schuster Speakers Bureau can bring authors to your live event. For more information or to book an event, contact the Simon & Schuster Speakers Bureau at 1-866-248-3049 or visit our website at www.simonspeakers.com.

Interior design by Jaime Putorti

Manufactured in the United States of America

10 9 8 7 6 5 4 3 2 1

Library of Congress Cataloging-in-Publication Data is available.

ISBN 978-1-9821-7138-4
ISBN 978-1-9821-7139-1 (pbk)
ISBN 978-1-9821-7140-7 (ebook)

For Piggy, who can't read.
And my parents, who can.

CONTENTS

CHAPTER ONE

THERE *IS* NO EXCUSE FOR YOU . . .

I was barely six years old when the fastest, dumbest boy in kindergarten called me the n-word. (Jeez, Kal, what a way to start your book.) It was late in the school year—May, possibly June. Unseasonably hot for late spring. Miss Withers's entire class was playing freeze tag on the playground, and agile little Randy Finn was "it," powering through the muggy air, happily trying to tag the rest of us. This devil child resembled a splintered toothpick—skinny, with tiny arms. He came at me with his fingers outstretched, and I took off, resigned that he'd catch me quickly. The gravel crunched faster under his feet behind me, his breathing getting louder and louder. This kid was *close*.

Just as he got within reach, we came up to a jungle gym, a crossroads. Randy's skinny knees reminded me of cartoon doorknobs. Time for a cartoon trick! "Look!" I shouted dramatically while pointing in the direction from where we came, "what is that?!" Nobody ever falls for this stuff outside of cartoons. Randy stopped. He fell for it. He turned to see what I was talking about. "What's *what?*"

By the time he turned back, I was twenty glorious feet away. Not because I was fast, but because Randy was so very dumb.

Hands on his hips, the kid caught his breath. I got a good, satisfying look at him: such a diminutive frame swimming in the ocean of an oversized T-shirt, trying to make sense of what just happened. As the realization dawned on him—that I just outran him by out*smarting* him—Randy's face contorted. He glared. Anger was building from a place deep inside. I glared back, unafraid. This silent staredown probably lasted five seconds—a kindergarten eternity. And Randy broke it with words that forever altered my understanding of the world. "You," he said confidently, "you're a %@*#!&!" Fast, dumb Randy Finn called me the n-word.

Every kid within earshot stood astonished. A white girl named Holly started to cry.[1] I didn't know exactly what the n-word meant, but I quickly understood its gravity from the other kids' reactions. An awful feeling erupted in my gut—whatever this word means, this is what I am? And that's bad? The sea of tiny, shocked faces quietly disbanded to the various swing sets and monkey bars.

I didn't tell any adults what happened. I knew I wouldn't get in trouble because I hadn't done anything wrong. I just didn't want to be part of someone *else's* bad behavior. I could dismiss Randy's name-calling since he was so dumb. But he had succeeded in defining me as *different* in a way I didn't yet understand. Being different wasn't something I wanted to draw attention to. I didn't need to be one of the cool kids—but I did want to blend in.

First and second grade were uneventful insofar as—super-low bar here—I don't remember getting called any racial slurs. I quietly sat decked out in clothes from Sears and did what was expected of me.

---

1   My first time witnessing white guilt.

By third grade, a Persian kid named Araz moved to our suburban New Jersey town. He was better-dressed, and looked nothing like me, but the teachers suddenly started mixing us both up. This fascinated me. I hadn't yet experienced the repeated behavior I'd come to know as "all look the same–ism," so the fact that teachers—who were the smartest people in my whole wide seven-year-old world—could get confused by two boys who only shared a vague brownness, fascinated me. It was almost as if Araz and I alone knew what the other kids didn't—that the teachers weren't actually that smart. And for that I felt kinda bad for them.

Fourth grade was the year I first recognized that I was way more different based on how my brain works rather than anything else, and I remember the first time I felt this way. For show-and-tell one Friday, I brought in a G.I. Joe jeep. It was boxy and green and probably about the length and width of this book. Before I stood in front of the class to talk about my jeep that morning, I had a compulsion to make up a complicated story. I pointed to the four wheels and confidently told the class that each one had tiny suction cups on them (total lie). These special suction cups were activated, I said, by remote control (another lie), so I could drive it anywhere—including on the ceiling (also a lie! Why was I doing this?!). I staved off any requests to see the jeep in action by announcing that I couldn't make it go upside down *right now* because it was out of batteries. (True, but only because I had removed them.) The kids thoroughly enjoyed and believed every part of my made-up story. This was my first acting improvisation, and it was both terrifying and exhilarating.

Also in fourth grade, I'd find myself zoning out while the teacher was talking. I'd stare through the window, thinking up crazy worlds and scenarios. (One of my favorites was the movie *Back to the Future*, which came out that same year and which I was totally obsessed with.

I imagined what it'd be like to be a fourth-grade version of Marty and Doc. Instead of a DeLorean, I imagined the monkey bars as my time machine; I could climb on top and pilot it anywhere I wanted to go.) The downside to discovering an overactive imagination was that when report cards went home, my teachers would always write to my parents, letting them know I was the only kid in class with this strange mix: "is very conscientious but daydreams a lot."

Being different meant my mind wandered. My imagination came up with endless scenarios throughout the day—sometimes to cope with boredom. Other children responded to boredom by acting out, but my first reaction usually was—and today still is—curiosity. If something didn't make sense, I needed to ask why. I always wanted to know more. And if I wasn't able to find the answer, I'd just make something up in my head.

In fifth grade our teachers thought that *immersion* was the best way to teach history, so they took us to a place that would become my favorite field trip destination outside of New York City. Old Sturbridge Village is a living history museum set in 1830s Massachusetts. All the people who work there have to dress, act, and talk like they're living in that period. They put on olden-days accents and say things like, "Hoo-where is Ezekiel? Behold! He has been churning the butter 'fore the sun shone its warm face this blessed morn." (I offer zero distinction between the speech of 1830s reenactors and, say, pirates.) It was on trips like these that it dawned on me: This was an actual job someone could have—showing up every day and pretending another moment in time was reality. I fell in love with Old Sturbridge Village because of this suspension of disbelief that the dressed-up employees maintained.

Without fail on these kinds of trips, somewhere around the

time when Ezekiel stopped churning butter to show us where his wife, Temperance, keeps "chamber pots for whence we must make waste," some bold, dumb kid (usually Randy Finn) would test the museum actors' ability to stay in character. "Hey Ezekiel, can I use your *phone*? That *Big Mac* I ate gave me the runs, I gotta call a *doctor!*" Ezekiel would rebut as best he could, "I'm afraid I don't understand, pray tell who is Big *Mac* and hoo-whatever is a phone and a doc-tore?" The absurd commitment! I couldn't get enough of it. Temperance would try to distract us kids (and in my opinion won the reenactment Oscar): "Poor child! When I find myself with such ailments I must thrice pare thin the yellow rind of an orange, unto which I will mix an amount of bitter brandy as prescribed by the *barber.*"[2]

On the way back to the buses on that first trip, we stopped at the gift shop (which was disappointingly not run by old-timey people and charged modern-day prices). Our school had earmarked a couple of bucks for each student to buy something, and all the kids went straight for the personalized items: license plate key chains that said "Ryan," large pencils pre-engraved with "Tommy," little glasses that said "Randy" and seemed useless to drink from because they only held one and a half ounces of liquid—what good is that? I knew from previous experiences in gift shops down the Jersey shore and in the city that personalized items never included my real name, "Kalpen." I always checked anyway. Always held legitimate hope that maybe *this* was the place that had a "Kalpen" mug. I'd go straight to the K section: Kacey . . . Kagan . . . *Kareem.* Then, willing to settle for a misspelling, I'd do the same with the Cs: Cain . . . Caleb . . . *Cameron.* No dice. They never had any variation of my name. I was too different. Maybe the next gift shop . . .

---

2   I have absolutely no idea if anything I describe here is in any way historically accurate.

*   *   *

An early spring afternoon that same year. Three p.m. School was dismissed. Ryan Sokolowski and I walked past the flagpole just as Zita Guardino's mom sped up to the turnaround in her jet-black Trans Am with the windows down. Bon Jovi played through the speakers. Mrs. Guardino was the cool mom. She was younger than the other parents, wore formfitting jean jackets, tight leather pants, and the same dangly earrings and teased bangs as her daughter, who everyone had a crush on. Everyone. Zita Guardino was a fifth-grade version of Mrs. Guardino, who, by the way, looked much more like a fun older sister than somebody's mother, and how this happened was one of the great mysteries of our eleven-year-old lives.

Ryan and I smiled and waved. Zita hopped in, and the Trans Am peeled out just as fast as it came in. With "You Give Love a Bad Name" fading down McClelland Avenue, Ryan confidently asked, "Doesn't Zita's mom look like such a hooker?"

Now look, I had no idea what a hooker was. But I could tell from Ryan's face that I was *supposed* to know. That it was *cool* to know. Whatever this hooker business was, it seemed like Ryan finally made sense of the mystery of Mrs. Guardino's youth. (A hooker, yes, that explains it!) "Totally!" I shouted, with too much enthusiasm. "I was actually just thinking that!"

The next day on the playground, I was super eager to share this cool, secret piece of information I had about Zita's awesome mom. So, when a bunch of us were at the monkey bars, I covertly announced, "Hey guys, did you know that Zita's mom looks like a hooker?" Randy Finn was standing within earshot. His eyes got so wide he looked like a frog. This excited me. Whatever a hooker was, Randy *clearly* knew, too, and he couldn't believe I was cool enough to be in the know.

After recess, when Randy tried to start a humming contest in class, the teacher busted him quickly and threatened to send him to the principal's office. In a desperate gambit, he stood up and declared to the entire room, "Well, shouldn't Kalpen get sent to the principal's office too? He said that Zita's mom is a hooker!"

Stunned silence. "That's it, Randy!" the teacher screamed. "To the principal's office! NOW. You can apologize to Zita and Kalpen later." As Randy stormed out the door, I was *horrified*. I looked to Ryan Sokolowski for guidance. He avoided my stare. Whatever a hooker was, in this fragile moment it had become obvious that it was *not* the answer to the mysterious creature that was Mrs. Guardino. I panicked. I wanted to cry. "It's okay, Kalpen," the teacher said, "I know he's lying. I know you would *never* say something like that."

I was so distraught and guilt-stricken when I got home from school that day. What was so bad about being called a hooker? I didn't intend to say anything mean about Mrs. Guardino. I was just trying to fit in. *Is Zita's mom a hooker, or is she not a hooker? Is being a hooker a religion? A job? Does it involve a hook?* I needed answers, which meant I needed to ask somebody, fast.

"Mommmmmm! What's a hooker?"

"Where did you hear that word?!" she asked in shock. At *school!*[3] Mom explained that a hooker is someone who sells her body. It's not okay to ever use that word or refer to anyone by it. And that was that.

The explanation created more questions than answers.

What parts of her body does a hooker sell?

Also, how can she sell her body? Doesn't she need it?

WHAT IS THE HOOK FOR???

---

3 This is why they moved to America, so their kid could learn the word *hooker* in fifth grade.

It was clear I wasn't getting any more info, so I didn't ask. I didn't feel any less guilty. In my heart, I knew I'd have to come clean the next morning. I'd need to tell the teacher that Randy—the fastest and worst-behaved boy in fifth grade—was actually telling the truth this time, and maybe didn't deserve a week of detention alone. I would admit that I didn't know what a hooker was when I said it on the playground. I had merely repeated it to fit in.

On the walk to school, my thoughts wandered back to the time Randy had called me the n-word on the playground. *I should have said something to the teacher then too*, I thought to myself. *That was not okay.* Facing my moment of truth and realizing I had the upper hand here, I felt my first tinge of vindication. I walked into the classroom and confidently kept my mouth shut. I let Randy take the fall for the hooker comment.

At the age of eleven, my curiosity led me to learn the power of words. The beauty of imagination. And the consequences of silence.

By middle school, I looked like this:

I'd be sitting on the couch laughing at *The Fresh Prince of Bel-Air*, crushing over Candace Cameron in *Full House*. I'd mimic Steve Urkel in *Family Matters* with zero sense of irony, thinking, *Nobody has glasses that thick in real life* (I must have been blind). What a photo! You likely have one of two reactions to how I looked. You're either in the category of "Oh man, I can totally relate, middle school was cruel to me too," or you're saying, "Hahahaha, you were the kind of kid I used to pick on!" If you're the latter, then you loved middle school, and I urge you to google all the people you made fun of as a kid just to see how much more successful we are than you.[4]

As a newly teenaged nerd struggling to find his place in the world—or at least in Marlboro Middle School—I regularly got book-checked in the hallways, tormented in the lunchroom, and picked last in gym class. Every time. I was also lucky to grow up in a diverse New Jersey town, with kids from lots of different spiritual backgrounds.

At thirteen, this meant that I was an active participant in the Central New Jersey bar mitzvah scene. I attended countless bar and bat mitzvahs over the course of my middle school years, interacting with large families who were a lot like mine: They were boisterous, liked to eat, and loved asking deeply personal questions in as loud a voice as possible.

"Are you Jewish?" Aviva Finkel's eighty-year-old grandmother shouted to me across the rectangular wooden seder table one Passover. "Because you look like ya could be *hay-uff*."

"No, Bubbe,"[5] I said, "my parents moved here from India, remember?"

---

4   Yes, I've had a chip on my shoulder since adolescence. My therapist says it's part of what makes me a good artist. I don't necessarily agree?

5   Yiddish for grandmother.

"Well," she complimented, "you could *pay-uss* for Sephardic."

My friends' families were so relatable, so wonderful. My own grandparents taught us to be proud of who we are. They regaled us with stories of marching with Gandhi and being thrown in jail by British soldiers for participating in acts of nonviolent civil disobedience. When a section on Gandhi appeared in my sixth-grade history book the year before, I processed for the first time the direct connection between Gandhi and Dr. Martin Luther King Jr.: that King had taken Gandhi's model of nonviolent disobedience and applied it to our civil rights movement.

We were assigned an accompanying class project, and I jumped at the chance to record a video interview with my seventy-eight-year-old grandfather. I put a glass of water on a beige, oval folding table. Grandpa (Mom's dad) walked with the help of a stainless-steel cane that had a brown plastic handle. He moved slowly. At five ten, it took him some extra time to comfortably tuck his legs around the chair.

I had heard bits and pieces of the stories as far back as I could remember. My grandparents had a framed photo of Gandhi on the wall of their humble one-bedroom apartment in Mumbai. The house was where my mom grew up with her three siblings. When we'd visit during summer vacations, I remember gazing at the photo as we'd fall asleep under a mosquito net on the cool tile floor of the main room. In the mornings, I'd ask for stories about the man in the photo. When our grandparents stayed with us in New Jersey, their tales of marching against British colonialism were used to coerce childhood-me into eating my vegetables at the dinner table. I thought all of this was just normal. I grew up oblivious to how extraordinary my grandparents were.

This time felt different. I was the one asking to sit down with

Grandpa, recording his answers, tying his experiences so explicitly to a history that I was automatically a part of. I asked what it was like to fight for his freedom. And, in a way, for mine. My grandfather lifted his pant leg to show me a long, deep scar from where a British soldier beat him, and broke down in tears. I had never seen him cry before. Fifty-five years on, the emotional marks seemed much fresher than the physical.

It would be decades later, as a young adult, when I'd connect my mom's father's sacrifices to those of Bapaji, my dad's dad, who had not been a freedom fighter. Bapaji was a tall, talkative man with a fascination for travel, riddles, and spelling. When he was ninety-two, I visited him in Ahmedabad, the largest city in India's western state of Gujarat. Dad's mom, who we called Ba, had passed away some years prior, so Bapaji lived there with my aunt. On this particular visit, I asked Bapaji if he'd like to come along for a rickshaw ride to Gandhi's nearby Sabarmati ashram.

The ashram is a gorgeous, well-maintained compound set on the bank of the Sabarmati River. From there, Gandhi led many of the activities that resulted in Indian independence. Today, it includes a museum, a small bookstore, and plenty of information displayed on signs in Gujarati, Hindi, and English.

Bapaji was both fluent and literate in multiple languages, but his eyesight was starting to fade. We walked around the ashram, chatting in Gujarati (a language I can speak, but can't read or write). He pointed to a small sign, asking me to read it to him: *"Ah soo lukheloo che?"* (What does it say here?) "Bapaji, that sign is in Gujarati. I can't read it," I replied. He pointed to the next sign, *"Ah soo lukheloo che?"* (What does it say here?) I told him, "Bapaji, that sign is in Hindi, I can't read it." Bapaji's frustration was building. He pointed to a *third* sign and hollered, "This sign is in *English*. Can you read *that*?!"

(I aspire to be this sassy when I'm in my nineties.)

I continued to translate signs from English to Gujarati, and as we wrapped up our visit, Bapaji—who was not known for reminiscing—casually remarked, "Well, it was good to see the ashram again. Brings back some memories of when we marched together."

I couldn't believe it. "Bapaji, you marched with Gandhiji too? Why is this the first that I'm hearing of this?"

"It was a long time ago," he replied simply.

I prepared for an unexpected and deep conversation about his role in the struggle for freedom, complete with tears, lessons, and morality, just like all those stories Grandma and Grandpa had told me over the years. I started firing off questions. "Bapaji, I can't believe I didn't know this about you. What would you say your biggest motivation was? Why did you decide you had to stand up and make your voice heard? Why did you ultimately march with Gandhi?" Bapaji shrugged his shoulders and, as was typical of his in-the-moment personality, matter-of-factly said, "I just felt like it."

Many of my Jewish friends' grandparents taught a similar pride—having been through hell, surviving the Holocaust, showing us the permanent markings of concentration camp tattoos. Some were quite vocal and emotional. Others more understated and quiet. Together, our grandparents were so brave and resilient. They were so strong. And despite their hardships, still so warm and kind. Their presence in our lives was a constant reminder of the need to fight the evil that is inherent in too much of humanity. I revered my grandparents. I loved that they lived with us for long stretches of time. I also loved getting to know other people's grandparents. And there was no better place to do that than Bar Mitzvah Saturdays.

*   *   *

Bar Mitzvah Saturdays would begin by mingling with friends' bubbes before a service at a synagogue. You'd hear from a friendly rabbi, who would make eye contact with every member of the congregation while delivering a usually funny, uplifting sermon. This was different from the impersonal Sanskrit, Hindi, or Gujarati prayers shouted by pious men at our local Jain or Hindu temples. Don't get me wrong, I liked that our *pujas* were so casual (literally you could walk around and talk in the middle of it and nobody would think twice), but I *loved* bar mitzvah ceremonies for the stories.

One of my favorites was about (you guessed it) someone's bubbe. A rabbi said that once upon a time there was a sweet, old bubbe who used a baking pan that *her* bubbe had given her (passed down from the bubbe before that, and so on) to make challah. This prized family heirloom had been moved around the world, through strife and triumph.

Sadly, a scatterbrained granddaughter lost the pan one afternoon, and the family went manic. Nobody wanted to tell Bubbe—she'd be absolutely inconsolable. The family began to mourn. Their ancient challah tradition was lost forever. Everyone kept the sad secret from their family matriarch for weeks, until the day Bubbe set about the entire house, trying to find the pan for her baking. When they finally confessed to her that the heirloom was gone for good, she intensely looked them in the eye, burst out in an elated laugh, and said, "I hated that pan! Finally, we are free of it!" Confusion reigned. "The family challah tradition," she clarified, "had nothing to do with that terrible pan! I know the recipe by heart, I just didn't have the guts to throw away what my grandmother gave me. Let's go buy a nice, new challah pan!"

The moral of the story is that traditions are deeper than a material thing, that it's okay for them to evolve, that we shouldn't be afraid to ask questions. Everyone could relate to this because most religion is rarely questioned.[6] Like my friends' experiences in Jewish households, our Hindu and Jain traditions were also both religious *and* cultural. Every Saturday morning was a chance to hear a new story from a Jewish perspective.

After synagogue came the party. Bar mitzvah parties were generally fancy affairs like a sweet sixteen or a wedding, even, with a theme chosen by the thirteen-year-old host. (In the early '90s, baseball, cupcakes, and hockey were especially popular.) You'd enter the venue to find a small card with your table number, make a pit stop at the bar for a Shirley Temple, and squint to find your chair under the colored mood lighting. The food was always delicious and always "kosher-style," with meals accordingly topped off with an endless supply of chocolate soy ice cream served tableside (seconds were available for those who made the trek to the dessert station on the far side of the room, where brown-paper-wrapped tubs sat over dry ice).[7] You'd dance your face off, hoist your friend up on a chair, and go home at the end of the night with either a bag full of top-shelf candy or a bar mitzvah T-shirt on which a pun connected to the theme of the party was written ("Peter's Bar Mitzvah Was Out-of-this-World" under a cartoon rocket, or "I had a sweet time at Amy's Bat Mitzvah!" scrawled inside a giant pink lollipop).

Every once in a while a party was so excessive that it blew every-

---

6   "That's why it's called faith!" says the T-shirt at a gift shop that wouldn't have my name on anything.

7   Scandalous tidbit here. "Kosher-style" means the food isn't *technically* kosher. As a friend of mine recently put it, "We lied to Grandma about it. And that fake ice cream was so gross."

one's minds. Deah Fishman had one such bat mitzvah. The faux-gem-studded addendum card accompanying the pink, glitter-infused invitation said it all:

> Buses depart synagogue ~ 4:45 p.m.
> Boat leaves dock promptly ~ 5:30 p.m.

A BOAT?!

For an entire evening, Dr. and Mrs. Fishman had rented a party boat that cruised up and down the Hudson River. The excess made me feel like I was in an MC Hammer video. On the water between Manhattan and New Jersey, eighty-five thirteen-year-olds had a DJ booth, a large dance floor under a double-height ceiling, and an endless supply of nonalcoholic cocktails, all to ourselves. The signature drink? A Deah Daiquiri. (This was actually a virgin piña colada. Deah hated strawberries but loved alliteration.)

My parents would never host a glamorous party like this. They and most of their friends are hardworking, middle-class Indian immigrants who save their pennies. They were not showy, and I just couldn't fathom a scenario in which hiring a party boat on the Hudson was in the realm of possibility for them. The Indian version of getting out on the water would be bringing a picnic lunch to a nearby state park and renting paddle boats.[8]

(There *was* the occasional outlier. My dad's friend Tapu Uncle once bought a brand-new emerald-green four-door Mercedes. He drove it to our house forty minutes down the Garden State Parkway just to proudly show off the gigantic built-in car phone. "As a cardiologist," he opined, making sure we understood there was some-

---

8   Still one of my favorite activities.

thing practical behind his extravagance, "my patients rely on me to stay in constant communication and arrive very fast." He snapped his fingers for emphasis. "Very fast.")

For the first hour of Deah's party, we drank our Deah Daiquiris, admiring the intimate view of the Statue of Liberty from the outdoor deck. As the sun set and dinner was served, we scattered to find our tables. I was relieved to be seated between Praveen Ramachandaran and Ed Cheng. I guess in any other scenario it might look a little racist that the three Asian boys were put at the same table, but Itay Borenstein, Andrew Spielvogel, and Tamir Jones were seated there too because we all happened to be in band together (I played baritone sax). Waitstaff brought around our previously selected "chicken, beef, or veggie" plates and I ate slowly, watching wealthy seventh-grade metrosexual Jason Gross to see which fork to use for which dish, and whether my water glass was on the left side or the right.

After dinner, everyone returned to dancing, which is when things really took a turn. Deah and her crew of besties had kicked off their shoes. They jumped around in their various-sized polka-dotted (as was the fashion) dresses, energized by the upbeat music. At some point they huddled together for some urgent negotiations and, with mischief in their eyes, strode confidently to the DJ booth. A song was requested. Moments later, the opening beat of Billy Idol's "Mony Mony" burst through the speakers. "Here she come now sayin', 'Mony Mony.'" Deah and her friends interrupted loudly, taking advantage of the two measures of music ahead of Billy's next lyric by chanting, "Hey, hey slut, get laid, get fucked!" before the speakers blared, "Shoot 'em down, turn around, come on, Mony—"

WHAT DID THEY JUST SAY? I felt a pit in my stomach.

"That's not part of the song," whispered Praveen, decisively.

"What's happening?" Ed Cheng asked. He looked shaken.

We had no idea how the girls learned this surreal refrain, because nobody we knew ever spoke this way in real life.

As the second verse approached, it became clear that Deah expected all her friends to join in the vulgar off-script chant, including me, Praveen, and Ed. Praveen and I were a hard no from the start. I wasn't about to repeat my "hooker" mistake. Ed started to recite, "Hey, hey . . ." but then he noticed the videographer and he clammed up. While we wanted to be supportive of our host, the only words of *Hey, hey slut, get laid, get fucked!* we felt comfortable saying were "hey" and "get," so the three of us feigned thirst and quietly escaped to the bar area for another Deah Daquiri.

At that very moment, I glanced across to find Deah's disappointed mom leaning over the railing one deck above us. She looked so elegant, holding her white wine with freshly manicured pink-glitter fingernails,[9] a little diamond in the middle of each one. The chagrin on her face was unmistakable. *This is it*, I thought, *Mrs. Fishman is going to pull the plug on that DJ and turn this boat right around. No more MC Hammer immersion.*

Ed, Praveen, and I watched with morbid curiosity as Mrs. Fishman steadied herself on the top rail. She took an extra-large swig of her wine, shooting the chardonnay like a sorority girl, and sarcastically shouted, "Nice language, ladies! Very nice language!" Mrs. Fishman then turned back to her friends, who refilled her glass, and Deah's crew *continued* with the rest of the song, obscene chant and all.

I couldn't believe what I was seeing. First, unbelievable that Deah

---

9   The color matched the invitation card perfectly.

and her friends had somehow learned this chant (and this was before the internet). Second, unfathomable that they had the guts to request the song from the DJ. And third, completely and totally incomprehensible that they *sang it in front of their parents and other adults*. And I'm sorry, Mrs. Fishman's inscrutable reaction was "Nice language, ladies"? That's it? Are you kidding me?! If a group of us Indian kids chanted, "Hey, hey slut, get laid, get fucked" in front of Bhumi Auntie at Janvi Jhaveri's sweet sixteen, all the parents would have drowned themselves in the Hudson River out of shame.

I was in total awe. Here was Deah Fishman. She had her own boat, her own DJ, and she could shout her own filthy made-up verses to well-known songs at the top of her lungs because this was her bat mitzvah. This. Girl. Had. It. All! At the age of thirteen I had discovered a whole new world: an envy-inspiring universe of white folks, where adults would merely offer opinions, and instead of enforcing consequences, they'd make observations and go back to their wine.

Deah's parents allowed her certain independent choices that I was still a few years away from exercising in my own right. Coming off the boat that night, I felt simultaneously invigorated and frightened. It was like the first ocean swim where you force yourself just a few feet beyond where your toes can touch the sand, terrified and exhilarated by the possibility that your reward for this boldness could be a rip current that sucks you out to sea.

Navigating the fear and freedom of independence as a teenager was the grown-up reality that we were all barreling toward—and Deah Fishman had gotten there first.

Okay, so middle school wasn't all party boats. I got bullied a lot. This was back when bullying was just something that happened, and not yet the subject of congressional commissions. Some of it was more "bullying lite," like when the popular girls would purposely bump into me:

ME: Oh, excuse me.

POPULAR GIRLS: Ugh, there *is* no excuse for you!

Popular Girls storm off laughing.

It was demoralizing in the moment, though I suppose character building in the long run?

Then there was the kind of bullying that wasn't mild or instructive, even with the benefit of hindsight. Kids like me or Praveen or Ed would get taunted because we were supposedly the weird, ugly, fat, skinny, dark, fill-in-the-blank-different kids. Harshad Shah, who was both Indian *and* fat, got a double dose. An extra target on our backs came from not wearing designer shoes or jeans. (This is how I learned that Sears did not classify as "designer.") It wasn't uncommon to get spit on or beat up between classes, usually with a side order of whatever movie or TV show quote the bully happened to be motivated by.

Chilled monkey brains![10] A whack to the face.

Hey Apu! Thank you, come again![11] Some asshole's spit lands in your hair.

Long Duk Dong![12] Your books and folders have been thrown sky-high and papers are raining everywhere. (Why didn't these kids watch wholesome things like *The Fresh Prince of Bel-Air* or *Back to the Future*?!)

Teachers knew this was going on. Most chose to ignore it. One

---

10 From a scene in *Indiana Jones and the Temple of Doom*, in which the Indian characters eat monkey brains (and bugs).

11 *The Simpsons.*

12 The name of the exchange student in *Sixteen Candles*.

outlier was our kind music director, Mr. Manziano, who freely gave bullied kids passes to "practice music" whenever we wanted. This meant that instead of the hell of a middle school cafeteria, we could retreat to Mr. Manziano's practice rooms, which is where I ate my lunch most days.

For the bullies at Marlboro Middle School, reciting those catchy lines from some of the most popular mainstream movies and shows weaponized them. *The Simpsons*, *Sixteen Candles*, and *Indiana Jones and the Temple of Doom* had something in common: stereotypical, dehumanized Asian characters who fueled the bullying.[13] *Short Circuit* had all that *and* a sweet robot named Johnny 5. Picking up my papers in a crowded hallway with spit dripping from my hair was an intimate way to learn that images of what we all watched on television crept into our thinking.

Aside from movie quotes, more direct slurs were thrown around, too, albeit none of them were especially creative.

Hey dothead: A reference to a bindi, or dot, that some Indian women (and Gwen Stefani) wear. In Jersey City at the time, a gang called the Dotbusters was thriving. These racists would go around harassing, assaulting, and even killing Indian people. A man named Navroze Mody was murdered by four men who were ultimately only sentenced to between six months and ten years. It was a scary time. My aunt lived in Jersey City. My grandmother would stay with her

---

13   Good time to point out something that I'm told is not always obvious if you aren't Asian American. Shows like *The Simpsons* certainly "make fun of everyone," but when the white (okay, yellow) cartoon characters are the only ones well-developed and fleshed out, and when the Indian ones are the only ones whose racial signifiers are mentioned, that's where the stereotypes come from. You might think to yourself, *What about characters like Barney who are drunkards?* Well, the reason they don't count is because the leads themselves are also white (okay, yellow!). If *The Simpsons* had brown lead characters whose racial signifiers didn't drive their character's plotlines, it would offset what they did with Apu and the resulting depictions would be multi-faceted.

often. Grandma regularly described how she'd hold her head high as groups of young men taunted her on afternoon walks. I guess after marching with Gandhi, a bunch of morons in New Jersey seemed pretty B-list, but it was all terrifying to me.

Speaking of Gandhi, they managed to turn this into an insult too. Which obviously never made sense. *Are you comparing me to the guy who nonviolently kicked the British Empire's ass—and inspired Dr. King and others in the American civil rights movement—because you're trying to insult me?* These kids confused nonviolence with being docile. Confounded use of force with strength. And why wouldn't they? Our favorite TV shows were riddled with racist tropes, and one of Navroze Mody's murderers only got six months in jail.

I don't recall much of the Indian community's reaction to Dotbusters, but I remember there being more fear than shock. This sort of racism was a fact of life. It was up to the community to look out for itself, which was harder with big newspapers like the *Jersey Journal*[14] giving a candid platform to these terrorists and their hate crimes:

> We are an organization called dot busters. We have been around for 2 years. We will go to any extreme to get Indians to move out of Jersey City. If I'm walking down the street and I see a Hindu and the setting is right, I will hit him or her. We plan some of our most extreme attacks such as breaking windows, breaking car windows, and crashing family parties. We use the phone books and look up the name Patel. Have you seen how many of them there are? . . . You said that they will have to start protecting themselves because the police cannot always be there. They will never do anything. They

---

14　Their website is literally NJ.com.

are a week [*sic*] race Physically and mentally. We are going to
continue our way. We will never be stopped.

                    "Jersey City Dot Busters,"
            The Jersey Journal, September 2, 1987

Anyway, that's the message I was getting. An entire brown lifetime is worth six months.

Something that made middle school a little more tolerable[15] was
drama club. I know what you're thinking. "How can this be? Drama
club kids are teased mercilessly at middle schools across America."

The crazy thing about drama club meetings in our town was that
the school thought it was a good idea to hold them during soccer practice on a stage inside the gymnasium, directly across from the locker
rooms. That meant the athletes (aka the worst offenders of bullying)
would catch the beginnings and ends of each rehearsal as they jogged
to and from the practice fields outside. In a bizarre twist of arrogance,
the soccer players were so into themselves that for better or worse,
little attention was ever paid to anything the drama club was doing.
So, we had the creative solace of an after-school bubble, *buttttt* had to
endure the late-bus ride home with them. You had to really love drama
club to put up with it.

In the spring of eighth grade I was cast as the Tin Man in our
school's musical, *The Wiz*. For two hours each day after school, the
six weeks of rehearsals were everything I'd wanted: an escape from
the frustrations of the day, discovering artistic expression, being able
to play a character who was confident when I was anything but.

---

15   Besides bar and bat mitzvahs.

I couldn't wait to sing his iconic song, "Slide Some Oil to Me." I was going to kill it!

A week before *The Wiz* was set to make its evening debut on the illustrious middle school stage, our director enthusiastically gathered the cast together. "Guess what, everyone? We're going to be doing three scenes from the play for the whole school at a special assembly on Thursday morning! Your peers will get a little teaser of the musical to entice them to come see it in the evening!"

Now, look. Doing a play in front of a hundred gracious parents who willingly paid $4 a ticket to watch thirteen-year-olds put on *The Wiz* was very different from 750 obnoxious and entitled middle schoolers forced to watch a show. The bullying was bad *before* the kids saw parts of our play. When I imagined what it would be like after, I wanted to slide something else down my throat.[16] There was *no way* I was going to say yes to this nonsense. The rest of the cast agreed with me: We were a hard pass.

"If you guys are too scared to go up in front of your own school," the drama teacher scolded, "then we aren't going up at all. I'll cancel the play."

We didn't have a choice.

The special Thursday assembly rolled around and I was convinced it was the end of my existence on Earth.[17] As the kids started to arrive, we could hear the jeers all the way backstage. "Doro-THEE!" Ben Garber yelled. "Nice TITTIES!"

The vice principal grabbed the mic. "Rude and disruptive behavior will not be tolerated because our school community is based on respect and kindness toward each other."

---

16 Cyanide.
17 I sometimes was, and still am, very dramatic. I AM!

"PPPRRRRRRRR!!" David Cohen made an annoyingly loud fart sound with his mouth. To follow up, he put on a talentless Indian accent, yelling, "I am excited for dee Tin Man!"

I heard him from backstage and wished I could go out there and slice his throat open. One of the drama-nerd stagehands saw the look on my face, knew exactly what rage I was feeling, and said, "Don't waste your energy on them. We can't let that bring us down. Let's just get through this. Remember, the whole reason for this journey is for you to get *courage!*"

"That's the Lion. I'm getting a heart."

He shrugged.

The curtain went up on the first scene. Everyone was—surprisingly—respectful. Second scene: also fine. Third scene: my turn. After the Wiz gives the Scarecrow some brains, here's what was supposed to go down:

> TIN MAN: *(Realizes he finally has a heart, crosses downstage, poses with ax blade on deck, handle in his right hand.)* All you fine ladies out there . . . ha ha ha . . . *(He kicks the ax blade with his right foot, sending it up to land on his right shoulder.)* Watch out!

Since this was an eighth-grade production, we couldn't use a real ax. Mine was made out of plastic and cardboard, spray-painted to look as metallic as it could on a middle school budget. But flimsy, fake axes cannot be kicked and landed on shoulders. So, during rehearsal I decided I would instead *point to the audience* and say the line.

> TIN MAN: All you fine ladies out there . . . ha ha ha . . . *(He points to the audience.)* Watch out!

Except that's not what happened either. Have you ever heard an actor say something like, "I don't even remember doing that, the *character* just made that choice? I was in the zone!"? When the Wiz gave the Tin Man his heart, I was *deep* in the zone.

As directed, I posed with the ax and then turned to the audience, saying, "All you fine ladies out there . . . ha ha ha . . ." but instead of just pointing to the audience, I grabbed the ax with both hands, held it horizontally like handlebars, and enthusiastically delivered a single, vigorous pelvic thrust toward the crowd while saying my last line: *"Watch out!"*

Everyone went *nuts.* I had no idea where this came from. They were cheering for the Tin Man! He got his heart. He showed them he deserved it. A force to be reckoned with!

When we got on the late bus after tech rehearsal that day, all the athletes burst into applause. It wasn't sarcastic either! After the torment of the daily rides home, these genuine claps and cheers were a most unexpected turn. As the dummies eventually quieted down, one of them turned to me and said, "Man, why didn't you guys tell us *that's* what you were doing? That was *awesome!*"

His question sat on my chest like a hundred bricks. Why didn't we tell them that's what we were *doing*? Meaning it was *our* responsibility to make ourselves worthy of not being taunted or beaten up? Was Navroze Mody's big mistake that he didn't tell people what *he* was doing?

I stared out the bus window. I was relieved to know that another spitball would not land in my hair that day, and yet, my brain was busy sorting out what had happened. Kids were complimenting our performances, reenacting their favorite lines. (My in-the-zone pelvic thrust was the clear highlight—something even assholes loved.[18])

I felt like I had discovered a superpower! While watching our scenes, these guys forgot their preconceived notions, and did some-

---

18 Pun intended.

thing they didn't think they would: They laughed with us. The very same kids who spit on us and kicked our asses while quoting Apu and *Indiana Jones* . . . we just changed their minds using the same techniques those TV shows and movies used—humor and art. Comedy can bring people together and change how they feel! This magical realization continued when friends and parents—mine included—watched and applauded when the show opened that night. It was the first catalyst in my passion for acting.

So, Randy Finn, Ben Garber, and David Cohen: Thanks for teaching me that there is a way to reach dumb-dumbs like you. Because hey, twenty-five years later, that seventh-grade dothead you bullied was one of *People* magazine's Sexiest Men Alive. I told you to *pelvic thrust* "Watch out!"

CHAPTER TWO

WHAT HAPPENED TO THE OTHER THIRTEEN POINTS?

(and Other Questions That Don't Have Answers)

We have a dear family friend named Pushpa Auntie. She's a sweet, quiet woman with exceptionally long black hair tightly wound into a single braid, interrupted only by a bright red rubber band. She's like an Indian Rapunzel, except, instead of being sadly banished to a tower, she happily enjoys the freedom of shopping at Target in suburban Passaic County. Pushpa Auntie's conservative look accentuates her innocence: Two things she always wears? A *salwar kameez* and a smile. Her childhood friends gave her a fun nickname because she was so virtuous: They shortened *Pushpa* to *Pushy*—since she's anything but.

Many languages, including Gujarati, have multiple s-sounds, which leads some folks to incorrectly pronounce the *sh* in *Pushpa* as a more dainty *s*, an unflattering *Poo-spa*. This type of transference can make the word *action* become *ack-sun*. And it turned Pushy Auntie's nickname into . . .

"Come downstairs, Pussy Auntie is here!"

The other aunties would call this out to us as her cream-colored Ford Taurus station wagon pulled up to our house. We'd descend the stairs amid the mouthwatering scent of samosas sizzling, listening to the uncles' jovial greetings,

"Hi Pussy!"

The aunties—wholesome immigrant women—never could figure out why the kids snickered and giggled every time Pussy Auntie visited.[1]

Pussy Auntie was hardworking, like most of my parents' friends. She's a pediatrician who came to America in search of a better life, and she was adamant that her kids—and her friends' kids—study hard and pursue careers in the sciences. To an outsider, it might seem a bit invasive to hear that family friends would take such intimate interest in the personal lives of kids who aren't their own, but that's not really how the Indian community views things. Culturally, having your parents' friends dispense advice about how you should live your life is supposed to feel far less like an imposition and more like the blessing of extra community support—from their perspective at least. I had the benefit of love from people we called aunties and uncles—not related by blood, but by an even closer bond of immigration experience, language, and culture. Like my parents, they risked it all, sacrificed, and worked toward a better life for their kids.

But as a teenager, having so many concerned adults around just felt like extra pressure, and these family gatherings grew tricky for me to navigate given my growing interest in the arts. On one hand, all the parents would encourage me to do a monologue or stand-up routine (which usually consisted of a John Leguizamo sketch I had memorized). That was always the clear high point of the evening for me. After that things went downhill.

Pussy Auntie was known to corner the high school kids in small groups while other aunties and uncles watched her orchestrate an

---

1   The uncles knew.

impressive quizzing on which *practical* plans they had. Here's how I remember it:

PUSSY AUNTIE: What's the latest, kids? Where is everybody applying for the college?

VARUN: Well, my first choice is Princeton for premed, but my safety is Hopkins.

I roll my eyes. This kid's fucking *safety* is Hopkins?

PUSSY AUNTIE: Very nice! So many choices. When we were young, we did not have so much choice. Aarti?

AARTI: I'm still a junior, Auntie, but I want to go to Boston University . . .

Disappointed nods from several aunties and uncles while they share concerned looks around the room.

AARTI: . . . for their seven-year combined medical program!

Dramatic sighs of relief, followed by excited nods of affirmation.

PUSSY AUNTIE: Wow! We came here with nothing, and you are going for seven-year medical program! Good plan, good plan. Nikhil?

NIKHIL: I got into Yale early. I'm premed.

This dude is worse than Varun.

PUSSY AUNTIE: Wonderful news! Very practical. Kalpen?

All eyes on me. Do I lie? Do I tell the truth? At sixteen, the pressure feels ridiculous.

ME: I um . . . I think I want to go to NYU or UCLA. I'm going
to become an actor and filmmaker.

Freeze frame, record scratch. Everyone stares at me for what
feels like forever. Pussy Auntie bursts out laughing.

PUSSY AUNTIE: Very creative! Very creative response!

Her smile curtly disappears. Her eyes narrow.

PUSSY AUNTIE: Seriously, what are you going to study in college?

Like a great many immigrants, the Indian American community
considered my passion for the arts a perfectly nice *hobby*—an uncomfortable phase that I'd God willing grow out of when I became older
and sensible. Sort of a professional puberty. The pressure to conform to
their aspirations of careers in medicine or engineering was enormous—
anyone who wasn't pursuing these professions was considered to be
going after "a nontraditional field." And it was strange how intimately
these professions were tied to the community's shared identity.

Whenever I'd talk about my love for film, I'd hear, "We don't do
those things. We are *Indian*." Why was being Indian mutually exclusive from having a career in the arts? If I became a professional actor,
would they suddenly not call me Kalpen Modi?[2]

This is probably a good time to talk about the sacrifices my parents and their friends endured to make it in America. My dad, Suresh,
was born a small blond boy in Kansas and adopted by an Indian family in Mumbai. No, he was born a black-haired boy in a small village
in Gujarat, India, and raised primarily in a studio apartment in Mumbai with four sisters.

When I say Dad and his sisters grew up in a studio apartment, I'm

---

2   Okay, bad example.

being generous. It was closer to what we might call a tenement. Each of the two identical buildings in their complex had four stories. Each story had thirty, one-room units. The front of the room had two single beds and a door that opened onto an outdoor walkway lined with entrances to the other studio apartments. This overlooked a courtyard. The walkway and courtyard were where the kids from the units in both buildings would play together; I loved hanging out with them when we'd visit Bapaji and Ba over the summers. Toward the back of the room was a kitchen area with a narrow ladder that led to an open-railinged platform with a double bed and small closet; it was my favorite place to sleep because you got a bird's eye view of the apartment. The unit had no toilet. For that, you had to walk out the back door next to the "kitchen," pass the large drum used for storing water (running water only came for a couple of hours a day), and go down the length of the rear outdoor walkway, where you'd come to a room subdivided with communal concrete holes in the floor (squat toilets, *sandas*) for each level's thirty studio apartments to share.

When you did have to use the *sandas*, it was a whole ordeal. For starters, you'd have to put on slippers specifically set aside for the purpose. Toilet paper was a luxury that was hard to come by in India in those days, so after putting on your *sandas* slippers, you'd need to stop at your unit's drum and fill your own bucket of water, which you'd carry with a bar of soap and small plastic cup to wash your little butt with. Anyone you passed would know exactly where you were headed. There was—obviously—no privacy anywhere, which I guess explained why years later, when I was a teenager, my dad would knock on my closed bedroom door and say things like, "Why do you need privacy? You are fourteen." I'm lucky he never said, "Why do you need toilet paper? We have running water."

Anyway, that's what life was like when I'd stay with Bapaji and Ba, and how Dad lived until he immigrated in the early 1970s to pursue a graduate engineering degree at Stevens Institute of Technology, just outside New York City. The day he left India, a contingent of extended family members—aunts, uncles, and cousins—joined his parents and sisters at the airport to see him off. They came dressed in their best suits and freshly pressed saris. The entire family's hopes, dreams, and finances were resting on my father. He *had* to succeed in America.

The story goes that because Bapaji was a manager in the accounts department of Air India, my father managed to get a free flight to the States. Among the first in our family to leave India, he landed at JFK Airport with the equivalent of twelve dollars in his pocket and dreams of opportunity that were only possible in America: financial stability, new discovery, access to the best education for his future children. The first few nights, he stayed with a college friend who had immigrated earlier, before finding a small, shared apartment in Hoboken, New Jersey. Dad lived simply, eager to study and work hard—both full-time. He patiently climbed his way up the ladder of the American dream, toiling and saving so that he could build a life for himself. After graduation and a little over a year into his first professional engineering job, he followed an adventurous streak and took a six-month sabbatical to backpack through Europe on a microbudget. After resuming work in the States, he would periodically return to visit his family in Mumbai. On one such trip, he met and married my mom in a beautiful, if hastily put together by today's standards, ceremony. (Hey, Dad had to get back to America! Work was waiting!)

Mom had grown up in that one-bedroom apartment in Mumbai with the photo of Gandhi on the wall. She had three siblings of her own. Their apartment had the luxury of a separate kitchen, but like Dad's apartment, no steadily running water or toilet.[3] She had completed her master's degree in chemistry and was working for an international company when she left Mumbai to join my dad in New Jersey a few months after they married. It was Mom's first time living anywhere else. That's how my parents began their modest lives together, hoping to save up a few bucks and push out a few American anchor babies like me one day.

Their story is classic: It's the journey of immigrants who come to America with nothing but an education, a mammoth work ethic, and a willingness to sacrifice. When they make it—when they finally achieve some hard-won stability after years of uncertainty—they'll fight to make sure nothing jeopardizes it. For a lot of Indian immigrants, *stability* came from careers in medicine and engineering. As you may have heard, this is entirely because of genetics.

The three things scientists have found Indians possess in greater numbers are: 1) a predisposition to excel in the sciences, 2) a high tolerance for tremendously spicy gossip about other Indians, and 3) exceptionally large testicles.

As much as I would love to let you buy into this, the real reason for all those Indian doctors and engineers is that the US government changed immigration laws in the mid-1960s to allow people from Asian countries to fill dire labor shortages in fields that didn't have enough native-born Americans. If you were from one of these countries (like India) and wanted to pursue a degree and career in a field in which we needed professionals, you could come to the United States. Together, America and the sciences gave my parents and their friends a home,

---

3   The better part of my childhood summers was spent pooping in communal toilets and washing my tiny butt with bucket water.

a job, a life. Given how they got here, and how much their new community of recent immigrants shared, it must have been impossible to
divorce their professional identities from their ethnic ones. Even more
improbable that their large-balls child would gamble it all on a career
in the arts. Of course, I didn't understand immigration laws or sacrifice
as a high school kid. I didn't even understand basic geometry.

I have always been awful at all things math and science. I could pull
a solid B in those subjects. It's just that by brown people standards,
a "solid B" is an "Indian F." In early childhood, I was used to bringing home minor disappointments in the form of all those recurring
report card comments about daydreaming in class. As I got older,
showing my parents my grades would usually go something like this:

MOM: A in history.

DAD: A in English.

MOM: What's this? B in geometry?!

DAD: Oh God.

MOM: How could you get a B?!

DAD: How did this happen?!

ME: It's not a bad grade, a B is like an 87.

MOM: Eighty-*seven*?!

DAD: Out of one *hundred*?!

MOM: *What happened to the other thirteen points?!*

Between my mom's master's degree in chemistry and my dad's in engineering, it was inconceivable that their eldest son could get anything other than an A in geometry, right?[4]

For my Bs, I wanted to blame my boring teachers—like Mrs. Teller, who stood five feet tall, was rumored to be ninety-four years old, and taught both physics *and* math. Mrs. Teller had tiny, arthritic hands—especially tiny, I should say, for an already diminutive woman. When I was bored, I would stare at her unmalleable fingers as she hobbled back and forth at the front of the classroom, admiring how the white chalk made her already pale and wrinkled paws look indecipherable from the hands of a mime. She once cut her thumb on the edge of a chair back and tracked droplets of bright red blood all over her desk for fifteen minutes before noticing. Several students, myself included, tried to get her attention, but she acknowledged neither our raised hands nor her cut finger. That's how observant she was.

The bigger problem with old Mrs. Teller was that she didn't enjoy curiosity. She'd drone on about abstract concepts without grounding them in anything concrete or interesting. This drove me totally insane. I'd take out my frustrations in a nerdy, productive way and raise my hand to ask if she could expand on a topic that I found fascinating. "Mrs. Teller," I'd say, "how do we know the theory of relativity is correct? How much are scientists still trying to prove?" She was always belittling, "My deah boy," she'd scold while cupping a little piece of chalk in the palm of her amphibious doll hands, "these are questions you will never need to know the answers to unless you intend to pursue a PhD in physics, which I assure you . . . you will

---

4 "You mean A-plus!" —Mom

not. The only thing you should be asking today is whether you have memorized enough fuh the test."

Back at home, "It's Mrs. Teller's fault. She's so boring! It's all memorization" didn't go over particularly well. My parents grew up without excuses. Coming from a country that is so highly populated, competition drove not just success but daily survival. Their parents sacrificed basic recreational comforts (they never so much as went out to the movies) in order to put their kids through school. So, when I'd blame my teachers, my dad's rebuttal was quick: "Mrs. Teller is right! You do have to memorize for the test! It's a multiple-choice test! The answers are right in front of you, you just have to circle the right one! If you can memorize lines for your school play, you should easily be able to memorize an equation. Why don't you at least *try*?" By tenth grade, this was an especially common tactic from my parents: If you can do it with your passion for acting, why are you *choosing* not to do it with science and math? *Why don't you at least try?*

If an exam had an essay component, I had a great shot at a near-perfect score because I could describe all the things I knew. Throw a multiple-choice test on my desk and I was totally stuck. *How can anyone possibly quantify the answer with just ONE of these choices?* I'd say to myself. *I can create a story in which a portion of each of the choices is true.*

I'd plead with my Dad to understand: "In acting, the stuff you're memorizing always makes total sense. Monologues and scenes have logical character arcs. Plot points motivate an actor's words. I *have* been trying! Why else would I ask Mrs. Teller so many questions? I want science and math to make sense to me so badly."

"Science and math do make sense," he said. "If the issue is the story, find a way to create a plotline or character for math too."

I began to process Dad's advice.

When normal people study something, they usually opt for rote memorization. In prepping for a dumb and useless geometry exam, for instance, they might recite "the area of a circle is pi r squared" and "the area of a triangle is one-half base times height" over and over until the formulas stick to the right part of their brains. The problem with me is, I don't have that part of my brain where formulas stick. It's missing.

When you memorize lines as an actor, you're really memorizing a story and a motivation. You're invested in it. In *The Wiz*, it was easy to memorize "All you fine ladies out there . . . ha ha ha . . . watch out!" because my character is expressing confidence after finally getting his heart. I knew what those words meant. They advanced a plot, *a story*. In fact, I understood their significance so deeply that I even added a pelvic thrust. What the hell does "the area of a circle is pi r squared" and "the area of a triangle is one-half base times height" mean? Nothing! It means nothing. And teachers would acknowledge nothingness saying, "There's no story here. You'll only understand how equations are applicable years from now, if you continue to pursue science." (But why would I pursue science if you're not telling me how the equations are applicable *now*?!)

I just couldn't memorize those equations. If I wanted formulas to make sense, I was going to have to take some of Dad's advice and define them for myself.

One night after a particularly huge Gujarati dinner of rotli, daal, bhaat, and shaak (colloquially referred to as RDBS), I was standing in my bathroom shirtless. Staring into the mirror in pajama shorts, toothbrush in hand, I noticed that my tummy looked quite large. *Oooh, circle*, I thought. *Maybe this is how I take Dad's advice. Maybe today I'll act math.*

Looking at my round belly in the mirror, I came up with a character: Sandra! I was massively pregnant—eight months on, *at least*. I revealed my two ginormous breasts; not because I was provocative, because of *geometry*. My belly was the circle I studied earlier: *pi r squared*. Each breast was a triangle: *one-half base times height*.

With my toothbrush hanging out of my foamy mouth, I strutted the length of the bathroom like it was a catwalk, rubbing my imaginary pregnant stomach, saying, "Oh *hello* pi r squared baby. Are you ready to come out of Mommy's belly?" Acting math was *working*.

I got deeper into the role. Asking myself character background questions: *Who is the father? What are our hopes and dreams for this beautiful little pi r squared baby?*

I grabbed my large triangle breasts tightly and screamed, "YOU WANT MOMMY TO FEED YOU HOT YUMMY MILK FROM HER ONE-HALF BASE TIMES HEIGHT BOOBIES?!" Just then, I glanced up to see my terrified parents standing behind me in the bathroom mirror.

"What the hell is going on here?! Stop this business right now!" Mom said. They had heard Sandra's commotion and saw enough to be concerned. "Finish your brushing and go study!"

I'm not cut out for math.

February 1992. I can't remember exactly where we heard about Mira Nair's film *Mississippi Masala*. It must have been either word of mouth or the Indian community newspaper. As the director of an Oscar-nominated movie called *Salaam Bombay!*, Nair was someone who excited me. Her new feature was about the daughter of an Indian *African* motel owner who falls in love with an African *American* carpet cleaner in Greenwood, Mississippi. I had to see it.

There we were: Mom, Dad, me, and my older cousin Shami

walking into the cold, dimly lit movie theater, unaware that my world would change forever. I was mesmerized from the start: Here were brown characters who looked like me, were played by brown actors, in a film written by a brown woman and directed by *another* brown woman! In 1992, the only time brown people would appear in film or on television was if they were a) actually white,[5] b) cartoon characters,[6] c) doing something deeply stereotypical, d) eating monkey brains, or e) some combination of the above.

Mississippi Masala sucked me into its beautifully crafted world immediately. Actor Sarita Choudhury's character, Mina, had a family that was a lot like mine. Boisterous, yes, but also relatable and well fleshed out in real ways: the overdramatic uncle obsessed with his car, the complicated immigrant parents navigating complicated lives. Plus, Sarita's character falls in love and has sex! With Denzel Washington! Sure, discovering my own sexuality was still a ways off, and sure, it was super uncomfortable to be a teenager watching a sex scene next to my then socially conservative parents, but you know what? I hadn't kissed anyone yet, and in my subconscious it was reassuring to know that falling in love and having sex with someone like Denzel Washington might be a real possibility someday!

None of Mira Nair's characters was one-note. They were all wonderfully flawed. For an hour and fifty-eight minutes, I was in the front seat of an emotional roller coaster. My parents seemed to enjoy the film too. I walked out of the theater, heart full. For all the spitting and hate I got from kids while they quoted Apu from *The Simpsons*, and *Indiana Jones* and *Short Circuit*, this was clearly the other side of cinema. This was an extension of the redemption I felt as the thrusting

5   In brownface
6   In brown-voice

Tin Man. This was what images could make people feel on a larger scale if done smartly, deftly, creatively, inclusively, and in a not-lazy way. This was magic.

If Mira Nair and Sarita Choudhury can do this, I said to myself walking out of the theater that evening, *maybe I can too!* That day changed my life because it was the first time I watched something and saw myself depicted as a human being.

With *Mississippi Masala* fresh in my mind, I spent the rest of the school year getting more involved with my public high school's arts programs, namely choir and drama club. I had already impressed the theater faculty with my small role in the fall play, *The Pied Piper of Hamelin*. (I played one of the creepy little kids who follows the Pied Piper around when he plays his creepy little flute.[7])

Like most underclassmen, that spring I was not expected to audition for one of the coveted slots in the musical *Godspell*. The unspoken code—*the spring musical is reserved for juniors and seniors and you'll have your chance when you're a junior or senior*—didn't sit well with me on account of the accolades I received for my breakout performance earlier that fall.[8] I auditioned anyway, "just for the experience." A week later when the cast announcement was posted on the drama club board in the main hallway of Freehold Township High School, my name was on it! Ensemble Member #3. An absolutely unheard-of feat for a freshman.

Teachers pulled me aside all day, congratulating me for getting cast. And not just the arts teachers, even the useless ones who taught

---

7 *Piccolo* doesn't sound as folksy.
8 I had no lines.

things like physics and algebra! My fellow students were happy for me, saying very complimentary things like, "That's phat!" and "Kalpen got cast in the musical . . . No duh."

The reaction at home that evening was not as inviting. I hoped my parents might be proud. That the next time Rekha Auntie called to remind everyone that Nikhil got into Yale,[9] they could brag that I was *Godspell*'s Ensemble Member #3. But my math grades were too low the prior semester, and they blamed it on my participation in *The Pied Piper*. *Theater is a very nice hobby, but it's not practical.* My parents didn't think I should waste time that way. That night, they forbade me from being part of *Godspell*. I was more heartbroken than angry. Not being able to act in the musical wasn't like a high school soccer player missing a goal and saying, "Aw shucks, I didn't score. Guess I'll continue to get straight Cs and bang my girlfriend this weekend." It was a real emotional devastation—like a piece was missing from somewhere inside.

As the dust settled through the spring and my grades didn't improve, it became clear that being forced to decline the role in *Godspell* had no effect. Despite remaining so awful at math, I somehow convinced my parents to allow me to attend a residential acting program that summer. The New Jersey Summer Arts Institute was less like a camp and more like one of those nerdy, intensive pre-collegiate schools where you all live and study together for five weeks, in this case at Rutgers University's Livingston Campus. I wasn't entirely sure why they agreed to send me. Maybe it was pure encouragement. Maybe they thought it would get the acting bug out of my system completely.[10]

---

9   "Did we mention that already? It is for premed. Early admission. He will be a neurosurgeon. *Anyway, how is Kalpen?*"
10   Spoiler: The opposite happened! And I am very thankful for their tacit support.

The New Jersey Summer Arts Institute was my first effort at taking the creative sparks I felt onstage and in the *Mississippi Masala* movie theater and turning them into something more. Living and working with people who thrived on artistic expression cemented everything I loved about making up stories. Our acting teacher, Joe Russo (white, smaller build, grayish hair, midfifties, raspy voice), and vocal coach, Yvonne Kersey (African American, midfifties, booming voice, stature of a Peeps marshmallow), were perfectly matched. Since this wasn't traditional school, Joe and Yvonne didn't have to conduct themselves with the same modicum of professionalism.

Joe openly chain-smoked unfiltered Camels from the back row of the theater while giving notes on our scene work. (This was viewed with some reverence by the handful of students who also smoked: "That's the last stop, man. Unfiltered. When the nicotine from regular cigarettes just won't do it for you. The laaaaast stop.")

Yvonne snuck her cigarettes under a tree outside and seemed softly guilty about us knowing that she smoked in the first place. Every few days she'd pat her chest and proudly remind us, "You have to take care of your instrument," before leading a group singing exercise of the gospel song "Go Tell It on the Mountain." This was all designed to build camaraderie and confidence, and you know what? It felt friggin' great.

The turning point of the summer came at its halfway mark, when I got to know the other kids well enough to realize they had missing math pieces of their brains too! What we didn't possess in the form of cranial rote memorization lobes,[11] we did possess in *other* areas. We *all* had the capacity to make up stories, create characters, and feel emotions. Our minds wandered all the time. I had become close with a kid

---

11   Not a real thing, I don't think?

named Nathan who wore Lennon glasses, had shoulder-length wavy hair and multicolored pants, and told me he *also* brought home report cards that said "is a conscientious student but daydreams a lot." An older kid named Ben—six one, bright red hair, well-built, aspiring US Marine—proudly recounted his own failed version of preggers geometry Sandra. There were other people in the world like me!

I felt empowered. By the art. By being around people who were as curious as I was, had varied interests like I did, and also found joy in the magic of telling meaningful stories. I wasn't as weird as I thought. At fifteen, I felt like I had found my people.

In fact, the only thing that seemed to be missing was a shared background. None of the Bens or Nathans were from immigrant communities. None of them grew up hearing "We don't do that. We're Indian." So, while I grew to feel grounded in who I could be as an artist, I also began to feel a strange distance from our own Indian American community because they seemed to take issue with who I am. It was a separation that wouldn't peak until college.

Toward the end of the Summer Arts Institute, Joe assigned me a scene from a play I can't remember the name of. All I can recall is that toward the end of the scene my character had to kiss a girl passionately, and I was completely terrified because a) I had never kissed anyone in real life and b) my scene partner was my timorous friend Jessica, who had kissed even fewer people than I had.

Joe had to have been aware of this awkward dynamic, which is presumably why he assigned the scene in the first place. Two of his favorite sayings were "You need to get outside your comfort zone!" and "Artists grow and succeed when we take risks!" No matter how I approached the beats of the scene, I couldn't crack how that kiss was supposed to go. I was too in my head about it. After about a week of excruciating rehearsal in which the class watches and critiques the dialogue and you don't actually kiss, Joe pulled Jessica aside for a private five-minute conversation. When they returned, we began the scene again. There was a strange fire in Jess's performance right out of the gate. Before I could get my first line out, she grabbed my face with both hands, pried my mouth open with her shockingly strong tongue, slithered it down my throat while filling my mouth with saliva, and banged her braces against my teeth. *Oh*, I thought to myself, *I guess I'm having my first kiss.*

After class, I described what the kiss felt like to Ben. I needed the expert counsel of an experienced friend who had witnessed it from the second row. "Oh man," he said, "that is NOT what it's supposed to feel like. She washed? Noooooo!" That phrase, *she washed*, was apparently in reference to her filling my mouth with saliva. He's the only one I've ever heard use that phrase, and it popped into my head every time I thought I might be about to kiss somebody for, like, the next ten years—which is pretty much how long it took me to kiss anybody again. Contrary to Joe's goal of teaching us that confidence comes from taking risks (a generally true and good lesson), his execution of that lesson had the opposite effect and scarred me for a long, long time. I'm not implying that this experience had serious consequences beyond kissing, but it's a good time to point out that my best-known on-screen love scene is with a gigantic anthropomorphic bag of weed, so there you go.

I came home from that summer program more interested in risk-taking, storytelling, and the arts, and much more confident in my own skin. I grew out my hair a bit, like Nathan. Tried to do some workouts Ben taught me (and failed miserably so I stopped that). I started dressing and acting cool: In the 1990s that meant I rocked jeans with holes in them, had a flannel tied around my waist, and said, "She's all that and a bag of chips" a lot.

I started to bank some quick teenage successes. By eleventh grade I had joined my high school's speech and debate team (Forensics) and consistently placed at the top of competitions, or meets, across the state. I auditioned for and got admitted to the Freehold Regional High School District's two-year public magnet program for the arts. After my standard morning academic courses, the Fine and Performing Arts Center (FPAC, for short) was where I'd spend the second half of the day, in intensive acting and theater study.[12] This was followed by the prestigious, publicly funded New Jersey Governor's School for the Arts, a crazy-selective summer program for incoming seniors that accepted the top five boys and top five girls in each arts discipline statewide. If you got in, you attended a free monthlong intensive residency where you took classes with top professionals in your specialization; in our case, we studied with instructors from David Mamet's highly esteemed Atlantic Theater Company. Governor's School felt like all-state for sports, except way more competitive and creative.

I was fortunate to live in a community where these rare public programs existed. Getting into them was a big stepping-stone, showing me that this wasn't just some random phase—my own state was saying I was actually good at acting. A hobby had become much more, and having these supportive signals of validation continued to offer me clarity: Turning my passion for the arts into a lifelong career was how I wanted to spend the rest of my life.

---

12 Modern, jazz, and tap dance classes instead of gym class. No more getting picked last!

CHAPTER THREE

YOU CAN'T HAVE YOUR CAKE
AND EAT IT TOO

My high school guidance counselor was named Mrs. Cummings, which I found as amusing then as I do now. As was customary for all students early senior year, Mrs. Cummings[1] called me down to her office to discuss my future. What were my goals? Where did I see myself in ten years? (Not kissing anyone yet, that's where!)

I had all the answers. I earnestly told her that I wanted to be an actor and filmmaker. I had also been so inspired by my grandparents—who basically instilled in us the idea of public service as a family value—that after my career got going, my goal was to add something civic-minded, like development studies or nonprofit work.

For the summer between the Summer Arts Institute and Governor's School, I had my eye on a few of the philanthropic international programs I saw advertised on the school library's bulletin board. I came home one evening and eagerly presented my dad with a color-

---

1 LOL

ful pamphlet about a "volunteer" opportunity that took high school students to Kenya for four weeks in July. He thumbed through it skeptically and laughed when he got to the last page: "Program Cost: $5,500."

"If you really want to volunteer in a developing country," Dad said, "I'll send you to India. Our friends Daxa Auntie and Anil Uncle run a small NGO in rural Gujarat called Action Research in Community Health and Development [ARCH]. You can stay with them there." I took him up on it. Each morning that summer I'd wake up early and shadow one of the various teams of ARCH specialists that could use an extra hand: doctors running an on-site medical clinic (which some patients traveled on foot for several days to access), environmental and social workers visiting tribal sites deep in the Dediapada rain forest, volunteers running sex education workshops on the street (bold for a conservative country).

I came back from India late that summer completely fluent in Gujarati—something I've managed to keep up, thanks to my parents and other relatives. I also returned with a basic understanding of 1) some important international development challenges, and 2) the reality that nobody wants to hook up with a sixteen-year-old American who came to rural Gujarat for a summer of volunteer work. (It was the exact opposite of the bucolic Maine sleepaway camps where my friends were getting repeatedly laid after Midnight Lip Sync Competition by the Lake Night.)

Mrs. Cummings knew about the summer volunteer work, and as I shared everything else that I wanted out of a future professional life, saying it out loud made my dreams feel more real than they had before. "So, that's what I want to do," I said eagerly. "Be an actor and filmmaker and do something in public service!" I was unprepared for her sudden, deep, from-the-belly laugh, just like Pussy Auntie's. "That's pretty much impossible," Mrs. Cummings said with a hint of condescension. "You know, Kalpen, you can't have your cake and eat it too."

She spent the next ten minutes bringing me back down to earth, telling me that my interests were too varied, my dreams too lofty and unrealistic. I was used to this scorched-earth tactic from the Indian community, having been recently asked at a family friend's house, "Are you not smart enough to get into medical school?" I just wasn't expecting similar discouragement from my guidance counselor too.

What a disappointment. Just like the elementary school teachers who couldn't tell me and Persian Araz apart, I mostly felt bad for Mrs. Cummings, thinking to myself, *Your grade-A, inspirational guidance counselor advice is "You can't have your cake and eat it too"? A cliché you probably read on a fortune cookie?*

"Something that might help get you on a more *realistic* path," she continued, "is a test we administer for students with varied interests." Okay, this was different from Pussy Auntie's "Be practical." I was listening. "It measures your interests and gives you a set of suggested careers to consider." This felt very promising: If an objective tool existed to figure out my future, that meant there was a way to know for sure whether something was going to work out, right? Maybe this test would give me special knowledge about how to blend my passion for acting with my interest in the social sciences, development studies, international affairs, and poli-sci. Maybe I'd never make it as an actor because my brain was actually wired for some other thing that I hadn't thought of yet.

Mrs. Cummings pulled a long multiple-choice test out of an envelope and handed it to me. I don't remember exactly what the questions were like, but I feel like they were more "Buzzfeed Quiz" than AP exam because I didn't stress over the choices. I quickly filled out the Scantron bubbles that would help me define my life, and returned to class, eagerly awaiting the results. Six weeks later, she called me back down to her office, and that's when my heart started beating fast. "Have a seat," she said. Opening this envelope felt like it took *forever*. I was sweating because I was excited about what it might potentially tell me about my future. What would be possible? What could I accomplish? I pulled out the results. On top, in bold letters, it read: **"Inconclusive. This student's interests are too varied for us to provide tangible recommendations."**

Mrs. Cummings laughed again, this time with genuine amusement. "I have never seen these results before," she said. "They *always* give you a specific set of answers." I broke the test. I was the anomaly, the oddball, the misfit. She sighed. "I guess no matter what you do, you'll be happy doing it."

Around the same time, the wonderful, caring director of my performing arts high school, Mr. Green, tried a different tactic based more on emotion than a test. "I'm going to flip a coin. Call heads or tails. Whatever it lands on, stick to that decision. If it's heads, you're going to drama school. If it's tails, you major in political science."

The coin landed on tails.

"You're doing political science. How does that make you feel?" he asked.

"I dunno, not great."

"You have to go with drama school then."

"Yeah, but I don't know about drama school either. I kinda want both."

Well-meaning tricks like the coin toss or a standardized interests test didn't work on me because I didn't see the world as binary.

Had I taken that test a few years prior, these results might have ruined me. *We're Indian. We don't do that.* Now, I knew who Mira Nair was. I had Nathans and Bens in my life. The confusing results were actually freeing. Maybe I could trust my instincts and become an actor. Or maybe I really *could* pursue a bunch of academic paths at once.

I kept my options open and applied to sixteen universities—some known broadly for liberal arts (with no clue what I'd specifically major in), and some for a BFA in theater, film, and television. Nothing with passion is ever as simple as heads or tails. Sometimes you're the guy who just wants a bunch of coins.

In addition to the standard university application, most theater programs require you to go through an audition and interview: pick two monologues, one classical, one contemporary (mine were from *Henry V* and *The Catcher in the Rye*), perform them, and then "discuss them with us while we ask why you want to major in theater, film, and television instead of becoming a doctor like everybody expected."

FPAC had a dedicated monologue study in the weeks leading up to college interviews. Since most of the class was applying to theater programs, the performance and critique sessions with our teacher allowed us to hone our skills when they mattered most. I was confident in my choices and had defended them in class several times.

The country's top theater programs hold satellite auditions for students who don't live close to the campus. This meant that my audition for the University of California, Los Angeles (UCLA) was held in New York City, not LA. As I did with my NYU audition a few weeks prior, I planned to take New Jersey Transit to Penn Station, then hop on the subway. Unfortunately, the night before, a massive blizzard plowed through the Northeast. Power lines were down. Ice was everywhere. Trains and buses into the city stopped working. I called a hotline that UCLA listed for inclement weather issues to find that since subway service within the five boroughs wasn't disrupted, the auditions were still being held. How was I going to get into New York City?

"Get dressed, I'll take you," my dad said. I was touched that he'd do this, in a blizzard, in treacherous conditions, just so I could audition for an acting program that he and Mom probably wished I wouldn't pursue in the first place. "I know how excited you are to audition for this school. Let's go, you'll be late."

On a good day, the drive into Manhattan takes forty-five minutes. That day, it took two hours. Plows were out in full force on the Garden State Parkway, but the snow was coming down so fast that an inch still blanketed the asphalt. We pulled up to the small black box theater in Greenwich Village five minutes before my audition slot. I jumped out and ran in while my dad went on a long search for parking.

I delivered my classical monologue first, then contemporary, in front of a well-dressed older man—round glasses, sweater, sports coat—sitting behind a folding table. I later learned he was popular UCLA theater professor Gary Gardner. "I've been doing this for twenty-two years and nobody has ever chosen a chapter from *The Catcher in the Rye* before," he grilled. "Why did you pick something from a *book* when the instructions clearly said to deliver a *monologue?*" I was momentarily intimidated, but it's not like I hadn't noticed the instructions when I chose it.

"Well," I began with an honest smile, "I love *The Catcher in the Rye*. Holden Caulfield is so different from who I am in real life, but when I read that book, I found that I could identify with him intimately. I probably won't ever get cast to play him—or to play any rich New England boarding school kid for that matter. But I assume there won't be a *Catcher in the Rye* movie anyway because Salinger has always refused to sell the rights. So, I figured this is the only time I would get to bring Holden Caulfield to life. And in the application, I noticed the instructions said the monologue just needed to be a contemporary piece, not that it *had* to be from a play or *couldn't* be from a novel. The whole book is written in first person. It's actually one amazing, gigantic monologue, and the beginning of chapter three seemed self-contained enough to make sense for me today."

Gary Gardner smiled.

I left.

My dad was in the waiting room when I got out of the interview, and we made the treacherous drive back home, where Mom was waiting with lunch.

I guess this is a good time to tell you about my spectacular rejection from Yale that winter, where I had applied early action. Mr. Green had encouraged me to apply early, as had my cousin Rita (then a second-year at Yale) and a couple of older friends and relatives sprinkled across different universities. They all thought I was the kind of well-rounded student Yale might be looking for. "Literally everyone here is great at multiple things," Rita said. "You'd fit right in. You can do both theater and international studies. It's not just about your SAT scores up here." The more I learned about Yale, the more sure I was that this was where I needed to be. I toured the beautiful campus (students seemed both motivated and social), completed the application (kind of fun because I like essays), went through an alumni review (stressful but quick), and then rushed to the mailbox every single day looking for the acceptance letter that my mom said she was certain I'd receive "because God told me in a dream."[2]

Instead, I got a tiny envelope rejecting me outright. I dramatically barked to my mom that she should ask God why he lied to her, went upstairs and shaved my head in the bathroom, while cursing Mrs. Teller for my own shortcomings in math and science. If that doesn't scream, "What a fucking crazy person! Obviously you need to become an actor," I don't know what does. Two weeks later, I had gotten used to my wonderful new crew cut and had refocused my attention on the fifteen remaining applications, which I had divided into broad categories.

As I awaited results from the other fifteen schools, I toured more campuses. They all had different things to offer—positives and negatives blended together: Earlham and Hampshire Colleges only have about two hundred and fifty students in each graduating class, which means lots of personalized attention, BUT Earlham is in a rural, isolated part of the country, and Hampshire seemed to have an insular student body. None of that exactly envisaged "boundless possibility." USC is in the middle of sunny Downtown Los Angeles and close to Hollywood, BUT since USC is in the middle of sunny Downtown Los Angeles . . . what if I get *murdered*?

The game changer came when I set foot on UCLA's campus and immediately fell in love. It all felt right—the picture-perfect East

2   She is *not* normally one of these people.

Coast look sandwiched into the west side of LA just a few miles from major film studios. It had the perfect balance of academia and the arts, and, for a theater and film student from out of state, was oddly far more competitive to get into than any of the Ivies.

I received rejection letters from two University of California campuses that should have been easier to get into, so I was bracing myself for a sound rejection from this one as well (and possibly another dramatic bathroom buzz cut?). When I called home from an after-school drama club meeting one afternoon to see if any letters arrived, my younger brother, Pulin, told me there was actually something there from UCLA. "Open it and read it to me!" I commanded. "Right now!" He got as far as "Congratulations! It is our pleasure to offer you admission to—" before I started yelling loudly down the main hallway of Freehold Township High School. I made my brother read that beautiful letter to me six more times before the pay phone cut us off.

By the very end of the college application process, my admission rate mirrored everything else until this point: Half the schools said yes, half said no, and one wait-listed me before rejecting me (such a Wesleyan thing to do, Wesleyan).[3]

I was determined to craft the life I wanted, and I knew UCLA would give me the space to find the perfect balance: arts and academia, proximity to the entertainment industry *and* a lower risk of getting murdered. Going to college so far from home was also a chance to move beyond the pressure of Pussy Auntie and her crew. The distance

---

3 In 2015, Wesleyan paid me a bunch of money to deliver a guest lecture on their campus, so we're cool with each other now.

wasn't something my parents had hoped for, but they recognized that the opportunity I had in moving all the way across the country to study in Los Angeles was in many ways not unlike the opportunity they themselves pursued in moving halfway around the world to start a life in America.

CHAPTER FOUR

WHY DO YOU DO THESE WEIRD THINGS?

The summer before I left for UCLA was an exciting time, and not just because I'd never have to take another boring class with Mrs. Teller. With the pressures of high school behind me (*yes, Pussy Auntie, I am going to be a theater major!*), I started planning for my life in Los Angeles. Film. Television. Hollywood! Opportunity! I would work my ass off to make it in the entertainment industry. Do whatever it took. I could apply all the skills I learned in those public arts programs to earn real roles in Hollywood. Maybe I'd even rub elbows with some of my favorite characters and actors. Did Will Smith really live in Bel-Air? Would I run into Steve Urkel at the grocery store? Would D. J. Tanner and Kimmy Gibbler be at the laundromat? (Did they even hang even out in real life? Did celebrities actually do their own laundry?!)

Before getting on the plane, I needed a summer job to save up for practical acting-related things like headshots, a gym membership, and (long-term goal) a car so I could get to auditions across sprawling LA.

I grabbed the local *Asbury Park Press* newspaper and circled jobs that seemed appealing: farmhand, water boy at a restaurant, a roofer—lots of good options. One job in the paper stood out: "Enjoy talking to people? Get paid to do it as a telemarketer!" I seemed eminently qualified for this: I *do* enjoy talking to people. I *did* want to get paid to do it!

Plus, wasn't this basically acting? I could pretend to be whoever I wanted on the phone, and the person on the other end of the line would have no idea that I wasn't *really* a pregnant lady named Sandra (pi r squared) selling stuff in my downtime. I also did have some prior experience.

As a weird child, I used to look forward to telemarketers disturbing our family dinners. It exhilarated me. The phone would ring while Grandpa was in the middle of *another* story about Gandhi (zzzzz[1]), and I'd race over to answer as my parents would yell out, "It's a marketing call, don't pick up!"

I'd always pick up. "Hello, is Mrs. Modi there, please?" a telemarketer would say. I'd pause briefly to put on my best high-pitched little-kid voice and say, "Mommy is sleeping . . . She hurt her head . . . There's a fire." They usually hung up right away.

Sometimes the telemarketer would have a particularly long-winded introduction before asking, ". . . So may I speak with Mr. Modi, please?" That gave me a chance to sigh loudly before gravely mumbling, "I wish you could speak with Mr. Modi. We all wish we could. He passed away yesterday."

"Why do you do these weird things?" my mom would ask.

The answer was the same compulsion as fourth-grade me making up stories during show-and-tell: entertaining (myself and) others,

---

1   Just kidding, jeez.

improvisation, making people laugh. I got all that just from answering telemarketers' calls, so why not become one?

I went in for an interview at the company's office in a gorgeous New Jersey strip mall, nestled between a pizza place and a pharmacy. Nine other prospective employees were also there.

The guy in charge of hiring looked like Big Bird from *Sesame Street*, but if Sesame Street was in a tough neighborhood. (Also, Big Bird doesn't undress you with his eyes.)

The group interview questions were a mere formality. "Raise ya hand if youz ever used a computer. Uh-rite. Raise ya hand if youz are familiar with the telephone. Uh-rite." Skeezy Big Bird hired us all on the spot.

On my first day I found out I'd be calling people on behalf of some sort of policemen's organization to ask for donations. This threw a significant wrench in my plan to play different characters on the calls. It would be one thing to create a fake persona if we were selling a timeshare or magazine subscriptions, but a policemen's association? That sounded serious. I didn't want to act my way into an "impersonating an officer" charge.

I'd have to test the waters slowly and be myself to start. The giant room was filled with rows of white plastic folding tables—two computer stations and headsets atop each. I was shown to my vacant seat and introduced myself to a portly guy named Peter, who sat on my left. My new desk buddy had a large hearing aid on his left ear that the headset went over. An auto-dialer did the work. All we had in front of us was the person's name and our script.

Every call followed an eerily familiar pattern. *Ring ring*. Long pause.

". . . . . Hell . . . -low?"

A two-hundred-year-old lady would answer.

"Hi! Is this Mildred?"

Mildred's voice perked up. She shouted loudly into the receiver.

"YES! HELLO? WHO'S THIS?!"

"Hi Mildred, my name is Kalpen. I'm calling on behalf of the Super-Helpful Policemen's Organization. How are you doing this evening?"

"YES! HELLO! SO NICE TO HEAR FROM YOU!"

If you recall from my Grandpa and Bubbe stories: I love old people. They've experienced things. They're chock-full of wisdom that too many of us take for granted. Lots of old people live by themselves. Sometimes one old person takes care of another old person. Their kids and grandkids don't call as much as they wish they would. Their old friends are no longer around, and they lose new friends every year because they're so old. Sometimes they're lonely.

Skeezy Big Bird knew that lonely old people wouldn't mind talking to an eighteen-year-old telemarketer calling on behalf of the Super-Helpful Policemen's Organization. My job, he explained, was to follow the script and keep Mildred on the line, chatting with her about all the super-helpful work the Super-Helpful Policemen's Organization supposedly did.

"How do you feel about the police in your neighborhood, Mildred?"

"I love the police. We should do more to support them so that we don't all wind up raped and murdered."

"Actually, Mildred, I'm so glad to hear you say that because you *can* do more to support them! I'm calling today to ask for your help in donating one hundred dollars toward the Super-Helpful Policemen's Organization Fund."

"Oh, I feel so bad. You see, I'm on a fixed income. I wish I could give one hundred dollars. I just don't have that kind of money."

Mildred didn't call me an asshole for asking for money. She didn't pretend she was a child stuck in a fire. The truly sad part was that even after explaining she couldn't give me the cash, Mildred didn't hang up. She was lonely. Why disconnect if there was someone willing to talk to her?

Skeezy Big Bird told us what to say when the person lingered. "Well, we understand you don't have one hundred dollars. The police keep us so safe . . . Maybe a fifty-dollar donation would be easier for you?"

"Oh, I really wish I could," Mildred would reply. "It's just that my Social Security check doesn't last all month. Since my husband passed away, it's been hard."

This was so awful—and it was happening hundreds of times a day in this hollow room full of cheap plastic folding tables in a Garden State strip mall. Rows of telemarketers soliciting money from a bunch of Mildreds who couldn't afford it. Each call would continue until someone *eventually* hung up or we succeeded in getting the Mildred to give *any* amount of money, usually five dollars. For someone on a fixed income, five dollars can be the price of a couple of meals.

This acting gig was starting to suck and it had barely been forty-five minutes. I didn't want to ask people for money, so I'd try to get off the phone as quickly as possible if the Mildred didn't enthusiastically offer up a $100 donation right away. I wasn't going to be a particularly good telemarketer, but I didn't want to be a terrible human.

Sixty minutes into the first shift, a break-time bell rang and a small guy in an oversized suit emerged from a back office. This was Skeezy Big Bird's boss. He was like a sad version of Joe Pesci from *My Cousin Vinny*. With considerable effort, Sad Joe Pesci hoisted himself up on one of the folding desks and in a thunderous voice launched into a motivational speech like they do in those Wall Street movies. "Every-bahdy! Pause ya' comp-yootahz and listen up!"

Portly Pete removed his headset, adjusted his hearing aid, and angrily whispered to me, "What did he say? I can't hear *shit!*"

"Pause your computer and listen up," I translated, fascinated that he could perfectly hear the meek Mildreds but not our boss's booming voice.

"A! First of all, Jackie ova here," Sad Joe Pesci began. "Jackie brought in tree-hundred fitty-five dollaz. Way to go Jackie! A! Anybody do better than her? Let's take a closa look." He glanced down at a hastily printed sheet of paper that Skeezy Big Bird handed him. "A! Phil brought in a clean two hundred. Good job! Who else we got?" He glanced again. "A! We got Joey with one-ninety-five. Not bayd not bayd!"

He'd go through the top five earners. Skeezy Big Bird would toss little pieces of candy out to them. Portly Pete, who felt snubbed, mumbled "Bullshit" as he fixed his hearing aid and put his headset back on. This didn't *feel* like a nonprofit in support of public safety. Just an hour in, I was feeling like maybe this thing was a giant racket.

All afternoon we called Mildreds. The bell rang again an hour later, and again Sad Joe Pesci got on the desk to announce the top five earners. Skeezy Big Bird threw the individually wrapped pieces of candy. Portly Pete grumbled.

There was another part of it that made me queasy. It didn't take much reflection—even from a recent high school graduate—to recognize that this was a rough place for adults to end up for a job. I was trying to make some money before college, but what about the other people in the room, like Pete? A lot of them were parents, with health issues and grown-up responsibilities like a mortgage. They seemed vulnerable too. And they were willing to suffer through the indignity of having candy tossed at them like children if it meant they could bring a few bucks home.

That night, the situation weighed so heavy in my stomach that I decided I'd quit the following morning. I would barge in there and tell Sad Joe Pesci right to his face that it was wrong to take advantage of people's grandmas. "What if someone did this to *your* grandma?!" I'd say. He'd be stunned. "I never thought of it like that," he'd say. "Thank you for opening my eyes. From now on, I'm going to be *Responsible Joe Pesci*." Then I'd make my exit to a standing ovation. Slow claps. Glory.

I drove my dad's Chevy Nova to the strip mall fifteen minutes before the start of the shift. I walked through the door with confidence. Skeezy Big Bird was standing at the front of a group of six people—all of whom had gotten there early too.

He calmly blinked at us a couple of times the way the real Big Bird blinks on regular *Sesame Street*, which was a little creepy. Before I could get a word out, he announced, "Raise ya hand if ya quittin' and ya here for ya check." We all raised our hands. Did this many people quit before the start of every shift? "The job's not fuh everybody," he said.

Sad Joe Pesci came out from his back office to distribute employment termination forms to the group. This was apparently the pre-shift ritual, taking care of everyone who quit from the day before. With an unexpected audience present, it seemed like the wrong time for my morality speech. *Sorry Sad Joe Pesci, you'll have to stay sad a little longer.* I signed on the dotted line, ending my illustrious telemarketing career less than twenty-four hours after it started. "We'll mail the payment to ya," Sad Joe Pesci said. "Take kay-uh."

I still felt skeeved by the whole situation, so I did the only thing I could think of: I reported them to the Better Business Bureau.[2] When my measly fifteen-dollar check arrived, I donated it to a local food bank. I wanted to wash my hands of everything, without profiting from any part of it.

When we think of amoral money-grubbers, we tend to imagine people who run shady corporations, corrupt politicians who give their children White House security clearances, or vile stockbrokers who defraud investors. But *they* are *us*. To some degree, we're enablers every time we buy products from companies and countries with a less-than-stellar human-rights reputation. We often point fingers at others while we ourselves contribute to a system that makes life tougher for someone else. This was the first time I realized that. That kind of amorality isn't just at the very top of the food chain— it's in the middle and at the bottom too, in a janky New Jersey strip mall, where Sad Joe Pesci is just trying to scam enough grannies to pay his child support. The telemarketing firm apparently did have a legit third-party contract with some type of law enforcement organization, and I'm still not sure if they were aware of the way money was raised. It didn't matter. I learned that a lot of people are motivated not by a sense of purpose, or love for their fellow humans, but by an ambition to grab dollars by any means—to scam better, harder, faster.

As for me that summer, I went back to the classifieds. That farmhand job was still open, so I took it. Working twelve hours a day in the hot sun felt like honest work. I loved being outside, and I saved up enough money to get those headshots. I didn't even need a gym that

---

2   I told you, I am a huge nerd.

year! Turns out loading boxes of vegetables into tractors all season long will turn you into a pretty ripped twink.

It was a weird detour to end my time in New Jersey, and a good lesson in getting clear about what my priorities were. A car was still far off, but I'd be heading to LA with a little extra cash and my integrity intact. For now.

CHAPTER FIVE

THE PANOCH

Flying to Los Angeles for college felt like moving to a different country. From the laid-back people to the crawling traffic, it was nothing like the aggressive New Jersey culture I had grown up in. My suburban hometown was always on the go. We filled each hour of the day with a task, a hobby, sucking the marrow out of life—or at least sucking the ricotta out of the cannoli—twenty-four seven. After my summer of Adonis-transforming farmhand work, I was ready to take this attitude with me to LA, ready to achieve my dreams.

My parents dropped me off at Newark Airport for my Continental Airlines flight to LA. I had checked a large green military-looking duffel bag with just the basics: clothes, sneakers, toothpaste, and a towel. My mom's close friend Hansa Auntie, who lived about an hour south of LA, would drive up the next day to help me sort out the shower supplies and bedding.

On my first day at UCLA I met Todd, my freshman orientation roommate. A super-relaxed blond dude from Orange County, Todd dressed and sounded like a movie version of a surfer, even though he had never actually surfed. He endeared himself to me quickly, because every time he spoke, his statements came out like questions: "Hi dude? It's nice to, like, meet you? My name's, uhhh, Todd?" Perpetually on-the-go New Jerseyans are a highly declarative people who speak very clearly, and with our hands, so this statements-as-questions thing was new to me. (You won't hear anyone from New Jersey say, "Go, like, uhh, fuck yourself?")

Like was a no-no in my world to begin with. Back at FPAC, my affable and demanding acting teacher, Mr. Kazakoff, had a laser focus on language. Kaz hated the word *like*. "If you can't introduce yourself to a director without using the word *like*," he'd explain, "if you can't have a conversation about the beats of a scene without using the word *like*, if you can't get through a *sentence in the English language* without using the word *like*, people will think you are stupid and they'll cast someone else. Your ability to communicate is *key*."

Using the L-word had serious consequences. The first time you said *like* in his classroom, Kaz would put your name on the board. Each time after that, he added a line next to it, the way cartoon inmates do on prison walls, or college students tracking the number of drinks they've had on their arms. From any other teacher, this might have been a pointless hassle. But Kaz was revered. With acid-washed jeans, ponytail, and wire-rimmed glasses, he cut a singular figure. Truly cool, respected teachers are rare, so a public shaming by one of the best is both highly amusing and very effective. Kaz taught us that you are what you say. Filler words weaken your speech. Flabby use of language could make a budding actor less competitive in the creative marketplace. By the end of the year, almost no one in the class said *like*.

On the West Coast, clear speech and fiery East Coast motivation were my secret weapons. Todd was far from the only person in California who talked like he just woke up from a nap. I'd show up to student-film audition waiting rooms full of preposterously attractive, chiseled dudes—and the "like" ratio was off the charts. Pretty soon casting directors were regularly complimenting me for being "articulate." Sure, some of them meant it in the casually racist way, like, "Where did you learn to speak such proper English, brown person?" But many of them also meant it in the actual way! Overusing *like* as a slang interjection doesn't mean you're stupid, but it does, like, make you seem a little flaky? In a city of Todds, I stood out.

Even with my no-"like" secret weapon and East Coast hustle, as I threw myself into the process of trying to become a professional actor, I knew that breaking into Hollywood was going to be a long, hard struggle. It is for almost everybody. My parents regularly called and encouraged me to have a fallback plan. I regularly responded by telling them with confidence that those who have fallback plans end up falling back on them, so instead, every Wednesday morning, I would walk from my dorm down to the newsstand on Gayley Avenue in Westwood to buy the *Back Stage West* trade paper and scan casting listings, circling any of the projects that I convinced myself I was *remotely* qualified for. I'd scribble notes in the margins that I'd turn into personalized cover letters, which included my brand-new pager number. (I learned early on that I couldn't trust Todd to accurately write down messages.)

I went through the same process with lists of prospective agents who were looking for new clients. Hours of my precious time and farmhand money were spent physically printing, cutting, and stapling headshots and résumés in my dorm room before walking the envelopes down to the post office and mailing them to casting directors for those unpaid jobs, and to agents for potential representation. If I had a little extra money that week and wanted to splurge, I'd take the stack of headshots down to Kinko's, where I'd pay to have the résumés printed. (This allowed me to use their industrial-size paper cutter, which saved hours compared to cutting each eight-and-a-half-by-eleven résumé by hand, getting it to fit the dimensions of the eight-by-ten headshot.)

Like thousands of actors, I went through this *Back Stage West* ritual every Wednesday in the hopes of even one audition, one phone call. I was hungry for experience! Anything that would allow me to build up credits on my résumé and work my way up the ladder to better, professional roles.

The problem was: I didn't have that car yet. Taking the bus to auditions took several hours in each direction, and my frustration mounted. In LA, traffic affects EVERYTHING. It may seem like a minor thing to readers unaccustomed to LA traffic and car problems, and how much all people who live in LA talk about traffic and car problems like I'm doing right now, but it's actually a really big deal. It's like a member of your family you can't stand but can't stop talking about. Like my cousin Raghav who caught gonorrhea during the pandemic.[1]

---

1   Okay, here's the deal. I love Raghav very much. We're super close. When he was in college, we started this dumb brotherly contest where one of us would try to throw water on the other's face at random times. There were a few botched attempts (like when I visited his apartment one morning and threw a full glass of water in his face only to quickly learn—amid screams of agony about his eyes—that it was a glass of gin his roommate left on the counter). Anyway, things escalated quickly after that. I used Facebook to convince Raghav's then-girlfriend to throw water on him in the dining hall and say it was from me. (Not the reason they broke up, shockingly.) From the safety of his dorm room in Ohio, he convinced his mom, my aunt, to throw a tiny and respectful bit of water on my face during—ready?—his *grandfather's funeral* in India, which I attended. That pretty much ended the contest. You can't top your grandpa's funeral. So, I had to do the only thing I could think of: write a book and tell everyone that Raghav caught gonorrhea during the pandemic. That's a total lie. He has never had gonorrhea. As far as I know. But most people don't read footnotes.

*   *   *

Halfway through freshman year, I had settled nicely into Rieber Hall room 507 and was regularly spending time with some of the guys in my dorm. We initially met when one of them knocked on my door somewhat at random. "I'm DLC," said a fun-loving bespectacled dude with tattoos and a wide grin. "This is my roommate Dennis. We call him Dennis Pennis. We're in the room above you. 607. You wanna get some food?"

"Sure," I said, appreciating the play on Dennis's name for the same reason I enjoyed having a guidance counselor called Mrs. Cummings.

"Tite," DLC continued. "I knocked on 707 first and they shut the door in my face."

"Isn't the seventh floor the quiet floor?" I asked.

"Yeah, but you ain't gotta be *shitty* about it."

After months of applying for internships and being rejected, I landed one! It was a coveted gig at *Star Wars* creator George Lucas's company Lucasfilm. Or rather, at the Lucasfilm satellite office in Burbank, about seventeen miles from campus. (The Lucasfilm headquarters is in Northern California.) The entire interview process was done over the phone, so I didn't realize that the bus trip from UCLA to Burbank—including traffic and transfers—would take about three hours each way.

I was a full-time student, with classes every day of the week. It didn't matter that I had a kick-ass internship for the people who created *The Empire Strikes Back*, there just wasn't enough time in the day to spend six hours commuting on top of school, so I had to quit on day two. I was disappointed that I had to walk away, but I was way more frustrated that I had moved to a city with such terrible mass transit. As I got madder and madder about the need for a car in a place that called itself a "city," I asked myself a critical question: Even if I could get my hands on a vehicle, where would I park it? I decided this was actually something I could have control over and should sort out as quickly as possible.

At UCLA there were way more students with cars than parking spaces on campus. You had to enter a highly competitive parking lottery to vie for a spot. If you were one of the few lucky winners, congratulations! What you won was the right to pay a few hundred bucks every eleven weeks for a permit to park in a lot. Everyone else had to fend for themselves, searching endlessly around Westwood, squinting at street signs.

Motivated by having to quit my Lucasfilm internship, I entered this parking lottery. You might be saying to yourself, *But Kal, you didn't have a car yet.* Correct. I *didn't* have a car. It was kind of like applying for a job that requires skills you don't have—you'll just learn them once you get the offer, right? Plus, I used my math brain to figure out that since the probability of winning the parking lottery was so low, if I entered it every quarter, my chances of getting a permit would increase exponentially as the years went on, so that by the time I could finally afford a car (which would likely happen in my third year of college), *probability* would dictate that I'd win the parking lottery and get a permit. Genius! Unfortunately, this is not at all how probability works, and I won the parking lottery on my first try.[2]

When word spread among the homies in the freshman dorm that

---

2   Good time to brag that I failed probability and statistics twice in college. I told you I was bad at math. Take that, stereotypes!

I had scored a permit but didn't have a car, Dennis Pennis knocked on my door with an offer.

DENNIS PENNIS: You want to share the Panoch?[3]

ME: What's the Panoch, Dennis Pennis?

DENNIS PENNIS: You've never seen the Panoch?

ME: I don't think so, what is it?

DENNIS PENNIS: The Panoch is the name of my car, man. I don't have a parking permit, so I always gotta look on the street. What if we join forces and share? You pay for the permit and your share of gas. I pay for insurance and my share of gas. You can drive the Panoch anytime I'm not using it.

ME: YES.

I *was* a genius!

As soon as our friends learned that Dennis Pennis and I struck a deal, they started rooting for us in a way that made me suspicious. "Maaaaan," said DLC, "your guys' deal sounds *super* tite. You think you've got what it takes to drive the Panoch?"

What exactly did it take? "Is it stick? I actually can't drive stick."

"Nah," DLC continued. "It ain't stick. It's the Panoch. The Panoch is super tite."

My college buddies—especially DLC—had an understated, shorthand way of speaking when something was up. I once stumbled upon a pair of handcuffs with the key inside (as one does), so I handcuffed DLC and our buddy Zach together as a prank and walked away. I intended for this to only last a few minutes, but I'm so easily dis-

---

3 Pronounced *pun-OH'ch*

tracted, I forgot that I had handcuffed them until about four hours later. "Oh, it's *all good*, man. You tite," DLC said upon my return as I sheepishly unlocked the handcuffs. Except it wasn't "all good"—the guys quickly jumped on me and carried me to a stairwell railing to which I was then handcuffed and left alone for four hours. (I clearly deserved it.)

Another time, I called DLC in a panic after playing Edward Forty-hands (a drinking game named for the movie *Edward Scissorhands*, in which players duct-tape forty-ounce bottles of malt liquor to each of their palms). It should probably be called Edward Eightyhands, since that's how much you're actually drinking, but in my case it was only Edward Twentyhands because I finished just half a bottle before real-izing something was wrong. I was perspiring. My heart was racing. The room spun and my mouth was dry. I ran home as fast as I could and picked up the phone for help because I was freaking out and this could only mean one thing.

"DLC," I said, "somebody put cocaine in my forty."

"What are you talking about? You're just drunk."

"No way man, I've been drunk before. It's never felt like this. Plus, I only had like half a bottle."

"Yeah, half a bottle of malt liquor. It can make you feel like that if you've never had it before."

"Are you *sure*? I've never had cocaine either, but this is what arti-cles have described it feels like."

He put me on speakerphone.

"Cocaine is *really* expensive, Kalpen Modi. Nobody put it in your forty, I promise. Go to sleep. You *tite*."

So, in hearing "the Panoch is super tite," I knew DLC meant either:

1) Dennis Pennis had been hiding something dramatically wrong about the Panoch or

2) Dennis Pennis had been hiding something amazing about the Panoch or

3) Both

It was both. The Panoch turned out to be a mud-brown-colored 1981 Datsun hatchback. When he took me to see it for the first time, Dennis Pennis opened the driver's-side door, which creaked like an elephant had stepped off a tall pile of rusted mattresses. He got inside, reached across, and manually unlocked and opened the passenger door. Was I about to share a car that had no power locks and a broken door handle?

"Welcome to the Panoch!"

The busted handle wasn't the only thing that made the Panoch "super tite." In addition to having no power locks, the Panoch had no air-conditioning, no power windows, no FM radio, no cassette player, and, obviously, no CD player. The only available music was on a few Spanish-language AM stations. I took French in high school.

"Titest" of all, the Panoch had *no power steering*. At low speeds—say, anything under fifteen miles an hour—changing lanes without power steering is the same as a high-intensity interval workout. You really have to use your body weight to pull the wheel in one direction to get it to move, then lean and push it back in the other direction to get it to stay. Because this was Los Angeles, you rarely achieved speeds above seventeen miles per hour. Every time I drove the Panoch, my arms and core got a little more ripped. Especially while parallel parking.

This had its challenges when it came to those *Back Stage West* auditions. Many people have a gym bag. I had a Panoch bag—with a towel, some water, deodorant, and an entire extra set of clothes (the first was to drive and sweat in, the second to change into just before a casting session). But I had access to a CAR! Subject to the continued durability of the Panoch—and the strength left in my arms—the opportunities for internships and auditions were suddenly limitless. Yes, the Panoch was, like, *super tite*.[4]

UCLA is a big school. It wasn't uncommon to be in a lecture hall with four hundred and ninety-nine other strangers. The University of California system is designed primarily for students from the state; very few nonresidents are admitted. This means that the School of Theater, Film and Television has an acceptance rate of about 3 or 4 percent. Nobody from my high school had ever gone to UCLA. In fact, the only other kid from my high school who went to California that year was our valedictorian, Nancy Adelman, up at Stanford. So, you can imagine my surprise when I was walking out of an American history class one day and saw a guy I recognized from home!

He already had an unmistakably LA vibe, and it impressed me that he learned it so quickly. He was about my height, close-cropped hair, *very* cool shoes. I felt like his name was Sean? No, Steven, yes, definitely Steven something, I just couldn't place him exactly. I thought he could have maybe been a year or two ahead of me in high school, and somehow I didn't know he had transferred to UCLA. Or did I know him from the farmhand job the previous summer? I followed him for a few

---

4 It wasn't until writing this book that I called DLC to ask, "Hey, what does 'the panoch' mean?" He laughed and explained, "It's short for *panocha* . . . 'pussy' in Spanish." Jeez. Would have been reeeeeealllly good to know that back in the day, when I'd offer people "a ride in my super-tite Panoch."

minutes, racking my brain. The more I walked, the more I noticed that Steven seemed to have a *lot* of friends. Definitely a big man on campus. With each intersection we crossed, more and more people would nod approvingly. I needed to just go say hello. Surely between the two of us, we'd remember exactly how we knew each other. I picked up the pace to catch up to him, trying hard to recall Steven's last name. I felt like it started with a U. *Umbila? Urwell? Urkel!*

"Steve Urkel!" I blurted out, before freezing and realizing what I had done. Holy shit, it's Jaleel White, the actor who played Steve Urkel on *Family Matters*. Dude is in my history class?! I ran around a corner to disappear. Hopefully he didn't hear it. Not because I was embarrassed,[5] but because I didn't want to be seen as the guy who Steve Urkel thought was uncool.[6]

Seeing someone like Jaleel White around campus was a good motivator for an aspiring actor like me. In moving to LA, I had hoped to rub elbows with the casts of my favorite shows at the grocery store or something. I hadn't really imagined that we'd actually be going to university together.

I only saw Jaleel on campus a few times after that. We never formally met, but my first actor sighting was an exciting highlight.

I assumed that being so far away from the likes of Panocha Auntie's reach would mean I was saved from the constant pressure of "Beta, be a doctor." Then I met Gita, Ravi, and the kids in the Indian Student Union.

I first noticed the Indian Student Union table on a walk through

---

5   I was deeply embarrassed.
6   Also a real consideration in the moment.

campus. "Hi Kalpen," the woman behind the table said as she watched me sign up for their email list. "Where are you from and what are you majoring in?" I made small talk about moving from New Jersey and majoring in theater. She laughed. "No seriously, what are you majoring in?"

It was unique for a brown kid to major in the arts—after all, I was the only Indian kid in the entire theater department—so I didn't take her laughter too pointedly. "Seriously, I'm really excited about it. I'm in the School of Theater, Film and Television!" With an evaporating smile reminiscent of an auntie who finds out you "only got an A minus in algebra," she ignored me with dead eyes, quickly shifting focus to the person behind me. "Hi! Where are you from and what's your major?" I never got added to their email list.

Gita and Ravi were part of the Indian Student Union crew. They lived on my floor in the dorm, which made them impossible to avoid entirely. They would often go out of their way to poke their noses in my business[7] by posing weird questions and then telling me how awful it was that I wasn't majoring in a science like all the other brown kids. "Aren't your parents disappointed in you?" Gita would say. "You're kind of a sellout."

What kind of selective cultural nonsense was this? I understood our parents' struggles, their immigration experience; the ways in which it was impossible for their generation to divorce culture from profession. What the heck did being Indian have to do with being a science major now? And why were they so obsessed with the fact that I wasn't one?

For every sacrifice or personal victory that first year, it seemed like Gita, Ravi, and their friends in the Indian Student Union were

---

7   Remember, Indians love spicy gossip about other Indians.

eagerly waiting to throw shade. On my way back from mailing head-shots at the post office one Wednesday, I ran into them in the elevator. Ravi eyed my backpack as we made small talk about where we were headed the rest of the day. "Library," I said. "Gonna grab my books and study for a bit. I can't really concentrate in my room."

"Why are you even studying?" Gita chimed in. "You don't take real classes. Aren't you just, like, *a theater major?*" *Ding.* The elevator doors opened before I could invite them to kiss—as Jay-Z says—my whole asshole.

The contrasts between my passion for the arts and the crappy brown students on campus continued to build. I saw a flyer one afternoon in the theater building and my heart stopped: Mira Nair, the woman who directed *Mississippi Masala*—the film that showed me brown people could be in movies—was set to speak on campus. For two weeks I planned how I might meet her. Do I find her hotel and leave a note? (Too creepy.) Follow her out of the venue after her speech? (Too sycophantic.) The move I decided on was to queue up *hours* before the event. That way I could get a seat toward the front and reach out before she walked off stage. I just needed to introduce myself, hand her my headshot, and tell her she's one of the reasons I'm studying acting.

As I was waiting in line on the north end of campus the day of Mira Nair's speech, a group of Gita and Ravi's friends walked by. *Cool,* I thought, *they're also standing in line early. Maybe this'll be my college version of the Tin Man thing and they'll understand that theater is a great major too!* But they weren't waiting for the event, they were just passing by. As they kept walking, one of them muttered, "There's that weird Indian kid from New Jersey," loudly enough for me to hear. "He's the one majoring in theater. Such a sellout."

As a working actor today, it feels silly to think that I let these people get to me. But that night, I sat by myself in the second row at the event. I hung on to every word Mira Nair said, took notes, raised my hand (but didn't get called on). The crowd was made up of mostly older, white film buffs, a handful of brown science graduate students mixed in. After the event, Mira walked through the audience to get to the outside door, and I pushed my way to the front. "Ms. Nair, I'm a theater student here. My name is Kalpen Modi. I really admire your work and I wanted to give you my headshot and résumé," is all I could quickly spit out in the rush of people swarming her. "Thank you," she said, taking my envelope before disappearing into the crowd of paler well-wishing faces.

I was honored to meet the woman who had inspired me, but I felt sort of lonely to experience it by myself.

For the next three years, thanks to my Panoch access, I racked up as many unpaid credits on my résumé as I could afford, with small roles in student films and microbudget independent projects. I became a Resident Advisor (RA) in the UCLA dorms for a while, which covered my housing and meals. I got paid $5 an hour as an extra on TV shows and movies when I wasn't in class, mostly so I could observe how big-budget productions work (and so I could continue to fund the parking permit and gas). I also set aside enough money to get my first cell phone. I bought it at McDonald's.

Look, there was nothing wrong with my pager—it worked fine, and it's not like I was getting so many pages about auditions that I was pulling off the freeway to urgently find a pay phone that often. So, when DLC knocked on my dorm door holding a thin, greasy piece of tray-liner paper with a photo of a blue plastic Nokia flip phone on it, it took me a second to follow along. McDonald's was running some sort of promotion. If you signed up for service through them, the phone was pretty much free. "Is it a toy phone, or real?"

"Real," said DLC. "Looks like it could be a toy though. It's pretty tite."

The catch when it came to the free McDonald's phone was that each minute cost a pricey fifty cents. I put the phone number on the top of my résumé so I would never miss the rare audition call. Everyone else could call my landline.

No matter what I did, I still couldn't land an agent, which meant I had no professional credits on my résumé at all. Dennis Pennis and most of the other guys I hung out with were science majors, following a well-marked path. Many of them were headed to graduate school and knew exactly what the next seven years of their lives had in store. For me, it was hard to figure out what the right catalyst would be. How could I get more auditions? Lots of the other drama students at UCLA had already secured agents—it seemed they were noticed because of the prestige of our program. I too was in this program—what was the best way to get an agent to notice *me*?

I had become friends with actor Jenna von Oÿ (who had recently wrapped the popular sitcom *Blossom*) through her roommate Jason, one of my UCLA theater department buddies. Jenna was super supportive of my passion and struggle, impressed by the hustle of the parking permit fiasco, and always eager to offer guidance and help. She offered to show her manager—who worked at a well-respected A-list company—some of the scenes I had shot in those student films. Maybe he'd agree to audition me and take me on.

When she got the rejection on my behalf, Jenna was both savvy enough to ask her manager why he didn't want to meet, and thoughtful enough to ask me if I wanted to hear the truth. Of course I did. Whatever it was that her manager didn't like, I wanted to know. Whatever it was I did wrong in those student film clips, I would immediately work to change so that I could earn an agent or manager just like so many of my classmates already had.

"First of all," Jenna said, "he told me that he watched your tape and thinks you're a really good actor. He's always brutally honest. He wouldn't have said that if he didn't mean it completely."

"Well, that's good!"

"He also said," she continued, with considerable hesitation, "that somebody who looks like you is never going to work in Hollywood. There just aren't enough roles written for Indian actors. He felt like you might play a cabdriver once or twice, but it wouldn't be worth his time and effort to represent someone who isn't going to work regularly."

Wow. I was very surprised that this manager was comfortable enough to straight-up acknowledge this intersection of business and bigotry. He could have made up any excuse he wanted about why he didn't want to meet with me ("He's too tall!" "He's too short!" "He's a bad actor!"), but he didn't. In a weird way, racism-truth felt so much better than being lied to. I was thankful for Jenna's true friendship and the accompanying willingness to tell me something so uncomfortable. Hearing it was both a slap in the face and a very welcome assessment of where I stood.

The quality of my performance in those student film clips wasn't the underlying issue.

A few months later, I had saved up enough money to get a new set of headshots. "The photographer is supposed to be really good," I remember telling the homies during one of our late-night food runs at Fatburger in Westwood. "I hope this time it'll lead to getting an agent."

My friend Marc Milstein spoke up: "You know what else might lead to an agent? A stage name. Did you know that Whoopi Gold-berg's real name is Caryn Johnson? Imagine if she went by that? No way would she be as memorable."

The idea of altering my name was something I had casually thought about since Jenna's manager said an Indian guy would never find steady work in Hollywood, but it's not something I seriously discussed with anyone.

"Chevy Chase's real name is Cornelius, man. Cornelius Chase. How tite is that?" said DLC. "You should come up with a stage name. I bet it would help."

My real name is Kalpen Modi. Kalpen is what most of my friends and family call me. In high school, kids sometimes shortened Kalpen to Kal as a nickname, the same way that Joseph becomes Joe, Rodrigo becomes Rod, and Pushpa becomes Pussy.

Between bites of warm fat fries, the wheels started turning. If coming up with a stage name helped those actors establish them-selves, it was a no-brainer—I would do it too.

So, what should my catchy stage name be? Should it be similar to Kalpen or totally different? Would a whiter-sounding name have persuaded Jenna's manager to meet with me? (Should I go by *Chad*?) Anyway, what's in a name? Wouldn't a brown person by any other name still play a stereotypical cabdriver and be called a sellout by his peers? Maybe not! Maybe coming up with a name that sounded a bit more like the names that casting directors were used to seeing *would* make me a little more viable in their eyes. This was a serious consid-eration. My friends' suggestions? Not so serious.

"What about Kal . . . Pacino?"

"How's Kal Ripken Junior *Junior*?"

The puns went on and on. That gave me an idea. "I could just split my first name in half and add an extra *n*."[8] My nickname is already Kal, and "Kal Penn" seems less dramatic than Cornelius becoming Chevy. The suggestion was met with resounding approval. It was now two forty in the morning, but our homework procrastination over munchies had yielded magnificent results.

That weekend I printed up my new headshots and replaced *Kalpen Modi* with *Kal Penn*. *Let's see what happens*, I thought, sending out the first of many more Wednesday batches to agents.

I was sitting at the desk in my dorm room a couple of months later when my blue McDonald's phone finally rang. "Hello, is this Kal Penn?" the lady's voice said. "Yeswho'sthis?" I said quickly.[9] "My name is Laura. I'm calling from Barbara Cameron and Associates. We received the headshot and résumé you sent in. We'd like you to audition for us, if you're still looking for an agent?"

I played it cool, but inside I was screaming, *YES OF COURSE I*

8   The extra *n* stands for "Not gonna play a stereotypical cabdriver."

9   Fifty cents a minute, guys!

AM STILL LOOKING FOR AN AGENT!! Maybe I even did say it out loud, I can't remember. FINALLY. It had been years of Wednesday-morning walks to the newsstand, three years of money spent printing at Kinko's and mailing packets at the post office, so many random audition inquiries sent, and finally, an agent *might* be interested in me! I scrambled to find a pen and wrote down the agent's address.

What motivated her to call, why now? Was it those new head-shots I had saved up for? Was it my new catchy screen name? Was it because the new catchy screen name was less ethnic-sounding and was attached to those new headshots I had saved up for? I didn't know, I didn't ask, and I didn't care.[10] It was time to focus!

I prepared for the audition by rehearsing two of my favorite Shakespeare monologues, putting all my energy into making sure I impressed this agent, whatever her reason for calling me. Three days later I grabbed my Panoch bag and drove out to her office in West Hills, at the far end of the San Fernando Valley. The whole way there I was running through my monologues: "Thou dost thy office fairly. Turn thee back. And tell thy king I do not seek him now . . ." I pep-talked myself, *I am Henry the Fifth!*

The address for Barbara Cameron & Associates turned out to be a small guesthouse-turned-office behind a suburban home in a completely residential neighborhood. My excitement switched to anxiety. *Isn't this how people get tricked into doing porn?* I buzzed the gate and stepped inside. The walls of the guesthouse office were adorned with promotional posters for *Growing Pains* and *Full House*. Just above the couch, a poster of my grade-school crush Candace Cameron and her

---

10   There was no way to know for sure, since agents toss out submissions they don't follow up on. Since I had submitted an old headshot to Barbara Cameron & Associates previously, it was presumably a combination of a new catchy name with a better photo that got me noticed eventually.

brother, Kirk. I glanced down at the piece of paper on which I'd scribbled the name and address. Barbara *Cameron*. Holy moly, could it be? Yes, agent Barbara Cameron, mom of Kirk and Candace Cameron!

On the one hand: Whew, this was probably not porn. On the other: What are the chances?! First Jaleel White in my history class and now an audition for my childhood crush's mom? My entire childhood flashed before my eyes. Was the Fresh Prince of Bel-Air around somewhere?

The audition itself was quick: I was asked to read a short script for a soda commercial and was out of there within fifteen minutes. (Turns out nobody will ever ask you to perform a Shakespearean monologue in Hollywood.) That afternoon, the blue McDonald's phone rang again. "Hi Kal, it's Barbara Cameron. You were fantastic in the audition and we'd love to have you aboard!" Was it professional to sound excited, or was I just supposed to calmly say thank you, play it cool, and hang up? While my brain was busy figuring out the right response, my mouth got ahead of itself and started woo-hooing ecstatically over the phone. I finally had an agent! "Can I call you right back from my landline?" I asked her. "This McDonald's cell phone is expensive."

Barbara and her associate Laura got me out for auditions almost immediately. It was a slow start to be sure, but I was borrowing the Panoch with more frequency now, toning my arms, sweating in traffic, and frantically running out to feed the parking meter if auditions ran overtime. I was on my way. Now I just needed to book a job.

CHAPTER SIX

HOW (NOT) TO PRODUCE MOVIES

Agent: ✓
Paid gig with actual lines: ✓
Panoch (super tite): ✓
Dope internship: TBD

By the end of winter quarter my junior year, I had gone on a handful of auditions thanks to my new agent. To my massive disappointment, most of them had been for stereotypical, one-dimensional roles in commercials. During these casting sessions it was not uncommon to be:

- asked "Where's your turban?" (I'm not Sikh),

- told "You speak very good English, wow!" (thank you), or

- questioned about "which country is that accent from?" (New Jersey. Go, ~~like, uhh,~~ fuck yourself?!")

So, when Barbara Cameron called one afternoon with a quick audition "to play a nerd on *The Steve Harvey Show*," I perked up. Forget commercials, I was going out for an actual TV show! The audition scene was only one line—the nerd (creatively called "Nerd" in the script) raises his hand and asks a question in a high school classroom. That's it, that was the whole audition. (I don't even remember what he asks.) Even though it was finals week, I reasoned that since my statistics grade wasn't going to determine my job prospects, I should abandon studying and go all-out. I got an ill-fitting plaid shirt and put tape on a pair of glasses—real high-end late-'90s sitcom stuff. I drove the Panoch to CBS Television City at the corner of Beverly Boulevard and Fairfax Avenue in Hollywood, parked in an area reserved for actors, and walked in.

Look, I am not a method actor. But you don't just dress like a knockoff Urkel and not embrace the character. From the time I exited the car, I committed to being this Nerd. When I signed in at the front desk, I spoke in a weird nasally voice to the security guard and got some smiles from the janitor who I high-fived (and purposely missed) in the lobby.

All of this for just one line, that's how badly I wanted it. When the doors to the small elevator opened, I saw there were already five people inside, coming up from an underground parking garage. Instead of waiting for the next one, I stayed in character, abandoned social norms, and awkwardly squeezed my way in. As we stood smooshed against each other, I said hi to each human, still in character with the weird nasally voice. I made a little small talk, excused myself at the third floor, made a left turn out of the elevator, and took a seat in the waiting room next to eight other prospective Nerds.

Ten minutes later a casting assistant called me into the audition room. I walked in to find . . . all of the people from the elevator! Turns out they were the show's producers. I thought about saying hello in a more professional manner, but after squishing myself into a tight elevator with them, I was just going to have to double down on this one and stay in character. "Hey, it's my friends from the elevator, hiiiiii! That guy has a warm shoulder."

I read my line and left. That afternoon Barbara called to tell me I got the part.

The way sitcoms work, you rehearse and block (nail down the stage directions of) each scene throughout the week and tape the entire show on Friday (usually in front of an audience). Since all of this was taking place right in the middle of finals, I had to ultimately drop my statistics class[1] and, after filming my one line, pull an all-nighter on a paper that was due at ten that Saturday morning.

I did not do well on that paper, and when the episode aired a few weeks after that, I got a big Hollywood lesson.

Our dorm oddly received the Chicago-based channel WGN, which meant we could watch some shows on central standard time— two hours before they aired in Los Angeles. WGN carried *The Steve Harvey Show*, so I planned to watch privately when it aired in Chicago, then watch with my friends in the dorm when it aired on the LA station.

It all happened so quickly: the Chicago feed on my small television, seeing myself on-screen, in that classroom, hearing the lead characters deliver the lines before mine, and then—*bam!*—a jump to the next scene. My line had been cut, and along with it, the potential for my first IMDb credit. I canceled the dorm gathering planned for later that evening, and asked Barbara to find out what happened. "It wasn't personal," she explained sweetly. "This stuff is common. The producers said they really enjoyed working with you, but they had to make some cuts for timing and commercials. That's just the busi-

---

1   The reason I failed one of the two times.

ness side of things, honey. We'll book another job soon." My first paid speaking television role had been anticlimactic, but it was a fast lesson that for all of my passion as an artist, I was also entering a business, whose producers had entirely different considerations and priorities from my own.

After winter break, with a newfound nervousness about what life would be like after graduation, I felt that I needed an internship more than ever. I wanted something that would give me valuable entertainment industry experience, academic credit, and an impressive résumé boost. I continued to use the Panoch for more (mostly stereotypical) auditions, but ever since the Lucasfilm fiasco, my weekly trips to apply for internships through the UCLA Career Center frustratingly brought no success. So, I was excited when after more than two years of searching, the assistant to the president of a production company based at a major Hollywood studio called me to come in for an interview with his boss.

We sat at a real picnic table in the middle of a fake sidewalk on a mocked-up New York City backlot set in Los Angeles. I thought this was the coolest thing in the entire world. The big-time talented CEO looked kind of like the older brother of someone from college—tall, skinny, sunken eyes peeking out from under the brim of his blue Dodgers baseball hat. And dude had a huge personality. For the first fifteen minutes, he talked nonstop about movies, his love of nice furniture, and the greatness of Los Angeles culture.

Then he pivoted to discussing his huge film company, and all the fantastic deals and relationships he had with other huge film companies all over town. "By the way," he threw in, "none of my interns get college credit. I really don't like all the paperwork." With access to the entertainment industry like he was describing, who needed credit? Not realizing that what he was proposing was—how you say—illegal, I agreed to this unpaid, uncredited "internship," and he hired me on the spot. I would start the following week.

I felt like I had hit the jackpot. I pictured the enormous bustling office I'd be working in and could practically smell the freshly printed pages of all the scripts he bragged about producing.

The job itself wouldn't involve the most glamorous work, but even getting people coffee, answering phones, and running errands would offer me the chance to learn about the industry I was passionate about joining. And who knows, maybe if I truly crushed it, a promotion could eventually be within reach?

The following week, I swaggered into the office for my first day. It was not what I was expecting. This guy's colossal "media empire" took up exactly one small, square room, with a tiny single window awkwardly positioned in the corner. Against the far wall, someone had shoved a very uncomfortable-looking couch that I suspected to be very expensive because of how hideous it was. *That's it?* I thought. *Yo, this is only about twice the size of my dorm room. Even the Panoch has six windows.*

The other intern (yes, there were only two of us) filled me in: The CEO who interviewed me was a trust fund kid from Beverly Hills. His dad was a big-time executive at the studio who had *gifted* his son the production company. Though the office real estate was small, this guy did have a first-look deal with a massive production company that spanned the remainder of the building's first floor. I was just five minutes into my new internship and was already learning a ton about bravado and nepotism. I was also in awe. People spend entire lifetimes building a career in the hopes of setting up a production company at a major studio. This dude got one as a gift from his rich dad. In my head, I started to call my new boss Captain Moneybags.

*   *   *

My first assignment for Captain Moneybags was to come up with a list of male and female actors to star in a horror movie remake. He gave me a set of instructions to guide my search: "Find me people who are known and accessible: someone who's hot—but not, like, DiCaprio hot. We need to be able to afford the person."

This sounded like a fun challenge. As an aspiring actor, I would get a taste of what life was like on the other side of the table: What exactly does a producer look for when casting a film? Hot, but not "pricey" hot. *Interesting.* I spent the next two days pulling together a pile of thirty headshots of actors who worked regularly, had a good following, and, per Captain Moneybags's guidance, weren't too expensively famous.

I pulled a chair up to Captain Moneybags's desk and handed him the stack of photos. He thumbed through them, making comments I'd have expected a cartoon version of a movie producer from the 1930s to make. "Nice teeth," he said, pointing to a headshot with a perfect smile. "This kid's got nice teeth." On to the next photo. "This one is a bit round in the face but there's somethin' about those eyes. Keep him in the pile, he'll shed a few pounds for us." It was jarring to hear a producer talk about prospective hires like a used car salesman assessing a new stock of vehicles. It was also a great eye-opener in the commerce of Hollywood: We sell actors, not cars, but in both, you're on the hunt for the right body, age, make, and model.

Captain Moneybags flipped to the last headshot. It was the actor Joseph Gordon-Levitt. At the time, Joseph was on the popular sitcom *3rd Rock from the Sun*. He was obviously very talented, and I put him in the pile because he probably didn't earn a superstar's paycheck yet. Hot, but not expensive hot. In other words, perfect.

Captain Moneybags looked at Joseph's headshot, and in his 1930s cartoon producer voice said, "What the fuck is this kid . . . fucking *Asian?*" Joseph was talented, respected, and in our price range. Was he *Asian?*

"I . . . don't know. Does it matter?"

Captain Moneybags quickly snapped back. "Of course it fucking matters! He looks *Asian*," he said. "I don't want any *Asians* in my movie, Kal. Bring me good. White. American. Kids!"

I took the pile of headshots back to my desk. CM's assistant didn't react at all, which told me this was all perfectly normal. I was completely baffled and phenomenally curious. Did it cross Captain Moneybags's mind that the person sitting across from him was not a "good white American kid"? I neither knew nor cared if Joseph Gordon-Levitt was Asian. Why did Captain Moneybags? Moreover, why was he so angry about it? I wanted to understand what went on in the minds of powerful producers. Specifically, in that moment, I wanted to understand: Were they confused, racist, or both confused *and* racist?

I let Captain Moneybags cool down for the rest of the afternoon. Before he left for the evening, I asked why it mattered if Joseph Gordon-Levitt was Asian. He answered simply, "Asians don't watch movies."

I didn't even know how to dissect that thought. First, confusion: *I'm* Asian American. I watch plenty of movies. Second, solidarity: I know lots of other Asian Americans. They *also* watch plenty of movies. Third, logic: You know why we Asian Americans watch movies? For the same reasons non–Asian Americans do—because movies are awesome.

I followed him down the hall, pushing once more, asking what he meant. As we approached the sleek glass door to the outside, Captain Moneybags shrugged. "Look at the data, Kal. Asians don't watch movies."

There was data on this shit? Now we were getting somewhere. I took advantage of my access to studio files by staying at the office long into the night, thumbing through a thick manual with raw data on the business of filmmaking. Around 2:00 a.m., I came across a chart that broke down moviegoing audiences by race and ethnicity. Next to "Asian Americans," there was just an asterisk.

I flipped to the appendix to see what it meant. As I read, a smirk crept across my face. The asterisk *didn't* mean that Asian Americans don't watch movies. The asterisk meant that Asian Americans weren't *asked* if they went to the movies in the first place. That's like senior year of high school, when Most Likely to Get Caught in an Auto-Asphyxiating Accident Philip Goldstein lamented to everybody, "Most girls don't *actually* want to go to prom," even though he never bothered to *ask* any girls to go with him. Captain Moneybags didn't *actually* have data to back up his claim.

I sensed a massive opportunity here. My excited mind wandered. Once Captain Moneybags learned about the glitch in the data, he'd be able to make better creative decisions. He'd probably go ahead and cast Joseph Gordon-Levitt in his movie, which would open at number one at the box office. It would make hundreds of millions of dollars and his company would expand. What phenomenal success! Naturally, I would be promoted to junior creative executive, reaping the benefits of a six-figure salary, beefed-up résumé, and more creative input. Maybe I could even get a Panoch of my own. All because I did this research for him and made these helpful recommendations.

The next morning, demographic charts in hand, I explained my findings with the confidence of someone giving a TED Talk.[2] Captain Moneybags looked at me, exasperated, and replied, "I don't care what

---

2   Except not irritating.

the asterisk means. If they don't *ask* Asians, it's because Asians don't watch movies. I'm telling you. They *don't* watch movies." This didn't bode well for Joseph Gordon-Levitt. It also didn't bode well for me or anyone else who wasn't a "good white American kid"—because if this was the way all big-time Hollywood people acted, then we were monumentally screwed.

It's one thing to be ignorant of the facts. It's another to be *willfully* ignorant of the facts. Had CM done any real research or bothered to put his hubris aside to understand what the data actually meant, he would have discovered a few things. The first is that Asian Americans, on the whole, have purchasing power at least on par with other demographics,[3] meaning, they have ample disposable income to spend at the movies. He also would have discovered something obvious, but important: You don't need an exclusively Asian American audience to cast Asian American actors.

Now, I admit, this took place before *Crazy Rich Asians*. And Harold and Kumar. And Justin Lin, Nisha Ganatra, Jet Li, Mindy Kaling, and M. Night Shyamalan. But it took place *after* Anna May Wong, George Takei, and Pat Morita. It took place *after* Bruce Lee, Keye Luke, and Margaret Cho. It took place, in other words, after generations of Asian American actors had proven that you could cast Asian Americans—and that audiences of all kinds would see and love them.

What's both hilarious and awful about Captain Moneybags's views on the matter is that he wasn't just stereotyping Asian Americans—he was stereotyping Middle America. He thought they (1) wouldn't watch compelling content if the characters were *not*

---

3   For comparison, here's a more recent statistic: https://www.forbes.com/sites /rosaescandon/2020/05/22/asian-american-consumer-market-is-now-12-trillion -and-what-that-means-for-digital-brands/.

white and (2) would watch crappy content as long as the characters *were* white. And he wasn't alone, then or now. Plenty of old-guard executives in Hollywood still buy into this view, and it sets up a Catch-22: Some in Hollywood sparingly cast Asian Americans because they think Middle America won't watch us, which results in there being few Asian Americans on TV, which results in Middle America not watching us, which results in producers not casting Asian Americans because they think Middle America won't watch us. Exhausting.

In the moment, I knew that trying to outline this would be like explaining to him that Bruce Lee isn't related to Jet Li. I wasn't going to change his mind on anything, so off I went to find good white American actors—and to wonder if the industry I had chosen was the wrong one for someone who looked like me.

As I spent more time in the office, I got to know Captain Moneybags better. My initial first-day impressions about him were correct: He wanted to be *seen* as a real player (whatever that means) without necessarily doing the actual work to *be* a player (whatever *that* means). He had someone else record the company's outgoing voice mail greeting to make it seem like he was such a busy, important person, he couldn't be bothered to record his own. Like rich guys in many different industries, I learned that CM could buy his way into and out of anything, with failures being papered over by daddy.

He would come up with dozens of crazy, expensive ideas that weren't at all related to producing movies. He'd often passionately monologue about his desire to make the company "pop" by spending money on things that seemed cool to him, like stacks of expensive business cards, a fancy watch that I didn't know the name of, and

"This gorgeous recamier," which "cost me $24,000." (Told you, ugliest couch I'd ever seen.)

Despite the obvious differences I had with my boss,[4] I still took my job seriously and sought to make an impact wherever I could. That's how I was raised: to work hard and have integrity. As long as I was interning there, I viewed the company's success as my own. I knew that even in this toxic environment I would at least learn what *not* to do, and I was determined to get as much out of the experience as possible.

Subversive piece of advice: If you parrot the language of an especially shallow boss, they will like you more, making your work environment more tolerable. I thought of ways to make CM's company "pop." Given his obsession with voice mails and business cards, I figured he'd probably love a sleek-looking website with his name in bold print at the top: **Captain Moneybags Productions**.

An online presence would allow us to consider a wider pool of talent because writers who didn't have agents could digitally upload scripts for us to consider. That could help us find better projects, since technology would let us tap into a talent pool otherwise closed off to us. (You traditionally need an agent to get a script seen by a production company.) It would also streamline a fair amount of paperwork, making my job a lot easier. So, while eating lunch at my desk one afternoon, I built CM a simple home page using a GeoCities template. It took all of twenty minutes.

Captain Moneybags strolled back from a fancy lunch meeting in an "I love myself extra hard today" kind of mood. I went to his desk and showed off my work.

"You made me a website?! We're gonna pop!"

---

4   This is how you word things politely in a professional environment.

"It's just a template for now. Yes, I did figure it could help the company 'pop.'"[5]

"Is this the internet now? Am I on the internet?!"

"The website will be on the internet, yes. And the most important thing is, it'll help with script submissions by—"

"Holy *shit*. I'm. On. The. Internet."

"Well, not yet, you still have to register the domain and after—"

"How much does that cost?"

"Ninety-five dollars."

"That's it?! I'll pay it!" He handed me his credit card. "Do whatever that thing you just said for the ninety-five dollars!"

"Okay."

"You are a GENIUS. I'm on the fucking internet! WE. ARE. GONNA. POP!!"

This Crazy Rich Caucasian had absolutely no desire to learn about how digitizing his script process could help his company do better. He spent the rest of the day calling everyone in his Rolodex, directing them to the janky-ass GeoCities link. On his way out the door that night, he promoted me to junior creative executive.

Please take a second here. This is important to digest. After all the grinding and actual work I had done for him, the reason I got promoted was not because I pulled business data, merged it with something creative, and offered him casting suggestions, like Joseph Gordon-Levitt, tailor-made for his feature film. No, I got promoted because I made Captain Moneybags something shiny with his name on it that "popped."

The promotion was essentially a vanity bump. I went from unpaid intern to unpaid junior creative executive, with the promise

---

5 I'm telling you, they love it when you talk like they do.

of a future salary; I would begin getting paid the day after I graduated. I was assigned more responsibility, like being empowered to search for new scripts on my own and hiring our new batch of interns. I realized I was in the right world because I was the first one to come in every day and the last to leave, and I was still taking a full course load at UCLA while working as a Resident Advisor in the dorms to pay for housing, making no money at the film studio, receiving no college credit, working for a wealthy narcissistic racist, and bizarrely loving that I finally had access to this incredible, creative world. The only perk that came with being an unpaid junior creative executive was a pass allowing me to park in a closer lot. (This may not sound like a big deal, but Hollywood people put the specific locations of parking spaces into their employment contracts. There's a detailed hierarchy that takes years to work through and generally culminates when you pull into your own personal parking *spot*. With your name on it.)

As a young man of color who knew nobody in Hollywood and whose Indian American peers at college chastised him for pursuing a career in the arts, I viewed my situation with the internship less as someone being taken advantage of and more as someone who was gaming the system with skill and sacrifice. Of *course* interns in Hollywood were a relatively homogeneous group: If you were lucky enough to know the right people in the first place, you still had to be able to afford working full-time for free. Now that I was in charge of hiring CM's interns, I could at least try to eliminate nepotism from the list of qualifications. I did an exhaustive search for the best and most diverse applicants, not just the ones who had family or school connections. My short list of candidates was an extremely talented group from around the country, including people from different demographic groups who didn't all come from Los Angeles or attend fancy private schools.

I was proud of this.

The last time I had gone through a pile of applicants with CM was when I brought him that stack of headshots (*Asians don't watch movies!*). This time, he leafed through the prospective interns, pausing at the third, fourth, and fifth résumés. I wondered what the issue was now. "Why are there chicks?" he asked. He could tell the question confused me, so he repeated it. "Kal, why are there chicks *in this file?*"

Was this dude kidding me with this shit?

"Every human in the pile is an exceptionally talented film student. Do you not hire women?"

"Nope. No chicks. You've heard me talk, right? I'm not trying to get sued for my filthy mouth. Don't hire any chicks." Then, with his 1930s smirk and wink, "Unless they're hot. Bring the hot ones in for an interview." I walked back to my desk, wanting to throw up.

The misogyny was inexcusable, and I didn't know how to handle it—they don't teach you that in film school, and there were no articles about it in those days. This terrible behavior also struck me as self-defeating to his company's entire bottom line. CM's "don't hire women because I'm an asshole" policy eliminated half the talent pool. He was writing off insanely creative people—people who could help him move beyond "pop" and into substance. And it was all because he didn't want to manage his own terrible sexist behavior in the workplace.

I should have fought him way harder than I did. At the time, I honestly wasn't sure how. If I went to the head of HR to file a complaint, Captain Moneybags would find out—the guy I would have complained to was friends with his rich dad. I continued to make my point, sending him the most qualified applicants of every gender and background in the prospective intern piles. I wasn't going to take any qualified women or people of color out of the running, even if he eventually did. What was he going to do, fire me? I was already too valuable to his empire.

I'd like to think that things have gotten better today, that people like CM are a rarer breed than they were when I was first getting into the industry. And I attribute this in large part to immense public pressure on the entertainment industry to change, and the high degree of social consciousness in the generations that followed mine. For all the crap everyone gives millennials for quitting jobs too soon and expecting sudden promotions without paying their dues, at least they and the Gen Zers don't seem to tolerate the bullshit we had to. Racist, misogynistic behavior no longer has to be an acceptable par for the course. That gives me a lot of hope.

That said, we're still not where we need to be. We must continue finding ways to expand the pipeline into workplaces in and out of Hollywood. When given a chance, talent and hard work will generally win out over misogyny and hackery, but only when the pool of truly qualified candidates isn't restricted to those with contacts or money (or those of a certain gender, ethnicity, race, or identity).

Want to know the best evidence I have that money and connections aren't enough to keep you in business? It's Captain Moneybags himself. Within three years of opening his daddy-trust-funded production company, he had produced only one project: a straight-to-DVD movie that took a massive loss. He eventually closed up shop and left the entertainment industry forever. The last I heard he was a struggling real estate agent in Florida.

I guess nobody told him that Asians buy houses.

CHAPTER SEVEN

AUDITIONING TO BE LATINO

Captain Moneybags wasn't the only one with weird ideas about people from Middle America. Now that I was going on professional auditions, I learned that Hollywood can be a place that sees you in ways you don't see yourself. Indians wear turbans and are terrorists. White southerners are slow and unintelligent. East Asians are timid, although they'll kick your ass at martial arts. Hispanic people are all Latinos, all Latinos are Mexicans, and all Mexicans make very passionate love, except when they're too busy being lazy. Makes perfect sense.

Against all of that, in February of my fourth year of college, I got a call to audition for a lead role in an ABC television pilot called *Brookfield*, created by future *O.C.* and *Gossip Girl* scribe Josh Schwartz. Set in a New England boarding school, the character I auditioned for was a half-Indian, half-Jewish bully named Kumar Zimmerman. This was a) the first Kumar I ever auditioned for and b) closer than I ever thought I'd come to entering a private school world like Holden Caulfield's.

I booked the part, quit my "job" with Captain Moneybags, dropped out of UCLA for the spring quarter, resigned as a Resident

Assistant, and flew to Greensboro, North Carolina, where we filmed for a few weeks. While the pilot ultimately didn't get picked up to series, shooting it was an eye-opening introduction to what might be possible in my career: well-fleshed out lead roles written by smart, funny people. The month I spent on location with such kind, focused people totally solidified that this was the dream I wanted to pursue: being in front of the camera, storytelling. Barbara assured me that booking the part on *Brookfield* would lead to a higher level of meetings and auditions that I might not have gotten if I hadn't been on an ABC pilot (even a failed one). I returned to finish college, eager to see what came next.

The reality by August 2000—a few months after my festive college graduation, which Mom, Dad, and Pulin flew out from New Jersey for—was that I had gone out for almost no new auditions. Barbara was successful in setting up just one general meeting. When she pitched me for projects, she was often told, "He was very good in *Brookfield* but I mean, Kumar Zimmerman? Who else could have played *that* part?," as if my talent was negated by the character's ethnicity (and mine).

Any momentum I expected from *Brookfield* turned out not to exist. The single meeting Barbara was able to arrange was with a vice president of casting at NBC named Sonia Nikore, who not so incidentally was the only Indian American network executive I was aware of. Our meeting at NBC studios was cordial. Sonia asked about my background and training. She told me a bit about the network and how they discover new talent. "How have you found it so far," she asked, "being Indian American in Hollywood?"

"I've definitely had my fair share of stereotypical auditions, but *Brookfield* got me excited about what might be possible."

"Glad you have a positive outlook. That's important."

"I have to be positive," I continued. "I know physicality is a factor. Actors lose out on jobs all the time because they're too tall or too short, too fat or too thin, too attractive or not good-looking enough. But being brown, I know I don't have the luxury of being too tall or short or fat or thin, too attractive or not good-looking enough. I'm just considered 'too ethnic.' I've got to stay positive to go up against that."

I was worried that I may have overshared in a professional environment. But Sonia put me at ease by recounting similar stories other ethnic actors had shared with her. As I got up to leave, she handed me her business card and kindly offered, "Call me anytime you need anything."

Later that summer, finally, an audition! *Sabrina the Teenage Witch* was a sitcom about a suburban family of witches and their talking cat. I was up for a small role: just a few lines playing a college student named Prajeeb in Sabrina's study group, but I was very excited. Though I had done *Brookfield*, it was almost impossible for an actor of color to get an audition for any of the big sitcoms, which were all purposely white: *Will & Grace, Friends*. Even *Seinfeld*.

Auditions can be a lot of fun to prepare for—I start by creating a backstory to the character, grounding who he is as specifically as possible, and developing his arc in the scene. I envisioned Prajeeb as a laid-back kid from Portland, Oregon, who was super into camping and small-batch organic coffee. I decided that he loves flannel button-downs like Eddie Vedder, so I wore one to the audition.

I did well in the first two rounds. As I walked to my car after the callback, the casting director came chasing after me. "Kal, the producers loved you and want you to read it one more time. Can you come back in with me?"

Hell yeah! It's always a good sign if they want another read-ing. On the walk back to the casting office, I daydreamed for just a fleeting moment: thinking about my little cousins who probably watch *Sabrina the Teenage Witch*. What a fun surprise if they ran-domly turned it on and saw me in an episode. I smiled confidently as I walked through the door to read for the six well-manicured faces another time.

"Thanks for coming back, Kal. We'd like you to do it again," the main producer said with a grin.

"I'd be happy to!" I said.

"This time with an accent."

For fuck's sake.

My game face was strong though my blood boiled. By then I'd experienced this bait and switch many times before—you don't bring anything stereotypical into an audition, and the producers ask it of you. This request wasn't quite as bad as some of the auditions for Indian food-delivery guys or store clerks that had been written in bro-ken English. It wasn't as nauseating as the woman who suggested I tie a bedsheet around my head if I didn't have a turban to wear to an audition. Still, I decided to not give them the satisfaction of knowing the sudden rage inside me.

This rage was based on two things. The first was very clear flash-backs to David Cohen spitting on me on the middle school bus after quoting Apu from *The Simpsons*. The second was because I have a low tolerance for stupid and boring things. An Indian accent, really? That's the *most clever* note a team of Hollywood producers could come up with?

I was proud of the two rounds of auditions I gave as Prajeeb from Portland, Oregon, who was super into camping and small-batch organic coffee! I wanted to play *Hipster Prajeeb*! So, if they wanted the kind of stereotypical Indian accent that wasn't on my menu, I was going to make them feel uncomfortable. I was going to make them look me in the eye. I was going to dare them to say it right to my face, by pointing out my talents, so that they could feel guilty and realize how terribly they were behaving. Hopefully it would be enough to change their minds.

"What kind of accent do you want?" I said deftly. "I can do Scottish, Irish, southern, Italian, New York . . ."

"Why don't we just stick to *Indian*?"

Yeeeeeesh.

I had less than five seconds to think through what I wanted to do. If I did the accent, I might get the role. It would look good to have a network sitcom job on my thin résumé. As I learned from *Brookfield*, I was going to have to work harder than white actors to build credits. The gig also paid about $700, more than a month's rent. If I didn't do the accent, I probably wouldn't get this job. Some other kid would get the credit on his résumé and the cash in his pocket, and I'd have to continue working odd jobs until I booked something else that may or may not be better than this.

I chose to read the scene again with an Indian accent.

I tried hard to remain grounded in the backstory I created for Prajeeb as I served up the ridiculous off-menu Indian lilt that many of the white folks in my professional life couldn't seem to get enough of. I barely got the first line out before all the producers' faces lit up with glee and they were laughing much harder than any sane person should laugh at a sitcom about a talking cat.

Forget the talking cat. I felt like a dancing monkey.

They proudly smiled as though they had accomplished a great feat and thanked me for coming back from the parking lot. I analyzed things on the drive home. It's not that I think an accent alone makes a one-dimensional stereotype. Lots of people have accents in real life, and lots of those people are cabdrivers and store clerks. A problem arises when we focus on the working-class nature of certain professions to protest a stereotype (oh man, he has to play a *cabdriver*)—as if being a cabdriver is inherently a bad thing, or that honest work is something to look down on. What really makes these roles onedimensional stereotypes is that the person's ethnicity or race is the focus of who they are as a character, which tends to be the case when it comes to the Hollywood version of cabdrivers and store clerks, or actors who are asked to put on hokey accents for no reason despite having prepared a full backstory for the character.

Racial signifiers are stereotypical because they're reductionist, yes. They're also artistically boring because they mean that a character rarely has any agency. Everything is tied to identity. Is the character hungry? Curry jokes! Sleepy? Probably because of a mystical Indian spell. Going shopping for clothes? Probably a sari. Zzzzzz. Those characters don't advance the plot. They just function to serve the arcs of the white characters. Stereotypical representation is dehumanizing when it removes the full breadth of what it means to be a living, breathing, multidimensional person with traits that are independent of identity.

Nobody was around when I got back to the house I shared with some of the homies, so I did some push-ups on the cold blue tile in the kitchen, contemplated making a screwdriver (the only cocktail I knew how to make), and dreaded what I assumed was the happy phone call coming any minute now.

When Barbara told me I got the part, I told her what happened. "Is there any way I could do it without the accent? There's no reason for Prajeeb to have one." A seasoned agent and talented stage mom, Barbara suggested that I accept the much-needed job and said I should ask the director in person when I got to the set. "These things are often better posed as creative conversations during production," she encouraged. It made sense to me. Besides, a month's rent.

During the week before the shoot, I was so nervous that I spent more time rehearsing what I was going to say to the director than I did my lines in the episode. I felt totally robbed of what should be the pure joy of booking a coveted television role. I so badly wanted to experience what the white actors got to experience when their agents called with the good news that they booked their first roles: excitement, dreams that come true, hard work that's paid off. I resented the fact that I instead found myself thinking about identity, about politics, about any of that shit. I just wanted to play the human version of the damn character.

On the morning of the shoot, I found the amiable director cozied up next to the coffee cart on the soundstage and politely made my case. "You have such a funny show," I told him. "I'm so thankful to be joining you for this hilarious little part! I was just hoping, you know, that maybe I could play Prajeeb without the Indian accent?" His mood turned so fast you'd have thought I asked for something crazy, like the scene in the *Borat* sequel when Tutar's father questions if his daughter can attend the debutante ball even though "her moon blood has arrived." The director wasn't shy about what he thought of me. "You're doing that accent."

I told myself maybe he's just not educated about this. Maybe if he just knew better, he'd agree with me. Sure, it didn't work with Captain Moneybags, but not all white producers and directors are the same, right? I brought up the creative backstory I'd crafted for Prajeeb, told him why I didn't think an Indian accent was necessary for the humor of a guy I purposely grounded in northwestern American values.

The flannel!

Pearl Jam!

His eyes narrowed. He was very angry. "We hired you to do the accent and that's what you're doing, got it?"

My final plea.

"I just thought it would be nice for my little cousins to see me in a role that wasn't a stereotype," I said, hoping to assure my participation wouldn't fuel a new generation of middle-school David Cohens. "Stereotypes are all I ever saw on TV growing up." He looked at me with laser-focused eyes, and for a brief moment I wondered if I had gotten through to him.

"Your little cousins should be happy you get to be on a TV show at all. And so should you."

I went through the rest of the day hating the job. It wasn't that I expected to convince him that Prajeeb didn't need an accent (although that was my hope and certainly part of the sting). It was the way I was being spoken to. The subtext of what he wanted. The complete awareness and purposefulness of the director's decision to require a stereotypical accent, knowing that it was reductionist and othering. I finally had another TV gig and I wasn't even enjoying it. That's what $700 was worth to me in August 2000.

The week before my episode of *Sabrina the Teenage Witch* aired, I anxiously called my ten-year-old cousin anyway. "Hi!" I said, with some excitement. "Do you watch *Sabrina the Teenage Witch*?" A true New York kid, he retorted, "If you're trying to ask me whether or not I know that you're going to be on *Sabrina the Teenage Witch*, *yes*, I know you're going to be on it, and *no*, I don't watch that show." Amazing. Even my little cousin had better taste.

A few months and several stereotypical auditions later, a big opportunity! Barbara got me in to read for the head of casting for the WB network (which is now defunct and was replaced by the CW). The network was looking for actors to play young marines on a new TV series, and I had a shot at auditioning for one of the supporting leads. I read the script diligently and worked hard on all five audition scenes nonstop for a week. Backstory. Character arc. The process I love.

I pumped myself up the entire drive to the studio. *I want this job. I am this character.*

I got to the waiting room very early and briefly clocked that all the other actors were white. Each one was given fifteen minutes in the audition room. The only open seat was between the sign-in sheet and the door, which meant I could size up my competition a little closer—glance at the other actors' résumés and see who their agents were. I found it interesting that they were all represented by the biggest firms in Hollywood, although almost none of them had any serious training—certainly not as prestigious as UCLA's School of Theater, Film and Television. I decided that this would bode well for me. *My training has to put me ahead of the pack, right?*[1]

An assistant called my name, and I walked into the audition feeling confident. I reached out to shake the WB casting head's hand. She retracted her arm, grabbed my headshot, and glanced back and forth between me and my photo with considerable confusion.

"You're Kal Penn?" she asked.

"I am."

"Okay, well uh . . . I'm not sure if they told you but we're only going to be reading the first scene today." *Only the first scene?* I thought to myself, *that'll take like three minutes, tops. Everyone else has spent at least fifteen minutes in this room.*

---

1   An interesting piece on the demand for young actors at the time: https://www.nytimes.com/1999/05/17/arts/for-all-the-tv-pilots-there-s-just-not-enough-youth-to-go-around.html.

There was clearly something about my look that the casting director immediately didn't like. She had decided not to cast me, before I even had the chance to audition.

As usual, I knew I only had a few seconds to decide how to react. A few seconds to take in the information, suppress the emotion. Against racism, my best device was professionalism. Just then, an angel popped up in the right side of my head. I'd seen him before. He was shouting, *You don't know that this is racism! Maybe she thinks you're just too tall or too short! Maybe she wants to cut the scenes because she has to run to a meeting! Maybe it's because you don't have a bigger agent! You're already here in this room, so do a kick-ass job anyway! Show her how good you are!* A tiny red devil popped up in the left side of my head, whispering nefariously, *Don't listen to him. You're the only one here who isn't white, buddy. Obviously, that's what this is about. Don't bother. You have no chance. Just go home.*

A lot of my early auditioning was a question of which voice to listen to on a given day.

Fuck off, Devil, I want this part. I would listen to the angel and I was going to give it my all, even if I only got to read that first scene. I took a beat. Peeked at my notes about the backstory. Channeled the character arc and began.

Two pages in, the WB casting head interrupted. "Thank you so much, Kal. I'm sorry. I just *have* to stop you before you finish the first scene. I just um . . . I just have to ask. What *are* you?"

"Huh?"

"What *are* you? . . . Like where are you *from?*"

"Oh, I'm from New Jersey. I graduated from UCLA's School of Theater, Film and Tele—"

"No, I mean like where are you *really* from? Are you Latin?"

The goddamn devil was right.

"I'm uh, ethnically Indian. I was born in New Jer—"

"You look like you could pass for Latin. Are you mixed, at least?"

"Mixed? Um, no—"

"Ugh, are you sure?"

There was now a miniature version of me standing on the shoulders of the tiny devil inside my own head. *Was I sure?* I thought to myself, *Lady, I already got myself a white-sounding stage name, I need to "at least" be mixed too?*

I hated the angel at this point but responded politely. Any sign of annoyance and they might think I'm difficult to work with.

"I got my training in the UCLA theater department, so I'm confident I can play a wide variety of roles! And yes, my parents moved to New Jersey, where I was born, from India—"

"Okay, right, so *you're not even Latin*. I can't cast you. I mean the role isn't written Latin, but that's the only way I could have cast you. You're a very good actor, by the way. You're *really* good. It's just too bad. That you're not Latin."

There was nothing to discuss further. I was the wrong kind of brown. The head of casting for the WB didn't want to waste her time auditioning me. Not when there was a room full of white actors with less training out there waiting for their shot.

Experiences like this were common and maddening, because they undermined my ability to make creative choices as an actor. While other newcomers got to create backstories, develop their craft, and showcase their talents with fifteen-minute auditions, I found myself kicked out after reading just one part of a scene, or relegated to playing tired stereotypes, regardless of how much I prepared. I felt like I was going nowhere artistically or professionally, and my cynicism deepened. An actor's job is to emote, but in the face of racism, it becomes necessary to put on what others see as a professional game face while burying feelings of anger and rage. It's emotionally draining, creatively suffocating.

I grew to expect bad behavior from casting directors as a rule rather than an exception. I learned to believe all producers would ultimately require a reductionist accent. When I did find a promising audition, I thought to myself, *Oh, they're bringing me in for the part of a guy named Ryan. I'll never get it since it's not written for an Indian American dude.* It was clearly a defense mechanism, something to take the sting out of the constant bullshit. Unfortunately, it was also turning into self-sabotage.

I felt so beaten up that I stopped my dedicated preparation routine. I no longer focused as much on doing well at auditions, because I knew in my heart I wouldn't get those parts anyway. Once I stopped giving one hundred percent, this pathetic self-pity only made the self-fulfilling prophecies come true: Without believing that my hopes and dreams were possible, I was not preparing. I hated every audition. Now that I was unprepared and hating every audition, I was not getting jobs. But most damningly, I was the one who decided—before the producers themselves had—that I was not worthy of a role. Even a stereotypical one that might have given me a coveted résumé credit or paid another month's rent.

Time went by. More odd jobs as a messenger or driver or production assistant or extra. A few months, then a few more. It didn't matter. I wasn't passionate about anything, so what difference did time make?

As one year of wallowing in self-defeating behavior was about to turn into two, I faced this reality: If I've already given up, *what is the point of wasting all this time?* I told myself to consider law school. Become a teacher. I took the bus to the library and checked out LSAT prep books. My parents sensed where I was at, and again urged me to consider a practical backup plan. This time I didn't oppose the idea. I read articles on getting a real estate license and spiraled even deeper into self-doubt. My friends didn't quite know what to make of things; they were at work all day so whenever I wasn't doing odd jobs to pay the rent, I was usually home alone.

Why had Kaz bothered encouraging me? Maybe I should have listened to Mrs. Cummings, taken another whack at the multiple-choice Scantron, and found something more suitable.

I was in the shower one morning when the devil and the angel popped back into my brain. They didn't argue with each other. This time, they joined forces and picked a fight with *me*. You've had a bad attitude for so long, they said. You've spent lots of time figuring out how to quit without actually *doing* it. What's the holdup? If you're going to leave acting, *leave*.

I listened to their bullying until all the hot water was gone, which is when I realized: I hadn't formally quit because I *couldn't* quit. I was more down and lost than I'd ever been, and in spite of this I could not really give up acting. As much as I'd flirted with the idea, I knew that if I walked away from chasing this dream—from my desire to tell stories that might make audiences feel emotion, bring them into worlds they might never have a chance to enter in reality—I would regret it for the rest of my life. That's the difference between a professional artist and someone with a great hobby: If I gave up on acting, there would be nothing to fill that creative void, which I love in the deepest part of my soul.

Also, for someone who needs to touch their pregnant character's breasts in order to learn basic algebra, the LSAT is a *really* hard test to study for.

*   *   *

I changed my mindset and developed a strategy. First, I couldn't afford to waste time and energy being upset with racist casting directors or bigoted producers. This didn't mean I was suddenly not angry when I encountered them. As much as I still wanted to scream and kick them in the throat, their bullshit didn't deserve all my energy.

Second, I embraced the difficult calculations I'd have to make. *I'm brown, period, and this is a white boys' game. If the best characters that writers, producers, directors, and casting teams can come up with are tired, unfunny stereotypes that we've seen a million times, it's a reliable sign that the individuals I'm dealing with are seriously short on talent themselves. This reflects badly on them, not me.*

Third, I had to differentiate passion from desperation. It was silly to view all job opportunities as equal. If something was a genuine, well-written part, I'd go all in. If I had to work ten times harder just to get the same shot as some dude named Braden from Iowa, I'd do the work. I couldn't change the number of frustrating casting directors or stereotypical auditions I was going to encounter—that part was out of my control. So, unless there was a potentially career-changing business or creative reason to participate, I would focus on things within my control and make a concerted effort to respectfully decline the one-dimensional roles. What I wouldn't do is show up to auditions unprepared and angry, as if I'd already lost the part.

I got my shit together and resumed going to auditions with my head held high.

CHAPTER EIGHT

ON FIRE

Barbara Cameron's associate Laura was beaming with excitement on the other end of the phone. We talked a few times a week and I had never heard her like this. "Honey, I have a fantastic audition for you! It's a big part in a teen movie called *Van Wilder*, come to the office *right now* so I can talk to you about the script and the character!"

My calls with Laura and Barbara were always very warm. An actor's agent ends up being everything from a math expert (you're not making enough money from acting to pay your rent) to a psychologist (get another job and don't spend so much on drinks—you can't even afford rent) to a moral compass (just take a Xanax instead).[1] It just wasn't common for them to ask for an in-person meeting. That's how I knew, whatever this *Van Wilder* movie was, it was huge. Getting to Barbara Cameron's (non-porn) guesthouse office at the far end of the San Fernando Valley during rush hour was a gigantic hour-and-a-

---

[1] Barbara was nothing but wonderful as an agent and friend. And not a Xanax pusher. Even though there were plenty of times I probably wished I could get some Xanax.

half-in-traffic pain in the ass. Though I had moved beyond my share of the Panoch (I saved up and bought a very-used Toyota Paseo with a salvage title after graduation), I was too excited to drive all the way out there. I needed Laura to tell me about this fantastic audition *now*.

"What's the part? What's the name of the character? Can you send me the script instead? Whatever it's about, I can't wait to read it!"

"The part in this movie is so great—it's a *supporting lead!*"

"Holy shit."

"I knowwwww! Come by the office!"

"Send it to me! What's the name of the character, so I can look for it when I get the script?"

"You know, I would love for you to just *come by the office* so we can discuss it!"

She was starting to sound a little like a Nigerian prince from a phishing email. I felt a tinge of suspicion.

"Laura, what's the name of the character? What's the role? I'll drive out to the office, I'm just too excited to wait!"

"Okay. The character . . . is . . . um . . . a foreign exchange student named . . ."

"Go ahead . . ."

". . . Taj Mahal."

I hung up the phone.

Laura called back immediately. "This is why I wanted you to come by the office!"

"I'm not coming by the office. How would coming by the office change anything? I didn't spend years training as an actor to play an exchange student named Taj Mahal."

Barbara got on the phone and the two of them broke it down for me. This wasn't any tiny old gig. It was a *supporting lead* in a Lionsgate studio comedy, starring two well-known actors: Tara Reid, who was a hit in *American Pie*, and Ryan Reynolds, who was one of the two guys from the sitcom *Two Guys, a Girl and a Pizza Place*. These were real Hollywood stars! If I earned this job, I would have a big film credit on my résumé.

"I know it wasn't the case after *Brookfield*," Barbara said. "But this is a movie, not a pilot. If you got this part, it would lead to more auditions." I rolled the options around in my head, going back to that promise I made to myself: *Don't sabotage an audition. Say no to stereotypical roles unless they could be career-changing.* Taj Mahal could be career-changing. Did I really want to turn down the possibility of building a résumé and one day getting better auditions?

I appreciated Barbara's business acumen and her candor. As much as I now believed in myself, it was difficult for her to get me auditions because of my ethnicity (well, because of Hollywood's reception to my ethnicity). The Brown Catch-22 was this: The only parts you could audition for were stereotypically brown. You couldn't read for non-brown parts unless you had more credits on your résumé, and you couldn't get more credits on your résumé because the only parts you could audition for were stereotypically brown. I had been hustling hard. The role of Taj Mahal (Taj Mahal Badalandabad, if we're using his full name) could give me a real shot, even if I had to swallow a bit of pride to take it.

I read the script. A few things stood out immediately: Yes, the character was very clearly a stereotype. A bumbling foreign exchange student speaking in an exaggerated accent, mixing up his metaphors, trying painfully to get laid by white girls—and failing miserably. They weren't breaking any new comedy ground with that.

I also noticed that the character was a stereotype of *every* eighteen-year-old college guy in teen movies—like Jason Biggs's character, Jim, in *American Pie*—trying to get laid at any cost, putting sexual experience over rational thought. The clichés weren't entirely racial.[2]

Most important of all—it was clear that Taj Mahal actually advanced the plot of the film. If he was left out of the story, the arc would not progress. In that sense, this was a real character. Without Taj, the movie wouldn't work at all. *Exciting.* I pondered this, trying to square it with my reservations about the name and the stereotyping. One of my frustrations had been that stereotypical characters never contributed to story arcs. Was this some sort of a baby-steps win? What to do?

I paced, barefoot and (creatively) pregnant, around the beige carpet of my San Fernando Valley apartment, staring at the office number of Sonia Nikore, the VP of casting at NBC, who had said, "Call me anytime you need anything" a couple of years prior. I had never been offered that kind of open-door policy from a casting director before, and never had a reason to take her up on it (what was I gonna do, vent about being *not even Latin?*), but now seemed like the right time—I needed real career guidance.

I wasn't nervous, I just wanted to make sure the words were precise. I dialed the number, and her assistant patched me through right away. I told Sonia about the character's name and background and my hesitations. She echoed what Barbara had said: "It's true. If you actually get this job, it's a pretty big deal for your résumé. I run into this challenge whenever I want to audition performers of color—their résumés are thin compared to white actors'. There are so few roles written for brown people. Almost nobody is going to audition you for a part unless it's *specifically* written as nonwhite, so if you get

---

2   Ayyyy, let's hear it for *all* kinds of heteronormative gender identity stereotypes!

this role, you'll have a credit on your résumé that you might not be able to get otherwise: SUPPORTING LEAD."

There it was—validation that the Brown Catch-22 existed. "I understand," I said. I think she could tell from my tone that while I heard her, I still had artistic reservations about a role that simmered with stale stereotypes.

Then she asked me an important follow-up: "When you read the script, did you laugh? Are parts of it funny?"

"Super funny. There are great gags and setups throughout. It's not all based in ethnic stereotypes."

"That's important. On the stereotypes, how many things in the script made you cringe?"

"I don't know—maybe thirty?"

"Okay, you get to pick ten," she said. "Pick the ten things in the script that you think are the most cringeworthy, and if you get the job, sit down with the writers and bring those ten things up."

Wait, I could do that?! Ten things? I didn't know I could do that! I mean, I had tried something similar with just *one* thing, and I definitely didn't want to get the "Prajeeb from Portland" reaction again.

"You shouldn't just say you think it's stereotypical and that they should change those ten things. You have to put in some work too. Come prepared with ten things that are *funnier* than what the writers came up with originally. Nobody is making this movie to purposely offend or degrade anyone. They're making it because they want audiences to laugh, to have fun, to spend money. So, come up with ten things that are *funnier* than what's scripted. That's part of your job anyway. Go be funny!"

This was new to me: the idea that I actually had some agency in the matter and that the creative work could be collaborative. My professional experiences so far taught me that I couldn't do much more than complain (exhausting) or refuse to audition out of principle (financially unsustainable). Sonia was mapping out how I could use my skills to make a project better and funnier, while building a résumé that could eventually lift me out of the Brown Catch-22. I had to get the part first.

With my new directive, *go be funny!*, I spent two weeks preparing hard for the audition, breaking down the beats of the script, getting off-book,[3] and developing a backstory for the character (Taj likes Barry White because Barry White has an absurdly deep voice. Taj loves his freedom in America but also finds it to be lonely. That sort of thing.). Despite the quick onset of a mild cold, I sat in traffic all the way to the casting office feeling *great*.

I walked in with confidence. I knew the character inside out and delivered what I thought was an exceptional audition. Nothing could stop me now. It was only a matter of time before the friendly, young casting director Barbara Fiorentino called the *other* Barbara (Cameron) and I would be sitting with the writers, impressing them with all my hilarious tweaks to the script.

I waited by the phone with nervous confidence the rest of the day. It never rang. The following morning I called Barbara Cameron's office to check in. "No word yet!"

I started to get even more anxious, eating lots of tacos in my pajamas and doing push-ups on the cold blue tile in the kitchen.

A full week later, a call. "Sorry, honey," my agent said. "The producers didn't really respond to your read. Maybe they thought you were a little *too old* for the part. You're not moving forward." I had been

---

3   Actor-speak for memorizing your lines. ("That's the easiest part of the job!" Kaz would say. Kaz was right.)

so presumptuous—I studied hard for this, I had overcome my hesitations about auditioning for the role, and I *expected* to advance to the next round. Out of desperation, I asked Barbara if there was any other way to get back into the room. "No. I told them you didn't feel your best because you had the sniffles, but they just won't see you again."

My confidence was shattered. I was confused: How could I be too old to play a character that was basically my age? It didn't make any sense! *Wait a second, was I actually not good enough to get a callback for the role of an exchange student named Taj freaking Mahal?* For two weeks I sat around, distraught. Part of pushing ahead as an actor is believing in yourself, believing that you're good enough to succeed if given the right opportunity. It was probably worth reassessing my life. A few weeks later, another blow to my ego. An acquaintance from UCLA forwarded me something: The *Van Wilder* casting director had sent mass emails to every Indian Student Union at every major university in the United States to solicit audition tapes. It was Barbara Fiorentino's first film. The role of Taj hadn't been cast yet, and she had gotten desperate enough to canvass random colleges to find someone brown. It didn't matter if they had any training.

Finding out that the casting team was letting random auntie and uncles' perfect science-major kids audition for this film made me feel like my eyes would bleed. Kids like Gita ("Why are you studying? Aren't you just, like, a theater major?"), Varun ("my safety is Hopkins"), and Aarti ("seven-year combined medical program!")—they could audition for this?! *Nikhil was going to Yale AND maybe getting the part of Taj Mahal Badalandabad?*

I couldn't let some sciencey Indian kid beat me out of this role. I couldn't slip back into self-pity. I had to dig into remembering what I loved about storytelling and the arts to begin with, channel those days at my performing arts high school, bring back some of my East Coast hustle, pick up my ax and thrust my pelvis out again.

I needed to go rogue: If they were soliciting audition tapes from anyone who was Indian—actor or not—then I would make a tape too and send it along with a note to the casting director. "Is that a dumb idea?" I asked my agent. I could sense her smiling over the phone. "What do you have to lose?" she said.

I spent the next couple of days working hard on the material all over again. A talented director I met through friends two years prior, Senain Kheshgi, was nice enough to help me rehearse and professionally tape the audition scenes in her apartment. Before sending it off, I wrote a heartfelt letter to Barbara Fiorentino, letting her know that although I had already come in to audition for her, I was sending a tape because unlike the people she was auditioning from Indian Student Unions around the country, I was a trained actor, confident I could do professional justice to the role. I sent it off in the spirit of a man frustrated, desperate—and motivated.

I didn't know it at the time, but over the course of that period, Fiorentino's frantic search of Indian Student Union aspirants had actually turned out to be a resounding success. She had gotten hundreds of audition tapes from Taj hopefuls all over the country. She hadn't slept in days, instead watching tape after tape of mostly abysmal auditions from every Indian man aged eighteen to fifty who had been forwarded her casting notice. She was relieved to *finally* find a premed undergrad from Stanford who was absolutely perfect for the role of Taj Mahal. The producers cast him, and everything was set to go. It was just a couple of weeks until principal photography was to begin. Unfortunately for Barbara Fiorentino, when Dr. Stanford told his parents that he had been cast in a movie and needed to take a semester off from college, they freaked out and forbade him from doing it. "What is this acting-bacting nonsense? You are going to medical school! You are going to be an oncologist!"[4]

She had searched the country and found what she thought was the right brown guy, only to be met with the dreaded Uncle and Auntie veto just as rehearsals and camera tests were set to begin. Totally exhausted and overcome, Fiorentino found herself crawling under her desk, crying on her office floor on her hands and knees while sorting— in desperation and defeat—through a late pile of VHS tapes that had been received in the days since she thought she'd found her Taj. Through wet eyes and intense fatigue, she opened a few of these new envelopes, including mine, the only one to include a letter. *I remember this kid*, she thought to herself. *He was really good. I don't know why the producers didn't respond to his audition.* She watched my tape and wiped away a few tears. *This is our Taj.* Suddenly, I was back in the picture. Fiorentino took the tape to the producers and told them they *needed* to audition me in person. With no mention of my prior rejection, I was sent straight to the final audition, known as the "chemistry test."

It was down to me and one other Indian actor I heard they'd found along the way. I knew nothing about my competition except that each of us would read scenes with Ryan Reynolds, and the producers and director would see which of the two Tajs fit best.

I was very curious for intel on my competition. What did he look like? Was this dude good-looking? Tall? Was he even a full-time actor like me? Or was he one of the many Indian college students who thought it would be fun to audition for a movie?

None of the above.

When I walked into the waiting room for the chemistry test, I saw that my competition was . . . a white dude. Wearing brown

---

4   Thank you, Uncle!

makeup. Though it was common, I'll let that sink in for a minute. I was up for the role of an Indian foreign exchange student named Taj Mahal against *a white dude in brownface*. Any reservations I had about taking the part vanished.[5]

I encountered brownface regularly enough in those days that I often assume everyone can relate to how widespread and not shocking it was. This is not to say it wasn't deeply maddening (it always was), but in writing the first draft of this chapter, for instance, I didn't anticipate my editor's notes: "This is quite shocking! And horrifying! Please give us some examples." There are too many to list. You can safely assume that any audition I went on, for a role written specifically Indian, included a number of white actors who (with the right makeup) could "pass" for Indian according to the producers. (To illustrate how not long ago this was with a frame of reference, the NSYNC song "Bye Bye Bye" had already been out for more than a year.)

Some of our most memorable shows and revered artists have utilized brownface. Most people know about Peter Sellers (1968), Fisher Stevens (1986), and Hank Azaria (today). Less-obvious instances, like Harvey Jason in *Jurassic Park* (1997), Max Minghella in *The Social Network* (2010), one hundred extras in *Aladdin* (2019), and Rob Schneider in a bunch of stuff, make you go, "Oh right. This is still a thing." The practice is still common enough today that I couldn't write this chapter without mentioning it. Given the widespread, systemic nature of it, it was

---

5   You've probably heard of "blackface"—the practice of white actors in black makeup doing horribly racist portrayals of Black folks, which was common "entertainment" well into the twentieth century. (If you haven't already, watch Spike Lee's *Bamboozled*.) We rightfully shame people who do that sort of thing nowadays, treating it like the awful historical artifact it should be. And yet, there I stood, in the year 2000, staring at a white actor who had covered himself in brown makeup to audition for the role of Taj Mahal in a major Hollywood movie.

impossible to hold personal beef against every actor who showed up in brownface. It made me angry, yes. Livid. It also made me feel lonely, with a decisive lack of support from the Indian American community, and the reality that every actor is just looking for a gig. The philosophy seemed to be: *It's super competitive out there. You do what you gotta do.*

For example, my stand-in on *House M.D.* was a really *really* nice guy who predated me on the show (he was a stand-in for other characters in seasons before I joined the cast). So, once I was in the picture, he was told to paint his face brown every morning by our cinematographer, who cited lighting as the reason he needed the brownface.[6] Back in the good old days (2009), this was just accepted.

As I sat across from the white dude in brownface in the *Van Wilder* audition waiting room, my head buzzed with the same questions I had in other similar waiting rooms. Did the other actor—in this case, let's call him Facey McPainty—put on his brown makeup at home before he left for the audition? Or maybe this dude got here hella early and locked himself in the bathroom for twenty minutes to get his brownface on. Was he rocking the makeup on his chest and hands in case they made us run a shirtless scene? Did any of this increase his chances of getting pulled over by the cops on the way there? I was super intrigued!

I also started to get a little angry. Facey McPainty could audition for ninety-nine percent of the other roles out there—he had so many more opportunities to get a supporting lead credit on his résumé than I did. I knew what I had to do. I stood up proudly and walked—slowly and

---

6   In reality, obviously this made no sense. The cinematographer also told the stand-in to do this to avoid a situation in which a brown stand-in (who wouldn't have to paint his face) could replace him. Nobody would ever ask a black or brown person to *lighten* their face as a qualification to stand in for a white actor. I should also note that the producers at the top didn't know it was happening. I share this to illustrate how systemic this stuff is. It was still early enough in my career—in an industry that saw nothing wrong with this—that I didn't even know how to have a conversation about it with anyone to begin with.

with purpose—into the bathroom. I decisively opened up my backpack and began to put on brown makeup too. Just kidding. I ran to the bathroom and composed myself. *Take all of this anger and channel it toward comedy, toward drive. Don't let this distract you. Use the fury as motivation.*

"Kal?" Barbara Fiorentino said with a welcoming smile. "Come on in, we're ready for you." I noticed the grand exposed-wood beams and hipster brick walls that lined the industrial loft as I walked into the audition room. It was longer than it was wide. Along with the lively novelist-turned-director Walt Becker, two young writers and a handful of producers were there. Including the casting team, there were probably twelve people in that room.

Ryan Reynolds was immediately super gracious (*Are you nervous?*), hilarious (*Don't fuck it up!*), and encouraging (*Hey, you're funny! Let's improvise a little on the next scene*). Walt asked us to play around with the material and color outside the lines a bit. The improvisation with Ryan was fun because I felt like I was being creative with an old friend—clearly we had chemistry, and because of that he just felt like my people. I was immediately put at ease. We even had a fulfilling conversation about Taj's story arc—the kind of discussion I hadn't had since I auditioned for the part of Kumar Zimmerman. I wasn't expecting everyone to be so young and approachable. I went home knowing I did everything I could to get this job. *Sorry McPainty.*

I should probably acknowledge that while the reservations I had about potentially playing a character named Taj Mahal vanished once I saw that my competition was a white dude in brownface, other misgivings had not. (If I landed the part, would everything work out like Barbara Cameron and Sonia predicted? If it didn't, would I get typecast moving forward?)[7]

---

7   I look back at that time using today's metrics and think to myself, *It would have*

The waiting period that evening was agony. I knew they were going to make a quick decision, so each passing hour felt like a week. I tried to distract myself (TV, reading, email; nothing could take my mind off this). When Barbara Cameron finally rang around 8 p.m., we talked over each other from the start. "Hel—"

"You booked it!"

I felt all the feelings—elation, joy, relief. And pure excitement. It was going to be *me* in this supporting lead role. It wouldn't go to some uncle and auntie's premed son or a white dude in brownface. I was going to be Taj Mahal Badalandabad.

After I officially booked the part, I made a checklist based on my conversation with Sonia: identify the ten most cringeworthy parts of the script and come up with funnier alternatives. I pored over the scenes. I replaced some existing formulaic lines that seemed basic (mostly tropes based on race or skin color) and tried to turn them into real jokes grounded in the character. A couple of weeks before shooting, I took a deep breath and planned to bring my concerns to the writers and director during rehearsal.

The day before that rehearsal, the producers asked me to meet with a dialect coach. "We want to make sure your Indian accent is authentic." I was very amused that people who decided to name an exchange student something as unrealistic as Taj Mahal were concerned enough for his accent to be right. In preparation for the audi-

---

been amazing to get the part, turn it down, and then have the studio explain why they hired a white actor in brownface to play the role. But today is not the year 2000. It wouldn't have mattered, and that dude would have gotten a credit on his résumé.

tion (and now the role), I'd already been talking to plenty of Indian immigrants with real accents (cousins and friends mostly). But if the producers were paying for lessons with an Indian dialect coach, I figured I might as well take advantage of it.

I drove to a house in the Hollywood Hills and was greeted at the door . . . by a white dialect coach named Nancy. *Jesus*, I thought to myself, *first I had to creatively eviscerate Facey McPainty and now White Nancy is going to teach me an Indian accent?* We started the work session and as it turned out, Nancy was actually really good! She had lived in India most of her life, was trilingual, and had a PhD in South Asian linguistics from Princeton, so her command of language was really quite impressive. I'm kidding. She was just some white chick from LA whose Indian accent was as bad as Peter Sellers's. I politely sat through the first session and then went home.

I canceled the remaining dialect coach meetings via email and instead prepared for the next day's rehearsal with the writers and director.

Thankfully, Walt and his writers (Brent Goldberg and David Wagner) were as nice in our conversation as they had been at the audition. They were all about finding deeper humor, were receptive to my thoughts about the script and character, and agreed to change a few of the more cringeworthy things: a few lines with the irrelevant religious references, the lame jokes about different foods, stuff like that.

Originally in the script, Taj was supposed to wear traditional Indian clothing. In the real world, most young exchange students try extra hard to assimilate, not double down by wearing ethnic attire. I pitched the idea that something like a collection of ill-fitting sweater vests was more realistic and therefore more charming and grounded.

While Walt and the writers were agreeable to this, one of the producers was *furious*. He ranted with a bizarre combination of bravado and
sass. Sassy Producer carried on about how he had been to India (once,
in the early 1980s) and was therefore an expert on all things Indian.
Taj *had* to dress in traditional Indian clothes, because the people Sassy
Producer saw in India in 1982 were wearing traditional Indian clothes.
End of story. I got the sense that this strange behavior was far more
about his own ego than the best way to ground my character.

I employed more of Sonia's advice, and stuck to explaining the
clothes as a way to make the character witty and more engaging.
More truthful could mean *funnier*. It worked. Sassy Producer eventually relented. The character's wardrobe felt like a win, however minor.
Sonia was right; practical compromises would help me keep some
artistic integrity. Of course, there's plenty of stereotype—ethnic and
otherwise—in both the role I played and the film in general. But I was
glad to have comedic bits beyond that, and happy to be working with
people who mostly respected and appreciated my creativity within
the confines of what we were making.

As nerve-racking as those creative conversations about stereotypes
were, on the first day of shooting, I had to do something legitimately
life-and-death terrifying. Keep in mind that this was my first real
major motion picture. It was the very first scene I shot for my first
real major motion picture. And it was my first sex scene. *Ever.*

In one of Taj's pivotal moments in the film, an enthusiastic
girlfriend comes over to his dorm room to hook up. While they're
getting naked in the scene's climax,[8] he nervously rubs massage oil

---

8   I couldn't resist.

on them both. He then—most unfortunately—leans too close to a scented candle, and his back catches on fire. Not the back of his shirt, mind you—the skin on his actual *back*, set ablaze just as he's about to lose his virginity. Debauchery. Hilarity. Nudity. (Told ya it wasn't all ethnic stereotypes.)

The producers couldn't light my skin on fire *directly*, of course (special thanks to our labor union, the Screen Actors Guild). Weeks before, I had been sent to a special effects shop in the San Fernando Valley where three guys with long hair and very cool tattoos stripped me down and took a plaster mold of my back. Out of this they built a prosthetic back, which was really just a very thin piece of silicone with small, hidden openings at the top and bottom. On the set, this silicone prosthetic would be affixed along the full length of my back and colored in to match my real skin before it was doused with a flammable liquid and set ablaze. Standing in the freezing special effects warehouse in my underwear while three strange men lathered me up in plaster felt like pretty good prep for this sex scene.

So, there I was, arriving at my trailer on my first day of work on my first real movie ever. I put down my backpack, took a sip of my coffee, and saw the costume that the wardrobe stylist had laid out for me: boxers and a pair of socks. That's it. It didn't take long to put them on, or go through hair and makeup. I showed up half-naked on set and saw that since there would be flames in the scene, the entire crew had been given special fire-retardant "just in case" jackets. Firefighters were also standing around, dressed in masks and hats, with tanks strapped to their backs, as if they were getting ready to put out a dangerous wildfire. This freaked me out. I was the guy they were lighting on fire in his boxer shorts. Any contingencies they were planning for would affect me the most. Firefighters? Special jackets? *Just in case of what?!*

A guy hollered from across the dimly lit room. "Kal Penn! Taj

Mahal Badalandabad!! How are ya, I'm Rod!" As Rod got closer, I noticed he had a quarter-inch-wide scar running the length of his face, from the top of his right temple, through his forehead, around his left eye, down his nose, ending below the left side of his cheek just after the border of his neck. "I'm your stunt coordinator. My primary concern is your safety. Just do what I say, and you'll stay safe. Promise."

Ohmygod.

Shouldn't a stunt coordinator have been able to avoid a scar like that?

Here's how the rest of the day went. Scarface Rod supervised the setup as two firefighters poured some gasoline on my silicone prosthetic back and lit it on fire before each take. When Walt yelled "Cut!" they'd smother the flames with a blanket. A third firefighter would then shoot ice-cold water through those hidden openings of the prosthetic and directly onto my real back to mitigate the heat transference. "We gotta do that quick," said Rod, "so the heat don't move through the silicone and burn off your skin." *Okay yeah, it seems like you should do that, Rod, thank you.*

I should have been scared, but I was running on adrenaline. I couldn't wait to tell my friends with as much humblebrag nonchalance as possible, "Yeah, of *course* I do my own stunts." The real challenge, it turned out, wasn't being lit on fire. It was the acting performance that followed: making moves on a half-naked actress as a virginal exchange student *while* on fire. My equally half-naked scene partner, the lovely and talented Ivana Bozilovic, thought the sight of me running around with flames shooting off my back was so hilarious (thankyouverymuch) that she busted out laughing in the middle of the first few takes. I had to get lit on fire over and over again until we got it right. *My first day on a studio film set and I was so funny that I was going to burn to death.*

*   *   *

During breaks that first day, I got to know the writers better and pumped them for information. Ever since auditioning for a character named Taj Mahal Badalandabad, I had wondered two things: 1) Why did they decide to make the character Indian? and 2) How did they decide on his last name?

It turned out that the choice of his ethnicity was somewhat random. There hadn't been that many Indian characters in movies, so this seemed like a fresh take to them. The important thing was that without Taj, they said, the plot wouldn't progress. I was happy to know that my initial assessment of Taj's creative grounding was solid.

And his last name? They just made it up. That was . . . *hilarious*. To those of you who don't speak Hindi, let me explain. The end of Taj's last name, -abad, could be taken from any number of generic cities—Allah*abad*, Ahmed*abad*, Abbott*abad*. It's common. But the first two syllables of *Badalandabad* were interesting. In Hindi, *bada* means "big." And *land*—pronounced *lund*—means "cock." They had no idea they had literally named this character Taj Mahal Huge Cock.

I *love* subversive, subtle things! After I explained what it meant to David and Brent, we all had a good laugh about how they had unknowingly named a character whose central problem in life was that he couldn't get laid—a Big Dick Baller.

In all, I was a Big Dick Baller who was lit on fire around a dozen times to get that first scene right. It was hard work, and I enjoyed it. As the day wrapped up, Ivana asked me, "Hey, do you know why they started the shoot with one of the toughest scenes? We're both naked, getting it on. You're lit on fire. A lot could go wrong." She raised a very good point. Why not shoot it later in production when we had better chemistry and communication?

I asked Sassy Producer that question. He was such an unashamed hothead, I knew he'd be straightforward with me. "Do you *really* want to know?" he asked, with super-sassy satisfaction. "If we lose an actor, we'd have to recast and reshoot everything. It's a whole process. By doing this scene on the first day, if we lose you I would simply have to recast you. I wouldn't waste money having to reshoot all your other scenes."

Translation: If something goes wrong with the fire and you burn your face off or die, I won't have wasted more than one day of my production budget. Still plenty of time to call Facey McPainty and see if we can light *him* on fire next!

Damn. Ice cold. But also, damn did I appreciate his honesty. I laughed about the twisted logic of it all the way home—just as with a car, if the actor burns, you replace the actor.

———————

After *Van Wilder* wrapped, my agent suggested I might want to hire a manager to help with career development, so she introduced me to a tall, fast-talking, quirky guy named Dan Spilo. Spilo had graduated from Columbia University Law School before deciding that he'd rather pursue his passion on the business side of the arts world. Talent managers are different from agents in that they help artists develop over the lives of their broader careers, and eventually produce projects. They also serve a more basic function as an extra person trying to get the artist a job—and if you're a performer of color you need all the extra pushes you can get.

Dan took a look at a few advance, rough-cut scenes the *Van Wilder* producers were nice enough to give me on VHS, and he burst out laughing. "I can see why you don't want to play characters like this, but I have to tell you, you're *really* funny, dude. Holy shit! I want to help make sure you really break out from this. I'm confident you can. You just need someone in your corner who can push for you." This was such a contrast to what my friend Jenna's manager had said, about an Indian actor not working enough to make it worth a manager's while. If this guy believed in me and was hungry enough to put in the extra work, it was worth a shot. Without meeting anyone else, I hired Spilo to be my manager.

Before *Van Wilder* finally came out, the cast participated in a bunch of promotional tours and interviews called junkets, the first of which was at a hotel in Los Angeles that was so fancy, they had printed up personalized labels for glass bottles of mineral water.[9] I was excited to be included in this junket—eager that maybe positive reviews and articles could lead to more work opportunities. Before I left the greenroom for my first interview, Sassy Producer pulled me aside and put his arm around my shoulder. "I just want to say how glad I am that the movie turned out the way it did. You're so good in it."

"Thanks, Sassy! Thank you for the opportunity."

"I know this is your first time answering questions with the press, and I just want to make sure you're happy."

"Of course! I'm really excited, it's my first studio comedy!"

"Good. You know, if they ask about what it was like making this movie, you were *always* very excited . . ."

At this point he started pressing down on my shoulder.

". . . We never had any disagreements about the character, or his name . . ."

He pressed down harder.

". . . or his clothes or anything like that . . ."

Now he was pressing down really hard.

". . . Right?"

"Right!"

"Great." He offered what seemed like a genuine, wide smile. "It'll

---

9 The ones that look like tubes, not even the ones that look like normal bottles!

be a good junket. The spicy tuna salad at lunch is really delicious. Have fun!"

It was so gangster. I've told this story to a few friends, and they've been furious on my behalf. "That dude was trying to emasculate you! He was bullying you!" To be honest, I was more impressed than intimidated, realizing that this isn't actually the ignorant behavior it's often excused as. It's purposeful. It's planned. Anyway, I got his message loud and clear. Don't rock the boat. Know your place. Don't bring up our internal conversations about race and stereotyping. Only say positive things.

That had been my intention anyway. I was excited to promote my first film.

Welcome to Hollywood, on all counts. It's a town that might have a reputation for dishonesty, and yet that first experience taught me the opposite: It can be brutally sincere. From the truths my agent told in breaking down why I should audition, to the systemic "business" considerations, and the frankness about why I was being lit on fire first, nobody was sugarcoating anything. They were all being as truthful as they could about the things they needed for the project at the time—sometimes bluntly and brashly, and other times with incredible nuance and kindness. (Thanks again, Ryan.)

I felt a step closer to one day beating the Brown Catch-22, hanging in the big leagues, and realizing my dream of having a fulfilling artistic career. Heck, this is probably a good time to mention that I eventually even starred in a movie called *Van Wilder 2: The Rise of Taj*. Hollywood, like all of us, has continued to change and evolve. I'm thankful for that. And hey, I'm thankful you kept me safe, Scarface Rod.

Even today, I do my own stunts.

CHAPTER NINE

OF SALINGER AND STRIP CLUBS

It was at least 3 o'clock on a Sunday morning when we stumbled into the Crazy Horse Too for Kenny Burton's Vegas bachelor party.

Ken was the first in our group of UCLA buddies to get married—he wed his wonderful college girlfriend, Stacy, a few years after graduation. After two solid nights of drinks, gambling, and roller coasters, Kenny wanted to hit a strip club. Our job was to take him to one.

At twenty-five years old, none of us were from the area, and most of us knew nothing about Las Vegas strip clubs. This was the same bunch of guys who stayed up all night cramming for sciency university exams. Someone decided to ask a cabdriver, and on the second of Kenny's four-night extravaganza, eighteen hammered dudes descended on the Crazy Horse Too in a caravan of taxis. It was festive, if that's an appropriate way to describe such an establishment being invaded by a group of nerds like us.

For those of you who don't know how ~~adult entertainment venues? dens of sin? Is there another phrase I can use to make my participation in this story sound less bad? no? okay then~~ strip clubs work, allow me to explain. You pay your entry fee at the front and walk inside. You can sit anywhere in the main room and watch the main stage. Women will approach you every so often and ask, "Would you like a dance?" If you say yes, they begin the ~~entertainment? Act of~~ ~~sin? Is there another phrase I can use to make this sound less shady?~~ ~~No? okay then~~ stripping. The stripper (actual job title) charges the strippee (not a technical word) a standard flat rate per song.

Strip clubs don't play the entirety of each song, only about a minute or two. That way they can charge you more. So, don't bother trying to request "Bohemian Rhapsody" because you think it's a good deal, you won't make it anywhere near "Scaramouch." I haven't attempted this. I'm just clarifying, on background, for the *educational* purposes of this story.

Our group sat watching the main stage, declining various lap dance offers, when a particularly striking and articulate young woman hovered over me. "Hey baby. I'm Sunny. Would you like a dance?"

"No, I'm all right, thank you."

Sunny leaned in. "Hey! I know who you are! You're Kal Penn! I'm a really big fan. Are you sure you don't want a dance?"

My buddies were floored, saying things like, "Dude, that stripper knows who Kal is. Unbelievable—he had one small part in that *Van Wilder* movie!"

"Come on, one dance?"

I again politely declined her offer. "That's not really my thing but thank you very much."

Sunny sized up our group and slid into the open chair next to mine.

"I'm just going to sit here and talk to you for a while then!"

"You're talking to me off the clock?" I clarified. (My immigrant parents raised me right.)

"Yeah, off the clock, don't worry. I just think it's so cool that you're here. I'm a really big fan of your movie. I'm Indian too!"

Oh shit! I thought. *That's amazing, an Indian American stripper!* A note for you, dear reader: For all the impressive headway the Indian American community has made in lots of professions—medicine, engineering, the law—there are shamefully few of us in Sunny's line of work.

For the next twenty minutes, Sunny and I got to know each other.

SUNNY: What was it like making *Van Wilder*?

ME: *(sweating)* I really enjoyed it.

SUNNY: What brings you to Vegas?

ME: *(sweating and smiling)* A college buddy's bachelor party!

SUNNY: Are your Indian parents supportive of your acting career?

ME: You know, my dad moved to America with twelve dollars in his pocket and other ideas for their son, but they're coming around! Okay, my turn. *(sweating and smiling and trying to be funny)* Are *your* Indian parents supportive of your stripping career?

SUNNY: It's more of a side hustle than a career, so I don't tell them about it.

ME: I figured; I was just joking.

An awkward pause.

SUNNY: Oh, so you think my life is a joke?

ME: No, not at all! I was totally kidd—

SUNNY: Relax, Taj, I'm kidding too.

Sunny winked.

ME: That was impressive. Pretty sure I just shit my pants, Sunny, thanks.

My buddies were watching every move in total amazement. One of my friends drunkenly reasoned that since I had started dating dudes recently, I must be having an excruciating time dealing with naked Sunny's fangirl questions and tried to *save* me. "Hey, you don't have to do this just to impress any of us."

I gave him a stern smile that umistakably conveyed, "Back off, Ryan, I am loving this! It's not every day a stripper tells me she's a fan of my work! (An Indian American stripper no less.) She likes *Van Wilder*! You can impress her with the Excel spreadsheets you crunch at PwC later. Don't cockblock my platonic moment! I am living liiiiiifffffe!"

ME: Sunny is a stage name, right?

SUNNY: Yup.

ME: Did you pick it because you're a *Catcher in the Rye* fan?

SUNNY: Umm . . . no. Sorry.

ME: "No, that's not why I picked it" or "No, I'm not a fan"?

SUNNY: No offense, but I've always thought *Catcher* was over-rated. *Franny and Zooey* is way better Salinger.

ME: My God, who are you?!

It turned out that Sunny was a psychology doctoral student from the Bay Area who flew to Vegas a few times a month to work at the Crazy Horse Too.

Look at me, I thought. *I really am a regular Holden Caulfield!*[1]

Sunny excused herself every few minutes to make her lap dance rounds. Several of the guys in our group ordered some dances as well, but she always came right back to the open seat next to mine. At some point around four thirty, the bachelor decided it was time to return to the hotel.

"Kal, it was so nice to meet you!" Sunny said. "We should stay in touch!" The guys had formed a semicircle behind her. *Did she just say we should stay in touch?*

"Sure. Let me give you my number." I wrote my digits down with a pen and handed it to her.

Sunny piped up, "It was really nice meeting all your friends too." She winked at me, then turned around and flirtatiously winked at the dudes. Sunny knew how to make a guy look *good*.

My closing had to be smooth. "It was really great hanging out with you, Sunny," I said as she turned to leave. "AND CAN I JUST SAY HOW REFRESHING IT IS TO MEET ANOTHER INDIAN AMERICAN IN A NONTRADITIONAL FIELD?"

Oh my God, why did I just say that? Ryan shook his head. Two of the guys put their hands over their eyes. *This is the big-time star of* Van Wilder? We quickly left.

The next morning I had no missed calls from Sunny. The guys imagined what the previous night could have been: *Sunny comes over. She falls in love*

---

1   In *The Catcher in the Rye*, Holden Caulfield hires a prostitute named Sunny and all they do is talk. Of course, a white American prostitute named Sunny is very different from an Indian American stripper named Sunny, but this is otherwise a fairly smart literary reference for such a dumb story and you should be impressed.

with Ryan's incredible math skills. What a great love story: a kindhearted accountant and a balanced, sex-positive PhD student, meant to be. It was pretty late when we left the club. Maybe all wasn't lost. Maybe she'll call today.

Our friend Raju threw cold water on our fairy tale: "You know that woman wasn't actually Indian, right?"

"What do you mean? Of course she was Indian. We spent like an hour and a half talking about being brown!"

"Nah, dude. She was just trying to get us to buy more lap dances. That lady was from El Salvador."

"Are you serious?"

"Yes. I heard her speaking Spanish to one of the other strippers."

"So? I took French in high school."

"Exactly. And you aren't fluent."

"What about the PhD program?"

"I'm pretty sure that part was real. But she was definitely not Indian."

I couldn't believe it. Yo, Latina Sunny was a good actor!

Today, the Crazy Horse Too is permanently closed. It apparently had a long history of mob ties. The shell of a building a few blocks west of the Las Vegas Strip shut down shortly after our attendance when the owner and some employees pleaded guilty to tax fraud and racketeering. Wherever you are, Sunny, I hope you got your PhD without getting caught up in all that. Your hustle still impresses me. I'd be down to grab a drink and talk Salinger sometime. And if you ever decide you want to put your psychology practice on hold to become a professional actor, I know a very high-powered casting director you should meet. She also can't tell the difference between Indian and Latin.

CHAPTER TEN

LIVING THE DREAM

"**D**on't you ever regret doing *Van Wilder*?" is a question I'm asked every so often, by a newer generation of South Asians who have the privilege of seeing the world through today's vacuum. Answering this question is exciting because it signifies the progress of the last two decades. Do I wish my first movie was an action film in which I played a super-hot marine who saves the world from bad guys parachuting out of the sky? Of course. But I'm pretty sure Chris Hemsworth did that in *Red Dawn*. Not only did I genuinely enjoy working on *Van Wilder* (naked back on fire and all), but without Taj Mahal Badalandabad, there'd be no *Harold & Kumar* in my life. I have no regrets. Here's why.

I was at an outdoor bar at the farmers market on Fairfax Avenue in Hollywood for the birthday party of one of the producers of the Jamie Kennedy film *Malibu's Most Wanted*[1] when my coworker

---

1 In which I played an *implied* terrorist named Hadji (a word that refers to a Muslim who has made the pilgrimage to Mecca and is also used as a slur, depending on the intent and circumstance).

Billy Rosenberg (then jovial assistant to the birthday boy, now jovial powerhouse Hulu executive!) introduced me to two of his friends: "Meet Jon Hurwitz and Hayden Schlossberg. They just wrote a script called *Harold & Kumar Go to White Castle*—a stoner-buddy comedy about the adventures of two friends who go on an accidental road trip to quench their late-night munchies." (Okay, the way he actually said it sounded more casual.) I managed to say, "Hey guys, nice to meet you!" before Hurwitz blurted out, "Whoa, you don't have an Indian accent." I must have given him a pretty dirty look because Jon quickly clarified: He had seen me in *Van Wilder* and assumed the accent was real,[2] so he was doubly impressed that it wasn't. As we made small talk over a beer, we realized that we both attended public high schools in New Jersey in the mid-nineties, and Hurwitz asked, "Wait a second, did you do Forensics? I think I vaguely remember a kid who looked like you at the New Jersey meets." Being from New Jersey is like an ethnicity. This was instant bonding.

I thought their *White Castle* concept was potentially funny, and when the guys sent me their script the next day, my mind was completely blown. *Harold & Kumar Go to White Castle* was (and remains) the funniest screenplay I had ever read. The characters were smart and hilarious, and the humor was grounded in the friendship the title characters shared. The scenes were so absurd, in all of the right ways, with the two leads getting super stoned and somehow hang-gliding and riding a cheetah on their quest for hamburgers.

And of course, the biggest surprise of all: Kumar and Harold happen to be Asian American—without goofy accents, karate moves, turbans, or any other easy stereotypes. *That's* why Hurwitz was

---

2   Thanks, White Nancy!

excited to learn that I didn't have an Indian accent. This was the first time I had ever seen non-stereotypical Asian guys in lead roles, in *any* film script. Harold even gets the girl!

Why did two funny white guys from New Jersey write a movie with two Asian American lead characters? I called the dudes immediately. Jon told me that he and Hayden had a diverse group of friends in high school[3] and college. Whenever they'd watch movies together, they thought it was weird that the Asian or Indian characters would barely speak. So, they just wrote them as leads in a movie themselves.

Respect. Unfortunately, these sweet, naive newbies didn't understand Hollywood the way I did. "Guys, this script is really awesome," I told them, "but you're new to LA. There's no way a studio is going to buy this thing." I was trying to be helpful. A few years earlier, two Asian American writers I knew were offered sour deals—told by studios that their scripts would be purchased as long as the Asian and Indian lead characters were changed to white ones. In both cases, they said no, opting instead to scrape together the cash to self-finance their films. "When nobody buys *Harold & Kumar*," I told Hurwitz and Schlossberg, "let's just do it ourselves. I'd love to help raise the money to make this independently. It's the funniest thing I've ever read."

The guys shut me down hard. "Kal, the script goes out to the market next week. We *are* going to sell it to a studio. And we're not going to change any ethnicities, or the spirit of the characters. We want to make *Harold & Kumar Go to White Castle*, not *David & Jason Go to McDonald's*."

A week later, Hurwitz called me. They had actually done it: *Harold & Kumar Go to White Castle* was sold to a company called

---

3 Jersey, baby!

Senator, with New Line Cinema distributing. Nobody asked them to change the ethnicity of the characters, and nobody would have to scrape together cash to fund the film independently. That's because two junior executives at New Line (one white, one black, both young) were given the opportunity to green-light and develop a lower-budget comedy. This is what they chose. It was perceived as a business risk, but they understood the characters and the world being created.

I'm wrong about a lot of things, and this time being wrong about the sale of the *Harold & Kumar* script made me happy. Knowing a film like this would exist in the world felt like a huge leap of progress, whether I could ultimately be involved in it or not. (But really, I needed to convince them to let me play Kumar.)

Just because I knew the guys who created the characters obviously didn't mean I was going to be handed the part. The auditions for *Harold & Kumar* were lengthy. Casting director Cassandra Kulukundis extended an especially wide net, getting submissions from around the world: New York, Chicago, London, Toronto, Sydney, Los Angeles. With plenty of qualified actors hoping to play the lead roles, the process was tedious. Opportunities like this hadn't just been few or far between for Asian American actors, they were nonexistent. This was the first. As the list narrowed, there were multiple rounds of callbacks held on the third floor of a black office building close to the beach in Santa Monica. Jon and Hayden were always there, along with director Danny Leiner, producer Greg Shapiro, and Cassandra's team. As with most callbacks, the closer you got to booking the role, the more people it seemed were in the audition room.

The opportunity to play a protagonist in a hilarious buddy comedy was a big part of my dream. I had never wanted a role so badly, so I intended to focus everything I had on earning it. Cassandra had given me a few character notes during the earlier auditions, which I wrote in the margins of the script (also known as audition sides). I'd wake up, work on the audition sides, go to the gym, work on the audition sides, make breakfast, work on the audition sides, shower, work on the audition sides. I felt like Rocky, except with audition sides. And a super-average body.

My experience and formal training helped me focus, and I pushed through the first four rounds. The last round was a chemistry test, like the one I had with Ryan Reynolds and Facey McPainty for *Van Wilder*. It came down to three actors for Harold and three for Kumar. All of us would sit in a waiting room together for an entire afternoon. We'd get called in—in pairs—to see who had the best chemistry: each choice for Kumar reading with each choice for Harold. They were looking for their perfect couple, their Brangelina, their Bennifer, their Haroldumar.[4]

Only two of us would get the gig. We had all been through lots of the same stereotypical Hollywood nonsense. Though we were competing, it felt like the end result would be a net positive for all of us. It was inspiring to be in a casting director's waiting room with these other talented Asian American actors vying for parts we knew we each had a fair shot at. Maybe I'd be too tall or too short in the end, but what a luxury that would be. My race wasn't a disqualifier or a knock against me. There was zero risk that the parts could go to some guys in yellow or brown makeup.

Ultimately, I was cast as Kumar, with John Cho playing Harold.

---

4   Never mind. That doesn't quite work.

I'll tell you guys a little secret that not even Cho knows as I'm writing this. Of the three choices for Harold, I felt the *least* chemistry with John in the audition room. This is such a ridiculous thing to have felt in retrospect. At the time, I was so in my head, I convinced myself that if they were to favor John for Harold then they'd go with one of the other choices for Kumar (and vice versa if they first decided I was the clear front-runner). Just goes to show you how completely insane actors can be. It turned out, Cho and I had the best chemistry. To this day, I have such deep love for that dude.

When it came down to getting cast, it wasn't just my audition being *marginally* better that got me the role of Kumar. I'm not trying to sell myself short here—I gave a great audition and worked like hell to prepare for it. But so did the other guys. Part of the reason the role went to me is because none of the other prospective Kumars had been cast in a studio comedy before. I was the only Taj Mahal Badalandabad, and therefore perceived as the more professional choice.

My agents, of course, had totally predicted this. That's why they pushed me to audition for *Van Wilder*. It's why they called back after I hung up on them, and it's why they encouraged me to build up a résumé and fight for auditions—even distasteful ones (see Hadji). It's what Sonia Nikore meant when she advised me to work at making scripts funnier, pay my dues, and build a career. All of that advice had been true. Do I wish I had a time machine with a magic wand inside that could make us live in a world where the industry was fair and equitable, and I didn't have to make those imperfect choices along the way? Well, yeah, obviously (mostly because that would be sick as hell, a time machine *and* a magic wand). But that world doesn't exist. Without Taj, I wouldn't have been Kumar. I don't regret playing my cards right.

A week before we began production on the film, Danny Leiner invited us to a debaucherous party at his house in the Hollywood Hills. A totally wasted young blond woman I'll call Rebecca slurred her way up to me: "Hiiiiiiiiiiiiii. I'm Ruh-BECCA, one of Danny's good friends, and I jussssss wanna say I'm so glad he cast you!"

"Thank you very much, Rebecca. I'm very excited about it all. Can I get you a water?"

"Shhhhhhhhh look. I saw the final-round audition tapes and I told Danny, I said mmmmmmake sure . . . mmmmmmake sure you hire the hot guy to play Kumar, he's very attractive."

"Thank you. I'm flattered."

"Ya, I said Danny don't hire the other guy. That UCLA guy from New Jersey? Don't hire him, he's definitely not good-looking enough."

Finally, I had the luxury of not being hot enough! And I managed to get cast anyway.

Harold & Kumar Go to White Castle takes place in New Jersey and was shot primarily in Toronto. I landed at Pearson International Airport and hopped in a car with someone from the show's transportation team who took me to the Minto Yorkville—an under-construction long-term furnished rental building in a fancy part of the city. That evening, as I unpacked my suitcases while listening to a Dr. Dre playlist (I make playlists for all my characters), John Cho knocked on my door. "Hey. We're supposed to be best friends. Let's grab a drink."

We headed over to an expensive-looking bar in our new expensive-looking neighborhood, where I ordered an expensive Amstel Light and John ordered some kind of scotch I had never heard of. We immediately hit it off.

"I'm really glad we're making this movie," he said to me. "I don't know how you feel about it, but I've thought a lot about how there's never been a film like this before. The script is *so* funny. And it's got two Asian American leads. That's two more than usual."

"Dude, I know! I'm so glad you feel this way too! When I read the script, I told Jon and Hayden it wouldn't get made unless someone financed it independently. But here we are."

We ordered another round and continued talking. John told me about a litmus test he had imposed on himself: the Twelve-Year-Old Me Rule. "Basically, how would the twelve-year-old me feel about the job I'm about to take? We didn't have anything like this movie when we were twelve. I think the twelve-year-old me is going to be pretty damn proud when it comes out."

I knew exactly what he meant. I told him I had a similar metric to judge things. I called it "My Middle School Me Rule," after those experiences getting called Apu and Johnny 5. How would middle school me feel today? Middle school me would have hated *Van Wilder*, but absolutely venerated *Harold & Kumar*.

"'My Middle School Me Rule' has a better ring to it," he conceded.

"But twelve-year-old me is more on point," I shot back.

Our evening was going well. I started to order us a third round of drinks, when John stopped me. "Are you seriously getting a THIRD beer? You don't like scotch?"

"I've never had scotch before."

"You've never had scotch before?!"

He made it sound like I confessed to a very shocking crime.

John turned to the bartender and announced, "He's never had scotch before! Forget his beer. We'll have two more of *these*."

When the scotches arrived, each poured into an ornate glass, I motioned to cheers John and do my shot. "NOOOOOOOOO! NO! NO!" he shouted, stopping me before the liquor touched my lips. "Jesus! This is not a shot! You drink it slowly." He then proceeded to teach me to sip scotch. The eventual buzz was kind of nice. Light. I could see why gentlemen in magazines dressed in fancy clothing would properly consume scotches during flowing conversations.[5]

My first big movie and my first big scotch. I was all grown up.

Our instantaneous bromance also meant that John and I became more like siblings than work friends. We were together on set almost constantly for the entire two-and-a-half-month shoot. A lot of the movie takes place inside a car, and about half of that was filmed in front of a green screen in a windowless studio. The downside was that we'd often spend twelve hours a day sitting in a parked vehicle with no air circulation. The upside was that we could get out to stretch our legs every so often, since we weren't actually on the open road.

Once, we were sitting in the car with our seat belts on while the camera guys adjusted something technical. "I'm cold," John said. "Can I roll these windows up until you guys are ready to shoot?"

After a minute with the windows up, he said he started to feel stuffy. "I'm going to step out." He opened his door and in sudden rapid succession: removed the keys from the ignition, loudly farted,

---

5 Still not sure why they all have mustaches in these magazines, but I do think that's kinda tite too. Gotta respect any mustache that comes close to looking like the Lorax's.

jumped out, hit the power locks, and slammed the door, leaving me seat-belted inside his airtight fart machine, with no way out.

I fucking love that guy.

H&K was every bit the dream job I hoped it would be, and each day on the set felt like a gift. Unfortunately, not the type of gift that would pay the bills. *Hold up, Kal. You're telling me you didn't make any money on* Harold & Kumar? That's not at all what I'm telling you. I made some money, sure, but I didn't make "never have to work again" money.

My gross salary for *Harold & Kumar Go to White Castle* was the equivalent of what the US Census Bureau called median household income.[6] After deducting the standard expenses—agent, manager, and lawyer fees; paying publicist salaries and taxes—what I was left with was good enough to live off of for about five months. To be clear, that's a huge victory. I had a roof over my head just from acting—I was supporting myself with my art, which meant that by my count, I was finally living the dream.

Having a publicist took some getting used to. I briefly had one after *Van Wilder*, and as a newcomer, I found her to be helpful in navigating things like those press junkets. Since I was now playing a *title* character in a movie, my manager, Dan Spilo, recommended I hire a way more established PR rep. The new publicist was sort of ridiculous. In the several months that I worked with him, I can't remember ever seeing his eyes blink. He always carried around an extra-large cup of coffee and popped either an Adderall or Xanax at spaced inter-

---

6 To put that into perspective, after initially opening to poor box-office numbers, the movie grossed at least $30 million in its explosive first two years on DVD (so the current number is way, way more than $30 mil). And no, we don't get any of that big money—those are the fairly negotiated breaks, kids!

vals depending on the time of day. If you met or talked with him before Adderall #1 kicked in, you'd know it because his eyelids would stay half-closed. He'd hold the side of his head with one hand, nurse the cup of coffee with the other, and tilt his neck slightly back so he could see you with the open part of his eyes. "Ugh. I just . . . I don't know what it *is* with me. The bottle of red wine I had last night must have been *spoiled*."

Once the pill took effect, his eyelids would fully retract, and you wouldn't ever see them again until it wore off a few hours later. During this time he'd talk very fast, about anything that came into his mind, from food trends to workout routines to serendipitous life events that he was sure had to do with either magic crystals or the position of Mercury.

On the plus side, he was always super nice to me and had a reputation for being a stellar publicist. The goal of hiring him wasn't to get my name out there for the sake of fame or attention, it was to get specific types of press that could lead to more acting work—articles in magazines and interviews on television that would make me more bankable in the eyes of casting directors and producers.

There were some immediate missteps. I naively followed his advice when he instructed me to "just make stuff up that you think sounds funny as your character" before an interview with *Playboy*. Days later I was horrified to read the piece laid out as if my made-up, improvisational riff was a real interview about my sex life.[7]

He would also leave me unbelievable voice mails ranging from "We need to partner you with a nonprofit. I can get magazines to publish pictures of you doing charity work," to "I'm going to send you a list of actresses who are up-and-coming. Let me know who

---

7 Then nonexistent.

you want to have dinner with so I can call the paparazzi and get some photos of your date in the tabloids." Was this how Hollywood publicity operated? I was always eager to invest in something that would get me more work, but this kind of stuff, what do you call it?—lying—wasn't for me. I let the publicist go.

With no real press to get no real jobs, those five months of living expenses didn't turn out to be much of a safety net, so I eventually needed to return to some temporary gigs. And I suddenly found that I couldn't get the kinds of day jobs I had relied on before. Production houses were hesitant to hire a somewhat-recognizable actor in an assistant role, because they knew I'd leave as soon as I got more acting work. And the service and retail industries wouldn't hire me in coffee shops, clothing stores, bars, or restaurants because they said I could potentially hold up business. "You won't be able to take orders as quickly if a customer turns out to be a fan." Apparently nobody wanted people's lattes getting cold if I was stopped and asked which special effects were used to light my back on fire in *Van Wilder*.[8]

Most people would think, Harold & Kumar *was a hit! Now it's on to fame, fortune, and fancy cars!* In real life, it was more like, "*Harold & Kumar* was a hit! Now you're not allowed to work at Jamba Juice."

That was real life: I was living the dream, but I was too recognizable to land a day job and too financially strapped to know if I would make rent in a few months. So, you can imagine my relief when Spilo told me I had an audition for the supporting best friend role in an upcoming Ashton Kutcher film called *A Lot Like Love*.

One of Ashton's friends was initially set to play the part until a bigger part in another movie came along for him. With the role open, they thought of me for the audition because the casting director's

---

8   None, it's real fire! I told you I do my own stunts, y'all.

assistant happened to be my good friend Lauren Grey. Finally, nepotism opening the door in my favor!

Completing *Harold & Kumar* allowed me to skip the first round of auditions and go straight to meeting the producers and director. Lauren greeted me in the waiting room and introduced me to the team: her boss (the casting director), the producers, and the very affable British director Nigel Cole. As Lauren videotaped, I read the audition sides. Nigel gave me a few character notes, and I read it a second time. Things seemed to be going well. Until . . .

"Kal, we'd like to see you do it again . . . this time with an accent."

It was Lauren's boss.

"Oh . . . the character has an accent?"

This was totally unexpected. I was reading to play a guy named Jeeter, Ashton's character's friend and business partner, who sells a company in a massive deal, charms a woman on their flight home, and buys an expensive car. Nothing in Jeeter's background indicated he might need to have an accent. The script was well written on its own.

I wanted to tell everyone in the room to fuck off and just walk out, but I knew Lauren vouching for me was why I was in there to begin with. I quickly glanced at her for guidance, and from the horrified look on her face, knew she had absolutely no clue this might have been coming.

"Sure. What kind of accent do you want?" I said, staring at British Nigel. "I can do *British* . . . Scottish, Brooklyn, New Orleans . . ."

The casting director interrupted. "Obviously, Indian is what we'd like to hear."

I read the scene once more with an Indian accent. A still-mortified Lauren looked sullen as I finished up and left.

As soon as I got to the car, she called. "I'm so sorry, Kal. I don't know what the fuck that was about. There was never any conversation about this character having an Indian accent. That was so racist. I'm so sorry. Nigel didn't even know that my boss was going to ask you to do an accent. They don't want this character to have one. You were great, and they're going to call Spilo to offer it to you later today. I just had to call to say I'm sorry. That was really fucked up."

"Wait, I got the part?! No accent?"

"You got the part, definitely no accent."

"Hell yeah!! Thank you!! And yeah, I don't know what was up with your boss, but that was really lame."

Shooting *A Lot Like Love* was a wonderful experience with very nice people. Nobody mentioned the audition incident on set, although Lauren and I will often reminisce about it. (She's now a casting director in her own right, and still very horrified about that day.) Ashton was an absolute gentleman, as was Nigel. And the quick scene in which I woo and charm the woman on the plane follows me around to this day. The part of that woman was played by a young fellow up-and-comer named Meghan Markle, and from what I remember of that enjoyable day of filming, we were as friendly as two actors of color with small roles could be.

A few weeks after my short stint on *A Lot Like Love*, I got an offer for a supporting role in Jamie Kennedy's next movie, *Son of the Mask*.

Jamie is an outgoing stand-up comic, with a perfect command of bizarre characters and ridiculous situations (like the time he played a waiter who had his mouth wired open and drooled on everyone's food on his hilarious prank show *The Jamie Kennedy Experiment*). We initially met on the set of *Malibu's Most Wanted*,[9] and we hit it off so well that when I booked *Harold & Kumar Go to White Castle*, we asked Jamie to play a weird disheveled guy in a suit who pees on a bush in a forest next to Kumar. So, when Jamie was set to play the lead in *Son of the Mask*, he recommended me for the role of Jorge, a computer techie.

The part was pretty straightforward. Jorge was just there to support Jamie's character, in scenes spaced throughout the movie. My salary would cover a few months' rent, I'd get to spend some time with my friend, and the film was shooting in Australia—a place I hadn't been and sounded exciting!

I landed in Sydney, took a quick shower, and went to my first rehearsal. I was greeted by the cheery director. He was short and—not to be a dick about it but—smiled a lot in a stupid sort of way. If there was a sound to go along with this director's grin, it would be one of those old Warner Bros. cartoon dogs, *uh-hoo-hoo-hoo-hoo*. This guy had a lot of energy. He wore two large hearing aids, a faded T-shirt, and comfortable-looking jeans with running shoes. My first impression of him during the audition was that he had a boring personality, which is rare for someone in a creative leadership position. This was confirmed once we sat down to go over the role. Because, as if this was the most goddamn brilliant genius idea any human had ever come up with in his life, he excitedly said, "So . . . I decided that Jorge should have an Indian accent! *Uh-hoo-hoo-hoo-hoo.*"

This bullshit again.

---

9   Where I met Billy Rosenberg, who introduced me to Jon and Hayden.

I put on a game face and did the three things I had become accustomed to doing in these situations: 1) Ask why my character needs to have an accent even though I knew the answer (*because it would make it so much funnier!*[10]), 2) Offer to instead help make the character funny on the merits of who he is, and 3) Pitch any number of *other* accents I could do besides Indian: Boston? Yiddish? Australian?

Director Original Ideas McGee had a predictable response: "No, that wouldn't be very *authentic.*"

I raised my voice a few times about why I didn't want to play this role with an Indian accent before saying to myself, *You know what, I just wrapped* Harold & Kumar Go to White Castle. *I didn't do* A Lot Like Love *the way the casting director hoped. I don't need to regress into a role with a reductionist accent, and I don't need to waste my energy getting upset.* I sent Dan Spilo a straightforward email: "Please call production and have them fly me home, I'm obviously not playing a role like this. Sucks to lose the money, but I'll figure it out. I'll be in my hotel room packing and will be ready to roll to the airport ASAP. Thank you."

We were supposed to start shooting a week later, and out of respect to my friend Jamie—for whom I wished success—I wanted to make sure Original Ideas McGee could cast someone else who was okay with the stereotypical accent he wanted. Surely there were other brown actors for whom this could be a way to break out of the Brown Catch-22.

Then my phone rang. It was Dan.

"Bad news. The studio is saying if you left, you'd be in breach of contract since they flew you to work in Australia already. This really isn't worth damaging your reputation over. It sucks, but you need to stick it out and do the character the way they want."

---

10   AKA: Because our writing is subpar.

"Damage *my* reputation? I'm not the asshole telling an actor to do some racist buffoonery because I'm not talented enough to come up with something better!" I was pissed. "Dan, I'm not fucking doing it. I've had it with this! I'm not breaking *My Middle School Me Rule!*" I hung up.

Reality set in with a call from my lawyer: Getting sued for breach of contract was a big deal, often designed as a deterrent. The studio could go after me for millions of dollars, which obviously I didn't even have. I had to suck it up and do the accent.

Once we started shooting I made it a point to perform as *light* an Indian accent as possible. I'm talking *barely noticeable.* No way was I going to give them a full Apu. If these guys weren't going to let me leave, I was at least going to fight creatively for a somewhat-grounded character. Maybe over time, the great chemistry that Jamie and I have could shine through.

We did a few takes of the barely noticeable accent on my first day, and Original Ideas McGee yelled, "Cut! Kal, I don't think I heard an accent!" He lifted his left hand to cup his ear just behind the hearing aid. "Did you do one?" The way he did this reminded me of Portly Pete, the older guy with hearing aids who sat next to me at my pre-college telemarketing job, exasperatedly asking, "What did he say? I can't hear *shit!*" any time Skeezy Big Bird and Sad Joe Pesci made a speech. For a moment, I thought about my day on that job, and how awful it felt working for shady guys who lied to old people all day long.

This gave me an idea: I could lie to this buffoon.

ORIGINAL IDEAS MCGEE: Did you do the accent?

ME: Of course I did—this accent is so funny!

ORIGINAL IDEAS MCGEE: I didn't hear it, Kal! Make it thicker and louder in the next take!

ME: Of course, of course! You've got it, boss. I'll make it thicker and louder!

We did another take. Instead of thickening my accent, I made my eyes much wider and bobbed my head the way other white directors had asked me to do in the past. Original Ideas McGee saw my minstrel nonsense and because he couldn't hear well, assumed I actually made the accent thicker. He was very delighted. This went on every day: I would do a light accent → he couldn't hear well and would ask if I was doing one at all → I would make my eyes wide without thickening the accent → he'd believe I was speaking with a thicker accent because he couldn't hear well and was boring and a bigot and probably has a tiny penis. *Uh-hoo-hoo-hoo-hoo.*

If you're a masochist, you can force yourself to watch the DVD commentary of *Son of the Mask* and, just after the fourteen-minute mark, hear a very candid Jamie recount to Original Ideas McGee: "We would argue with Kal between takes because he didn't wanna do an Indian accent. Because he's like [bad Indian accent], 'I am not trying to be an Indian,' and he got so mad. We went, 'Do it more Indian!' He got really mad at us. And we would, like, say, 'Just be Indian, it was funnier!' Anyway, he got mad."

Bottom line: It was super exhausting. When the movie wrapped, I went back to LA tired and frustrated. But I also had enough cash in my bank account to cover rent for a few more months.

With *Son of the Mask* mercifully behind me, I reconnected with John Cho back in LA. In addition to being an enthusiastic scotch drinker and talented farter, John is an avid reader. During production on *H&K*, he was horrified to learn that I hadn't read Jhumpa Lahiri's *Interpreter of Maladies*. He gave me a copy, and, of course, I loved it.

Lahiri's book won the Pulitzer Prize—especially impressive because it was the first she ever published. It's a moving collection of short stories, most of them set against a backdrop of immigrant challenges, her beautifully crafted characters living with one foot in two worlds.

Her next book, *The Namesake*, came out shortly after, and John and I read it around the same time. It's an emotional coming-of-age story about an Indian couple and their American-born son in Boston. It easily became one of my favorite novels. I loved *The Namesake* for the same reason I loved *Catcher in the Rye*—I wasn't a rich New England boarding school kid, but Salinger's writing was so vivid that I felt like I was Holden Caulfield.[11] Gogol, the lead character in Lahiri's novel, was written so beautifully, so intimately, that I *needed* to play him in a film adaptation of the book.

John and I tried to get the rights to turn *The Namesake* into a movie, only to find that someone else had beaten us to it. And that someone was . . . director Mira Nair. Mira Nair, you'll remember, was the woman behind *Mississippi Masala*, the film that pushed me toward a career in the arts in the first place. She's who I stood in line to see on UCLA's campus one day, so I could hand her my headshot and résumé.

We couldn't have been happier at the news: Who besides Mira Nair could do justice to a beautiful book like *The Namesake*? Adapting novels into films is a time-consuming process, so I made a mental note that she had the rights and figured I'd hear from my agent whenever the movie was casting.

---

11   Damn, Sunny was good!

Just a month later my mom called. "Kalpen, I read an article in *India Abroad* that Mira Nair is in preproduction on *The Namesake*—you should audition to be Gogol! You'd be perfect! Call Dan." How rad, Mom telling me to call my manager and go in for an audition.

I followed my mom's sound business advice and began an aggressive campaign to get cast in the role of Gogol. Dan was surprised to find that they had rather quietly been searching for actors; this project wasn't on his radar either. He called Mira's office several times. No one called him back. In Hollywood, as in dating, if they don't return your phone calls, they don't want you. That was frustrating. I *had* to have a shot at this role. I just needed to figure out how to break through to them.

At my manager's suggestion, I decided to go rogue, sort of like I did when I directly mailed a note and audition tape to Barbara Fiorentino, the *Van Wilder* casting director. The difference was, with *Van Wilder*, I was desperate for a résumé builder. For *The Namesake*, it was about the art—the story. I composed a platonic love letter, holding nothing back. I told Mira that her movies were a massive influence on my life. They were funny, poignant, and empowering. They had opened up a world to me where pursuing storytelling as a craft was an actual possibility. I told her how inspired I was by seeing *Mississippi Masala* in high school, how powerful it was to see people who looked like us onscreen for the first time. Now she was directing a film adaptation of my favorite novel. She *had* to let me audition. *Had to*. A part like this was a once-in-a-lifetime opportunity. I was unabashed: I told her that playing a role like this—my *Catcher in the Rye*—directed by her, was the reason I became an actor. It was all true.

A few days after I sent the letter, Mira called Spilo asking that I fly to New York to audition. This was my big chance! Hands shaking with excitement, I hastily transferred some money from my savings account to my checking account and used my debit card to bid on a plane ticket on Priceline.com. I was at the airport a week later. Getting the chance to audition for Mira Nair was a dream come true, and I was happy to spend some of my *Son of the Mask* money on it.

As I walked into the bright, lofty office just off of Manhattan's Union Square, her assistant greeted me: "Hi, Kal! I'm Ami." *Oh, hell yeah, Mira has a badass Indian American woman working for her! This is incredible!* "Can I get you some water or chai?" *Holy moly, Mira Nair's badass Indian American assistant just offered me chai. This is exactly how this sequence played out in my dreams. Focus. FOCUS!*

"I'm fine, thank you," I said. I took a seat in the waiting area and looked over the audition scenes one last time.

A few minutes later, Mira came in and hugged me warmly. "Your letter was so lovely, Kal, thank you so much. Did Ami offer you some chai? Ami, did you offer Kal some chai?" *What was happening? I'm used to walking into auditions and being told "Wow, you're so articulate! Thicker accent, louder!" and here I am being offered chai? Twice?! Is this what it's like for white people every day of their professional lives?!*[12]

Now that I was standing in front of her, post-hug, I was eager to tell Mira about the time I handed her my headshot at UCLA. No time for that.

"Kal," she said, "I have to tell you two things. First, my thirteen-year-old son Zohran is a huge fan of yours and wanted to meet you. He's in school until two thirty. Can you stick around until then? He'll come say hi."

It had never occurred to me that Mira Nair's son could be a fan of mine.

"Of course. I'd love to meet him!"

---

12 Yes.

"The second thing you should know is that the role of Gogol has already been cast. But your letter was so beautiful, and you said that I *had* to let you come and audition anyway, so here we are."

What? Damnit. Okay, calm down.

I was going to have to talk myself off a ledge quickly. *You're not getting this part, but you said it yourself, you wanted a shot to read for this project, and for her. You still would have used part of your savings account to buy a ticket to audition. Count your blessings. Focus. And crush. This. Audition. Anyway. She'll have other projects in the future, so still give it your all. Focus on your work and impress her.*

I read the first scene. Mira looked worried. I read the second scene. She looked even more worried. Third scene. Mira put her head in her hands. I was confused: If I was doing a good job, why didn't Mira Nair look happy? She spoke up. "I wish I had auditioned you before I put an offer out to someone else. You're fantastic."

Was she just being nice, or did this cinematic icon actually mean that she wished I had auditioned sooner?

"Look," she said. "The other actor, you should know, has the *offer* for Gogol but has not closed his deal. He might have a problem doing some of the sex scenes. If you were cast, would you have the same problem?"

"Oh, that would be no problem for me," I said, remembering being lit on fire in my *Van Wilder* sex scene and boning that anthropomorphic bag of weed in *Harold & Kumar*.

Mira brightened. "You are really fantastic. I'm glad you wrote to me."

It turned out it wasn't just my letter that got me the audition. For the previous several months, Zohran and his friend Sam, both huge *Harold & Kumar* fans, had been lobbying her to audition me. The two of them dragged her over to a computer, where they showed her scenes from the *Harold & Kumar* DVD, insisting, "You have to audition Kal Penn for the part of Gogol!"

This, she admitted, only hurt my case. "I saw you play that character and thought, 'He's totally wrong for Gogol.'" The roles were very different: Gogol is a subdued, Ivy League–educated, sensitive, New York–based architect. Kumar, on the other hand, is a larger-than-life free-wheeling stoner who rides a cheetah. (You're welcome.)

Because Zohran had pestered his mom to audition me, when she received my letter, she gave in and called. Knowing that, I happily waited, thanked him for his fierce advocacy, and went back to LA with mixed feelings. I had spent some *Son of the Mask* cash to fly myself to New York for a role that would never be mine. But if I was honest with myself, I was still happy. I had the chance to meet and audition for a director who had influenced me since I was a kid. Doing *Van Wilder* meant I got *Harold & Kumar*, and doing *Harold & Kumar* meant I got to audition for Mira Nair. You can't put a price tag on that.

About a month after the *Namesake* audition, I went into a recording studio in LA for some ADR (automated dialogue replacement, or dubbing) on *Son of the Mask*. ADR is a common process. Sometimes during a shoot, there's a little background noise over a few lines from a truck going by, or an airplane overhead, something that drowns out the audio. So, during postproduction, you stand in front of a fancy microphone and dub whatever lines they have laid out on a music stand in front of you.

The email about *Son of the Mask* ADR said only three lines needed to be fixed, and that it wouldn't take more than twenty minutes. When I got to the studio, the sound engineer and Original Ideas

McGee were there waiting, as expected. Next to them were a couple of guys in suits also waiting, as . . . well, that was unexpected. These turned out to be studio executives on the project. Instead of one sheet of paper with three lines of ADR, they had placed the entire hundred-and-twenty-one-page script on the music stand. Something was up.

I exchanged fake pleasantries with everyone about how excited we all were about this hilarious project (one of the worst movies I've ever done), how much fun we had in Sydney (truly hated it), and how cool it was to see each other again (I never wanted to see their faces after this was over). Then they dropped it. "Hey man, so as we were editing, we realized your character didn't really have as pronounced of an accent as we thought, so we need to take a couple of hours and dub all your lines in a really thick Indian accent."

This was a shakedown. The studio executives were there to try to intimidate me. By this point in my short career, I knew how to handle hubristic tiny-dicked guys like this. "That's hilarious!" I said with an enthusiastic smile. "You really didn't think the accent was thick enough? Well, I want the character to be as funny as possible, so let's make it thicker!"

They seemed relieved that I was so agreeable. "The only thing is," I said, "the email said this was just a twenty-minute session. I have three auditions today. Can you guys call my manager to set up a day when I have the time to be here for a few hours? I'm excited to come back."

They bought it.

"Of course," one of the suited guys said. "We'll call over there right away."

"Can't wait!"

Randy Finn taught me in kindergarten that I could always outsmart a racist. The reality was, I didn't have any other auditions that day. I had no other auditions all week. In fact, I never wanted to go on any auditions ever again because if *this* was the shit I still had to deal with after doing *Harold & Kumar Go to White Castle*, then I was done with this industry.

I got in the car—by that point, my mom's Chevy Cavalier . . . the Toyota with the salvage title had since died on the 405 Freeway—and called Spilo. I cursed and ranted the entire drive from the studio to his office, yelling about how I never wanted to work in this town ever again—this fucking town, filled with so many people who claim to be so politically progressive when in reality they're just racist assholes.

"Calm down. You're coming to my office?" Dan said.

"I am! I need to discuss this face-to-face!" I said, before continuing my profanity-laced rant about how I was going to leave entertainment forever. "I am smart! I have other interests! I did my own stunts! I can do anything else! Fuck Gita and Ravi!" Every grievance. On and on and on. I was losing it.

I got to my manager's building, parked in a reserved space where the powerful owner of the company usually put his silly Lamborghini, and barged past the receptionist into Dan's office. I gave zero fucks at this point. I continued my ranting for another ten minutes, covering every racist experience from *Son of the Mask* back to talking cats and dancing monkeys. I couldn't take it anymore. I was finished with acting, and he needed to know it. *I quit.*

With that, I finally stopped to breathe.

"Are you done?" Dan chimed in.

"I don't know! Why?!"

"Because Mira Nair just called. The other guy backed out. You got the lead in *The Namesake*."

I started crying in his office. "Congratulations, man. Don't worry about *Son of the Mask*. Fuck them. I'll get you out of it. You're about to work on your dream project with your dream director. You're doing a Mira Nair film."

CHAPTER ELEVEN

NO PRIOR EXPERIENCE

The empowerment I felt at the audition just from something as innocuous as Mira Nair having an Indian American assistant really paled in comparison to what it was like on the set of *The Namesake* itself. It was so totally different from any other project I'd had the chance to work on. For starters, I hadn't had the opportunity to be part of a creative team that paid such attention to detail. Every word of the script and each frame of each scene seemed stealthily commissioned. With a nominal budget, equally financed by American, Indian, and Japanese companies, the production wasn't fancy. There were no big trailers or huge setups. Our dressing rooms were in a honey wagon: one long eighteen-wheeler subdivided into ten small, narrow spaces by thin, plastic retractable accordion blinds. Each narrow area had enough space for a small bench and one tiny toilet that doubled as a chair, but it was below a rod for hanging clothes, so you couldn't actually sit on it. Didn't matter. It was all you needed to prepare for each day's scene work. Besides, Mira didn't have a room like this. She didn't even use a chair. On set, she just sat on a wooden box covered with a thin cushion.

As a director, Mira Nair gave her cast and crew the gift of both unlimited on-set chai and ample preparation time. The prep period for the film stretched for weeks. This allowed us to rehearse and really research our characters. When you're working on a film based on a book, you have the entire expanded world at your fingertips. I took the train from New York up to New Haven, tracing Gogol's fictional steps as laid out by Jhumpa in the novel. Which dorm room at Yale was it where I lost my virginity? Which ATM might my wife and I have entered the password *LULU* into? It can be rare for an actor to have this kind of time to prepare.

Once we began shooting, even more time. During a somber scene in which Gogol visits his father's apartment shortly after he passes away, I had several beats of silence before breaking down in tears. Mira allowed only the cinematographer and sound guy on set that day, and when it was time to begin the scene, they too stepped out of the room. "When you think you're ready," Mira told me, "just open the door so we can switch on the camera. Give it half a beat and then you can begin." On a film set, time is money. Mira Nair liked to spend both in ways that respected and facilitated her actors' performances. *The Namesake* remains the project of which I'm most proud.[1]

A few pretty exciting things happened in rapid succession over the next few years: After I wrapped *The Namesake*, I got a small role in *Superman Returns* (had an incredible time but spoiler: most of my

---

1   *The Namesake* super fans might notice that in the end credits, it says Kal Penn played Gogol Ganguli and Kalpen Modi played Nikhil—a subtle hat tip to having two names like my character, albeit for different reasons.

lines ended up getting cut). We also shot a sequel to *Harold & Kumar* (*Escape from Guantanamo Bay*). I hired a speaking agent and began doing paid guest lectures on topics ranging from diversity in film to the business of acting; one such gig led to an opportunity to join the faculty at the University of Pennyslvania, where I was hired as a visiting lecturer for a semester to teach a course called Images of Asian Americans in the Media. Around the same time, my manager lined up an audition for a series-regular gig on the TV show *House*.

The show's producers were adding nine new characters to play fellowship doctors in the first part of season four. Of the nine, three would stay on permanently. The makeup of the audition waiting room was like nothing I'd seen: women and men, young, old, of different backgrounds and ethnicities. Auditioning for *House* felt futuristic. I originally read for the part of a Mormon doctor (ultimately played by Edi Gathegi, who is Black). Curious about why the show's creator, David Shore, would be willing to let guys who look like me or Edi audition for a part written Mormon, I would later learn that he purposely cast a wide net for actors so that he could find the best talent. It sounds simple, but almost nobody does this, especially back then. The most exciting part of the *House* waiting room was that it showed me that smarter people in Hollywood tended to also be the most likely to embrace artistic diversity.

After a handful of callbacks, I got an offer to play a sports medicine specialist named Dr. Lawrence Kutner. It had been eleven years since I'd moved to Los Angeles to pursue this crazy acting dream. Now I was one of nine new cast members for a few episodes of a television drama. If I was further chosen as one of the three permanent additions, it could be my first steady job in Hollywood, playing a doctor[2]

---

2   "Finally." —Suraj Uncle

on a popular medical drama to boot. I was happy with the way things were taking shape. I eventually traded in my mom's Chevy Cavalier for a black Toyota Prius.[3] My new castmates and I got along really well. The start to the season featured those nine new fellowship doctors vying for a permanent job in the hospital. As actors, we were vying for a permanent spot in the cast, but rather than competing against each other, all nine actors embraced this rare opportunity and spent time getting to know one another. Olivia Wilde (Thirteen), Peter Jacobson (Dr. Taub), and I (Dr. Kutner) grew particularly close, and those friendships deepened when we three were ultimately hired on as the new series regulars. And with that, my parents finally stopped asking me to "at least" get a real estate license.[4]

The mood among the three of us on set was light and fun. During downtime, we would solve crossword puzzles, tell stories, and oh right . . . we'd also play something called Accidentally Fucked in the Ass.[5]

The premise of this "game" was introduced to us by screenwriter Sara Hess at two a.m. on a Saturday while shooting a scene in the Princeton-Plainsboro Hospital lobby. The rules are as follows: Each player enacts a scenario in which they're going about an everyday task (like making coffee). At some point, the player decides to get

---

3   I always thought it sounded cool when people say they "traded in" their car. In reality, Mom's Chevy Cavalier started making a very loud noise; it sounded like someone had attached three leaf blowers to the hood. I took it to a mechanic who said it would cost a few thousand dollars to fix, so I donated it (my first lesson in one-percent problems—you sometimes garner more benefit from donating something than selling it) and used some of the new money I had earned to buy a more environmentally responsible car.

4   If I remember correctly, when it became clear during college that I wasn't going to become a doctor, the further downward expectations went: At least go to law school ➔ No? Okay at least get an MBA ➔ No? Okay at least get a real estate license.

5   It probably should have been called "Accidentally Yet Consensually Fucked in the Ass," but the consensual part was implied.

"accidentally fucked in the ass" by their imaginary significant other—indicated by a crazy facial expression. For example, while Peter is in the middle of adding cream or sugar, his face quickly contorts—and that's the exact moment in which he is "accidentally fucked in the ass." It was not a very complicated "game."

The winner (usually Olivia) was the person who came up with the best nonchalant task, and the most extreme facial expression. Sara didn't invent AFITA. It was created by friends of hers to amuse themselves at parties where only they knew they were playing. On our set, however, everyone knew we played. The rest of the cast was always invited to join, but I think they saw Accidentally Fucked in the Ass as an absurdity for only the three new actors. (That said, I'm pretty sure we did convince Hugh Laurie to play once. Omar Epps was always an emphatic no.)

Not to be outdone by Hess's "game," Peter started a "competition" called HULLLLLL in which each player:

a) impersonates a castmate (castmate must be present) while

b) pretending to gag on a dick by performing a throaty choking sound (the length and intensity of which varied. Player's choice!).

This would always have to take place at a time when:

c) the castmate being impersonated was complaining about something.

Peter does a pretty solid impersonation of me, so when it was his turn at the "competition," he would wait until I had complained about something innocuous, like my burger being cold or not getting enough sleep the night before. He'd then push out his bottom lip, slouch the way I sometimes do, and say, "My name is Kal Penn and my food was too col—HULLLLLL!" (You either know this sound accurately or you don't.) Anyway, that's it. That's the whole "competition."

On the off chance you find this game disgusting or immature, you should know that Peter brought "HULLLLLL" to us from his days on Broadway. His understudy taught it to him when they worked on the Steve Martin play *Picasso at the Lapin Agile* together. From there, Peter HULLLLLLed his castmates at the very serious Atlantic Theater Company during his run of *The Water Engine*. (If you recall, David Mamet's Atlantic Theater Company is where I did my first professional workshop through the Governor's School for the Arts before my senior year of high school. It all comes full circle.) So, when Peter introduced this on the set of *House*, there was a lot to live up to.

The best "players" on our cast were the ones who would bait you with a long, misdirected setup. I once goaded Olivia with a setup about social justice, something we both care a great deal for. Knowing she had read the paper that morning, I played dumb and said, "I heard there's a *New York Times* article on greed and Big Pharma, have you read it?" For the next ten minutes, she passionately talked about economics and morality. I finally interrupted her, leaning in and saying, "You should write an op-ed. I think your take on drug prices with the recent economic data you cited was HULLLLLL!"

OLIVIA: Did you just set me up with that whole thing?

ME: I sure did.

I guess what I'm saying is that I was living the dream. Not just because I was paying my rent by acting, but because I had artistic contentment too. I had broken out of the Brown Catch-22. Roles would still be tougher to get to be sure, but I had built enough of a résumé to truly know that this was something I could make a career out of. I felt perfectly content living an entirely apolitical life doing an Emmy-winning medical drama while very stupidly dodging imaginary dicks at both ends.

*   *   *

Then one day in the fall of 2007, Olivia knocked on the door of my trailer. "Kal, do you want to come to an event for Barack Obama's presidential campaign next week? I have a plus-one! You'd love it." The primary season was kicking off in an especially crowded field: Since Vice President Cheney wasn't running for the presidency, there were more than a dozen viable candidates between both major parties.

"Nah, I like public service. Not politics."

"But you protested against the Iraq War!" she said.

"That's not politics; that's just being a decent human before both parties voted to kill innocent people for no reason," I opined in my kinda irritating soapboxy way.

Olivia saw her opening: "Exactly. Obama was against the Iraq War too!"

I had read Obama's book *Dreams from My Father*, and like most people, loved his 2004 DNC speech. But I detested politicians, and the idea of going to an event in support of someone running for president just wasn't on my radar, even if my friend was saying he was different from the rest.

Not one to take no for an answer, Olivia pleaded with me. "Obama is a real underdog candidate! He's the only major candidate to refuse federal lobbyist donations, and he's been trailing way behind Hillary Clinton and John Edwards—we're talking thirty points behind—all summer long in Iowa."

Iowa is the first state to vote in the primary process, so every candidate goes there early and often. It turned out that Obama was looking for bumps leading up to the Iowa caucuses; he was coming to LA for a two-day fundraising stint and was tacking on a special reception for artists.

"It'll be mostly actors and musicians," Olivia explained. "The senator wants to meet us, and he'll probably ask us to be *surrogates* for him—to do events on his behalf and help him campaign in Iowa. It's a small, intimate thing that Pantera Sarah[6] is putting together for him—it'll be fun!"

I was dubious: Lots of politicians make swings through New York and LA to ask for money, and I wasn't really interested in seeing one give a canned speech at a Hollywood recruiting event. Olivia was getting tired of my stubbornness. "You're coming with me! It'll be fun. We'll have a drink and see what it's like." The passion of my trusted friend was contagious enough—I accepted her invitation.

A few of the *House* writers caught wind of the event. Eli Attie (previously one of Vice President Al Gore's speechwriters) was excited for us and wanted a full report back. Peter Blake (active in Democratic donor circles) suggested we also attend a high-dollar breakfast fundraiser that Obama was doing the morning of our artists' reception. "It can be eye-opening to see what a candidate is like in front of his donors. Tickets are like $2,500 a plate."

Jesus! While Olivia had tried so passionately to convince me that Obama was different, Blake's invitation was exactly what the cynical side of my brain had expected—that Barack Obama was the same as all those other politicians, holding fancy fundraisers for rich people where he'd probably say whatever it takes to get more and more of their money until he gets elected and represents their interests. Also, what the hell kind of breakfast is served for $2,500?! I was confused but curious, like a college student who clicked on the wrong Pornhub link.

---

6   Pantera Sarah was a club promoter and is a talented organizer. A real progressive advocate with roots in Wisconsin, she was pivotal in helping Obama recruit artists to help out on his campaign.

Blake continued, "If you want to see what that world is like, I can get you in for twenty-five bucks. You just have to stand in the back, and you can't eat any of the food."

Wait, I could get a $2,500 ticket for only 25 bucks? My parents had raised me better than to pass up a $2,475 net value. "I'm in!" That morning, I drove my Prius up the Pacific Coast Highway to Malibu. I passed the valet parking line full of fancy Land Rovers, giant Hummers, and shiny BMW sedans, and spent twenty frustrating minutes searching for a spot on the street.

Once I finally parked, I paid my $25 and stepped onto one of the nicest properties I'd ever seen. It belonged to Ron Meyer, who ran Universal Studios. The view was insane. You couldn't tell from the main gate,[7] but the mansion sat on a cliff overlooking the Pacific Ocean. It was easily the most beautiful backyard and most impressive view from anyone's home I had seen in my life.

What a party! The sun had just come up over the house and was reflecting off the water, casting a beautiful yellow light over every affluent, manicured face. Each table was draped in a white cloth that seemed to have been painstakingly ironed. And there were utensils. Lots and lots of utensils. *Why did rich people need multiple forks at each place setting for breakfast?* Just like the time I watched wealthy metrosexual Jason Gross to see which fork he was using for which course at Deah Fishman's bat mitzvah, I scanned the whole place, bursting with next-level curiosity.

There was fruit—but, like, *nice* fruit. Papaya and pomegranate and stuff, not just plebeian oranges and bananas. There were a variety of eggs (maybe from a variety of birds? I dunno) prepared in different ways, a fancy spread of smoked salmon, a nicely laid-out bread

---

7   You know it's fancy when a house has a *main gate*.

bask— *Oh shit, there's Eddie Murphy!* Okay this was already worth the twenty-five bucks.

I was directed away from the tables and onto the outskirts of the backyard with a handful of other thrifty twenty-five-dollar donors. We exchanged the "game recognize game" nod and continued to observe how wealthy people lived.

As I continued to stare creepily at Eddie Murphy, a few people in suits and earpieces emerged by the sliding glass door to the house. Senator Obama was here, ready to kick off this bougie breakfast affair. Someone made brief introductions, and Obama hopped up in front of the crowd in slacks and a button-down shirt, sleeves rolled up. He grabbed a microphone.

As he started in on his speech, it was clear that Obama could read a room and land a joke, even if he'd told it a dozen times before. He spent most of the speech laying out his plan for universal health coverage, talking about pressing challenges in national security, and outlining a vision for the economy. Then he got to talking about clean energy and the environment. That's when everything changed for me.

Midway through a riff on climate change, he stopped midsentence and seemed to take in the vast space. As the $2,500-a-ticket crowd used dainty miniature spoons to stuff their faces with passion fruit–infused Greek yogurt, the senator went off-script. "I'm really curious about something," he said. "When my motorcade pulled up, I noticed there were a bunch of huge Hummers parked outside by the valet. Who drove a Hummer to a Barack Obama breakfast?"

The crowd knew what he was getting at—the Hummer is basically a rebranded war vehicle for rich people that gets terrible gas mileage. They laughed in that good-natured way in which people getting made fun of by a close friend laugh at themselves. *Wow, that's a fun burn*, I thought.

But the senator kept pushing it. "I'm serious, guys," he said. "Who drove a Hummer here?" The relaxed vibe in the backyard turned awkward. What was this guy doing? He was down thirty points in the polls! What was the upside to publicly calling out the rich donors who drove Hummers to his fundraiser?

The uncomfortable silence felt like it lasted for hours. "My point," he said finally, with the tone of someone who wasn't angry as much as he was disappointed in you, "is that if you can afford $2,500 to have breakfast with me, then you can also afford to buy a hybrid car. That way, we can incentivize American-made environmentally friendly vehicles, so that everyone will be able to buy them one day."

I had never heard of a politician risking their relationship with donors, yet here this guy was, calling out some powerful, deep-pocketed Angelenos directly for the gas-guzzling vehicles they drove *while simultaneously taking their money* AND making them love all of it, AND empowering them to feel like we each had some personal responsibility in making the world a better place for everyone. What a skill! Obama wasn't even angling for a good headline in the press the next day; this fundraiser was a private event, and no media were present. I was witnessing something rare: a politician saying what he really thought, even if it cost him votes and dollars. Could someone like this actually get elected? Would the system allow it?

I left that "don't eat any of the food" fundraiser feeling inspired (and super hungry). I drove back to my apartment, pounded some tacos, and spent the day reading through the policy papers on Obama's campaign website. In the evening, I showered and got ready for the reception with Olivia.

*   *   *

The artists' reception was held in a small room on a lower floor of the fancy-pants Beverly Hilton hotel. There were about fifty actors and musicians there, enjoying the wine-and-beer open bar. Obama rolled in a little late, announcing, "I've done my stump speech a few times today at our different fundraisers, so if it's okay with you, I'd like to just spend some time walking around the room, getting to know you instead. Any opposition?" Obviously not. "Before I do that, I just wanted to say one thing: I think what you guys do is pretty incredible. I like to think I'm a pop culture–savvy guy. I love music and film—my wife, Michelle, and I are passionate about the arts. Some of the work you guys do . . . that stuff is among our greatest cultural exports. Movies, television, film, music—these things capture the spirit of the American people: the way we live, the way we work, the things we love. They make so many people around the world happy."

Then Obama shouted out a few individuals he recognized, starting with Justin Timberlake (maybe Obama just couldn't see me from where he was standing?). "Justin. Because of you, a single mom somewhere is listening to your songs on her iPod and keeping her head up just a little while longer as she takes the bus to her third job. Olivia, because of you, a latchkey kid whose dad might be locked up and whose mom is working hard to feed the family can come home and take his mind off of things for a little while—you're the solace and the humor that brightens the day. You all bring hope to so many people. I'm here today to ask for your help in Iowa, so we can get elected and start to make these folks' lives better in a substantive way, by changing policy."

I was stunned. This dude was *definitely* for real. Here I was expecting a tamer, more hollow politiciany ask, and instead, Obama was making a genuine connection between the arts and real people's lives. He was inviting us to be part of a solution, and he was connecting our very privileged existence to something worthwhile in people's everyday struggles.

No matter what you do for a living, whether you're an artist or not, it's easy to get lost in the minutiae of the day-to-day. But in that split second, Obama reminded us about the audiences who watch and listen to what we create. He connected it to an opportunity to help. Like everyone energized by his campaign, it made us feel like we were invited to be a part of something bigger than ourselves.

––––––––––––

It's tough to explain that special moment on its own, unless you also have a sense of how more-traditional campaigns operated. Obama's pitch—genuine, heartfelt, sincere—stood in contrast to the more calculating way an acquaintance working on the fundraising team of another campaign had approached me. A few weeks earlier, she had asked me to consider speaking at an event designed for the South Asian American community in New York.

As you know by now, while I'm mindful that many demographic groups (like South Asian Americans) are underrepresented in media, entertainment, politics, and policy, I generally dislike things that are exclusively couched in race or ethnicity. So, I asked a few questions about this South Asian political event. My finance acquaintance didn't sugarcoat it: The reason she wanted my help was because there was "a lot of untapped money in the Indian American community." She didn't pretend that there were deeper reasons: It all came back to *You're a draw as an actor, Elections require fundraising,* and *You can help get the Indian money.* As always, I appreciated the honesty, but this seemed a bit patronizing, so I politely declined.

The political finance world can be icky across the board. Most campaigns across party lines hold demographic-specific fundraisers.

Like that South Asian political event, these are often organized by those demographic groups themselves. It's a way to exercise political muscle and serve real community needs. In my case, after spending the first chunk of my career having to navigate race in Hollywood, I didn't want to be a token brown guy for anyone.

Standing there at the Obama event, I thought about how a primary election offers a chance for people to not only air their disagreements and pitch bolder policy ideas but to show voters that an entirely different style of politics is possible.

Obama's approach at the time was so different—not only was he not taking lobbyist money, he wasn't pursuing Olivia Wilde's support in an effort to carry the women's vote, just as he wasn't courting me to volunteer because I'm brown.[8] His pitch was simple: Let's work together to make all our fellow Americans' lives better, to make the country we love even stronger. It was an authentic statement, and it was delivered in an authentic way.

That evening, as the senator made the rounds, people talked to him about sports, or music, or life on the road. I decided I wasn't going to waste time on small talk. I'd ask him a question about a recurring topic in those policy papers I had spent my whole afternoon devouring: biofuels.

I fancied myself a little wonkier than the others in the room. You see, I was enrolled in a distance-learning graduate certificate program in international security at Stanford University. (Yes, super nerdy to do a graduate program in international security as a *hobby*.) I had recently read an article in *Foreign Affairs* about the potential

---

8   Okay, fine, *technically* I wasn't even invited to this event, I was just Olivia's plus-one.

risks of ethanol and was sure this made me kind of an expert on the topic. Plus, if I applied my knowledge to what I read on his website, I could ask an actual policy question. In a room full of actors, that would make me look super smooth. I was sure Obama would be very impressed.

"Senator, I read your policy papers on clean energy," I said when he came around to where Olivia and I were standing, "and I was curious about something. Your plan talks about the importance of biofuels, but experts say the market doesn't currently distinguish between corn we grow for *human consumption* and corn for *industrial production*—you know, to be turned into ethanol for *fuel*. If we do invest in ethanol, won't it drive up the price of food for people in developing countries who eat corn?"

I was very satisfied with myself for asking my smart question!

"Yeah, I read that article from the experts in *Foreign Affairs* too," Obama said. "The point of my plan is to use corn-based ethanol as a bridge to cellulosic ethanol, so that we can eventually make biofuels from things like grass clippings and leaves."

Here I was, confident that I would be asking the most incredible question of all time and schooling a senator, and not only did he have a clear, concise answer, but he had also read the *same article* and knew that's where my outside information was coming from. (Weird, but I guess my graduate certificate in international security was just no match for a member of the Senate Foreign Relations Committee). Anyway, this all clinched it for me: the boldness of what Obama had said about the Hummers at the private rich people breakfast, his understanding of the arts and humanities, an approach to transcending race, and of course, schooling me on an article I had read while we had a casual convo about climate change. I disliked politics but was always passionate about public service. This guy knew how to merge the two, and I knew I had to be involved with his campaign. He was the real deal.

As Obama walked away, Olivia turned to me and said, "Hi, my name is Kal Penn and I have impressive things to tell you about biofuels. Did you know that I read an artic—" Olivia's face contorted into an "accidentally fucked in the ass" look as she finished with "—HULLLLLL!" Holy shit, a combo! That had never been done before!

I signed up to volunteer for Barack Obama that night.

The day Dad left for America, summer 1967. Above: My grandmother (Ba) and the women of the fam seeing him off at the airport. Below: My grandfather (Bapaji) and the men of the family. *Suresh Modi*

ABOVE: Lighting a sparkler with Shobhafoi (my dad's sister) at Ba and Bapaji's tenement in Mumbai. Diwali circa 1982. *Asmita Modi*

MIDDLE: Mom and Dad saved money by packing lunches to eat at rest stops on the way to camping trips. At the front of the table, Mom's parents (Grandma and Grandpa), who were active in the Indian Independence movement. *Suresh Modi*

BELOW: Elementary school class photo, happily wearing my Sears sweater.

ABOVE: At a living history museum, gleefully reenacting getting tortured for stealing my neighbor's horse. *Kalpen Modi/Modi family photos*

MIDDLE: Eighth grade me as the Tin Man in *The Wiz*, just before the life-changing pelvic thrust. *Suresh and Asmita Modi*

BELOW: Vegas trip with the UCLA homies circa 2000 (years before Sunny) in my salvage-title Toyota Paseo. *Ernest Filart*

ABOVE: John Cho and me with actor James Adomian as President Bush. *Jaimie Trueblood/ New Line Cinema*

MIDDLE: On set in Shreveport, Louisiana, 2007, *Harold & Kumar Escape from Guantanamo Bay*. *Jaimie Trueblood*

BELOW: A University of Pittsburgh 2008 primary campaign event. *Kristopher Radder*

On the set of *House* circa 2009 with my wonderful stand-in who was told to wear brown makeup "for lighting purposes." *Peter Jacobson*

With senior advisor Valerie Jarrett and her deputy Michael Strautmanis after my formal job interview, April 2009. *AP Photos/ Charles Dharapak*

In the Oval with Tina Tchen, Candace Chin, Bryan Jung, and Eugene Kang, before Whappy and Diwali, 2009. *Official White House Photo by Pete Souza*

ABOVE: The president and the pandit under the famous Lansdowne portrait of George Washington, who probably never thought a Diwali observance would happen there. *Official White House Photo by Pete Souza*

MIDDLE: Meeting NASCAR puppet Danny Hammerdropper, March 2012. (I blame Josh for all of this.) *Jeff Dubinsky*

BELOW: Backstage at the 2012 Democratic National Convention. *Dan Spilo*

With the president's videographer Hope Hall and senior video producer Thomas Kelley en route to New Delhi on Air Force One support, 2015. (Though a guest on the India delegation, I was excited to be put to work, too.) *Kalpen Modi*

On the tarmac in Riyadh with one of my seatmates, Bartlett Jackson, on the way back to DC.

After separate campaign events for Secretary Clinton in Ohio on October 13, 2016. *Official White House Photo by Pete Souza*

Shooting the *Sunnyside* pilot with director Oz Rodriguez, my cocreator Matt Murray, and actor Ana Villafañe, Los Angeles, 2019. *Romen Borsellino*

Coach Zach (holding the baseball) and his Hawaii Pacific teammate Steven Camberos after practice. Half my shirt is soaked in sweat. *Romen Borsellino*

Sunnyside's Thanksgiving episode! (From left, director Linda Mendoza, writer Ayo Edebiri, and cast Moses Storm, Samba Schutte, Kiran Deol, Sakina Jaffrey, Diana Maria Riva, Bernard White, me, Poppy Liu, and Joel Kim Booster.) *Romen Borsellino*

CHAPTER TWELVE

UTOPIA
(The Underdog, Part One)

A few weeks after Obama pushed me off the bridge to Cellulosic Ethanol, I was headed to Iowa with Olivia and *CSI: Miami* actor Megalyn Echikunwoke for my first political volunteer trip. Until this point I had been a regular voter (I registered as soon as I turned eighteen), but had never campaigned for anyone outside of attending a single event in support of John Kerry in 2004.[1] For the next three days, Olivia, Megalyn, and I would drive around the state, speaking primarily at college and university events as some of the Obama campaign's first surrogates.[2] But instead of carrying the senator's election baby in our tummies, we'd be carrying messages of freedom. That is, if we landed in one piece.

The Quad City Airport is small, which I'm told means the planes that land there have to be even smaller (math). A brutal winter storm

---

1 Kerry was not in attendance. A cousin spoke on his behalf.
2 Just a refresher, a campaign surrogate is someone who speaks on a candidate's behalf. In this case, we were the first nonpolitical surrogates, meaning we came from a world outside of politics.

was making for a choppy welcome. As we slid to a stop on the frozen tarmac, I looked out the window and thought, *This is the whitest place I have ever seen.* A sheet of ice covered everything in a glossy half-inch sheen, and all the weather reports warned that nobody should be on the roads except for essential workers.

We gathered together in front of the kind of white van that up-and-coming bands rent when they self-drive to shows in third-tier cities, and looked up in horror as the sky vomited chunks of sharp ice. An overly cheery Obama staffer said, "Don't worry, we won't let a little weather stop us!" Just as I was thinking how I didn't want to die in Bettendorf, Iowa, the overly cheery staffer introduced herself as Teal Baker, Obama's national director of surrogates, and motioned to a bearded, flannel-clad man in a mesh-backed baseball hat. "Meet Colby. He's a professional eighteen-wheel emergency truck driver. He'll be operating the van today. Cool?" Phew. A professional.

We piled into the campaign van with Colby at the wheel. As he was about to pull onto the ice rink of a highway, a young blond woman sitting in the passenger seat held up her index finger. "Wait a second." She turned around to face me, BlackBerry in hand. "Kal, I'm Erin Fitzgerald in Communications. Before we get going, I just—I'm reading something here from our state director . . ." She glanced anxiously at her screen and shook her head. "Ummmm, so I guess we're wondering . . . since these college events are all open to the press, you know, since journalists might be there . . . ummmm . . ."

I knew what Erin Fitzgerald in Communications was fishing for. "Are you wondering how I'd respond if someone asks me a question about marijuana? Because of my movies?" I had beat her to the awkward elephant in the room. "Erin, I can assure you I don't smoke weed." I smiled.

She relaxed a bit. "I only do edibles. They get you *way* more stoned and are super easy to sneak through airport security."

Erin looked like she was going to be sick. "Don't worry," I said. "If I get a weed question, I guess I'll say that movies aren't real life—it's just a character I play."

Her eyes returned to their normal size and she let out a deep breath. "Okay, great!"

Weeks later I found out how close I had come to getting shipped back to Los Angeles. Paul Tewes, Obama's Iowa state director, was late in reading a memo about our college surrogate tour and flipped out once he saw that the guy from *Harold & Kumar* was involved. He emailed Erin in a panic just as Colby was about to drive us to the first event, worried that my presence might fuel the ability of Obama's opponents to run distracting ads, saying that the campaign was promoting drug use among college kids. I always find it funny when people think *Harold & Kumar* promotes drugs. That's like saying *Silence of the Lambs* promotes eating people.

In hindsight, it's crazy to think that if Erin hadn't taken a moment to ask me directly, or if Paul hadn't trusted his team's judgment in the first place, I would have been sent back to LA, no questions asked, only to continue on *House* for its remaining seasons, playing a doctor, and making Uncle very, very happy.

Olivia, Megalyn, and I had a breakneck schedule ahead. Our mission for the three days—dubbed the All-Actor, All-Iowa, All-Star Voter Education Tour—was twofold: First, to educate college students about their opportunity to caucus ("Whichever state you hail from, if you're enrolled in a college in Iowa, you can caucus in Iowa, so long

as you don't also vote in your home-state primary!"). Second, to collect coveted supporter cards: colorful envelope-size index cards with
a photo of Obama and a place for someone's name, email address,
date of birth, and phone number.

Supporter cards served multiple purposes. They were used as sign-
in forms for people who attended campaign events (a way to collect
hard data). There was also a place on each card to sign a small pledge
saying that you commit to caucusing for Barack Obama. Signing this
at one of our events wasn't binding, but the information gathered was
key to building the campaign database and helping organizers persuade undecided potential voters to caucus for Obama. Interestingly,
there is behavioral science behind supporter card utilization. It shows
that when people sign something, the act of doing so—with their
actual signature—makes them feel more committed, and therefore
more likely to fulfill their pledge.[3] This was one of the ways Obama's
innovative tactics were a departure from campaigns of the past.

On this trip, I saw that Team Obama didn't take anyone's vote
for granted; if you filled out a supporter card, volunteers followed
up with you multiple times. ("You're going to caucus for Obama on
January third, right?" . . . "You're going to caucus for Barack Obama
on January third, *RIGHT*?" . . . "Hey, ON JANUARY THIRD DON'T
FORGET TO CAUCUS FOR BARACK OBAMA, *ALL RIGHT*?!")

Iowa is a weird state in that it has a caucus rather than a primary. (It's
also weird because a highlight of their state fair is a life-size butter cow
sculpture, which is exactly what it sounds like—*and* they don't even eat
it at the end.) So, what is a caucus? Instead of going to a polling place

---

3   Author Sasha Issenberg talks about this very thing in his book *The Victory Lab*.

and privately casting your ballot behind a curtain in a booth, Iowans meet up at designated locations to discuss, debate, and then publicly vote on candidates. They do this across the entire state. If this sounds insane to you, that's because it is, in fact, insane. If you tried to have a caucus in a place like New Jersey, it would quickly devolve into fistfights.

I think we need universal health care.

Oh yeah? I think ya mom needs universal health care.

Wuddid you say? Say it again to my face.

Uh-right. Ya mom. Needs. Universal health care. To fix her ugly face!

For Iowans, who live in a real-life version of a wholesome black-and-white movie, a caucus actually works. People bring homemade potluck food to the meeting site—often a church basement, school gymnasium, or cafeteria—and stand underneath the sign or banner that indicates their preferred candidate. *This is Hillary Clinton's sign! Come over here, eat one of these cookies I baked, and let me tell you why Hillary is better than the other candidates! No, come over here and stand under Bill Richardson's banner! If you have never heard of Bill Richardson, let me feed you some chili I made and tell you about him. Since I am the only one under this banner, you can eat as much chili as you want. Mmmmmm. Bill Richardson.*

If a candidate doesn't have enough support to be viable at a caucus site (to oversimplify, let's say there is no clear majority), the caucus-goers who supported that candidate will need to pick a backup. That's when people try to convince one another to join their groups for a second time. The people who get convinced walk from one side of the room to the other, to signal their support for their second-choice candidate. It's like a middle school dance, but instead of dancing, the middle schoolers are passionately debating whether

Dennis Kucinich or John Edwards has the better energy policy. It's a uniquely public way to vote and requires a lot of commitment on the part of caucus-goers to turn out—the process can take a few hours. Once everyone's under the right signs, they raise their hands and are counted for the final time.

In general, people who have voted in past elections tend to support establishment candidates (Clinton, John Edwards, George Bush). First-time voters tend to vote for the newer outside candidates who motivated them to participate (Ron Paul, Obama, Obama's successor). That's why in 2007, the Obama campaign focused on what's called "expanding the electorate": encouraging people who had never voted before to caucus. A huge part of ensuring Obama's victory was making sure these new voters showed up on January 3.

Each morning of the All-Actor, All-Iowa, All-Star Voter Education Tour began with a briefing from Teal Baker over a continental breakfast (included in the price of the room) before piling into Colby's college band van. We'd first make an appearance at a local field office to talk to supporters and give a special shout-out to the volunteers who had collected the most supporter cards that week. Next, we'd hit three or four colleges to make speeches and help collect new supporter cards, using the drive time to do interviews with local reporters. We'd wrap up each evening with a quick dinner at a local eatery, where we'd also shake hands and campaign, then stop at another field office before getting some sleep.

The short speech I wrote for these events opened with the Hummer story from the $2,500 fundraiser in Malibu (I left the Eddie Murphy part out). I then talked about Obama's opposition to the Iraq

War and how that related to an acquaintance named Brady in Texas. Brady was the friend of a coworker, and really wanted to go to college. He was working a minimum-wage job in the office of a trucking company hoping to eventually save up enough for tuition. One afternoon, Brady got a call from a huge corporation called Halliburton and was offered a salary of $90,000 if he agreed to move to Iraq to drive a truck. (Shout-out to the military-industrial complex!)

I was so bothered by the fact that this was Brady's choice.[4] In the richest, most powerful country in the world, you can go to college if you work for years in a minimum-wage job or earn $90,000 a year driving a truck in a war zone (presuming you made it back alive to enroll in school). What if we hadn't started this bipartisan war in Iraq and instead allocated that money toward making higher education more affordable? What if we elected someone like Obama, who proposed a doubling of the Pell Grant?

My speech was always well received, and it opened up a lot of great conversations about other people's experiences. The most common questions we and the staff got were about Obama's plans for health care, the economy, equality, and climate change. Marijuana and *Harold & Kumar* rarely came up. Turns out, when given the opportunity to talk with representatives of a presidential campaign, young voters will overwhelmingly ask about real issues that affect them. This is not to say there weren't disruptions. One speech at a high school event was interrupted by some kid who aggressively shouted, "Hey Kal! Will you suck my caucus?" His classmates shut him down quickly with boos and reprimands, and I ignored the whole thing and went on with the rest of my remarks. But as soon as that event ended

---

4   He ultimately decided not to go.

and our van door shut, I burst out laughing. "That heckler was hilarious. He was so embarrassed after his buddies booed him. Get me his
phone number, I want to make sure he signs a supporter card."[5]

Each time we delivered our stump speeches to crowds of enthusiastic young people, a thought crept into the back of my mind: *Yo,
what if Obama actually becomes the first African American candidate
to win the Iowa caucus? Could we really make history here?* Everyone
on his team was so positive about the work they were doing, and
the energy was contagious. "We're in this to win. And if we don't,
we'll have registered so many new voters that they'll be more likely
to participate in future elections. That's ultimately a really good
thing."

Our three-day tour was exhausting and exhilarating. When we
helped out at campaign offices each evening after our surrogate stops,
Megalyn and Olivia and I got to know the process of phone banking.
I helped with data entry, punching the info from supporter cards we
collected into a digital database. Until you've worked on a campaign,
you have no idea the amount of effort that goes into connecting with
voters—I certainly didn't. The Obama campaign was filled with a
conscientious, dedicated team, with no ego or arrogance about it.
The senator's staff—many of whom would go on to become some
of my best friends—reinforced what appealed to me about Obama at
those events in LA: integrity.

In contrast to my interactions with Hollywood liberals (like Original
Ideas McGee), Obama's campaign world felt like a postracial, post-
identity utopia. He was focused on hiring the most qualified peo-

---

5   He did.

ple, irrespective of what they looked like. I think my first example of this was meeting the campaign's head of rural and agricultural outreach—a guy named Rohan Patel. Spoiler in case you've never known one, Patels are brown. *Obama hired a brown guy to head up outreach in the whitest pockets of a state that's already ninety-two percent white?* I thought to myself. *Just because he's . . .* qualified? The campaign felt that Rohan was simply the best person for the job. They were willing to bet that voters overwhelmingly care about competence more than skin color and shouldn't be pandered to.

Added to that was the rarity of a high number of women in leadership positions—interestingly, more than the Clinton campaign had at the time. Senior advisor Jackie Norris helped lead the team alongside deputy state director Marygrace Galston, field director Anne Filipic, Get Out the Vote director Paulette Aniskoff, political director Emily Parcell, and policy director Karen Richardson.

To round out the ways in which Obama was walking the walk on his staff hires was a marine named Brian VanRiper, who served as both the Veterans Affairs *and* LGBT outreach coordinator. With Don't Ask, Don't Tell still in effect, the decision to make the LGBT and Veterans outreach person the same dude was a blatant embrace of intersectionality. Obama was focused on bringing people together to do the hard work, not caught up in tokenizing different groups or hiring people who "looked the part." Compared to my time in Los Angeles, each of the three days on the campaign felt like I was living in a far-off idealistic future, where people are uplifting, inclusive, encouraging, and also don't ask you where your turban is.

At the grassroots level of the campaign staff were the Obama For America field organizers, or FOs. FOs were in charge of organizing particular areas of the state, divided into regions. Most were in their midtwenties and had been inspired by the senator's message enough to put their lives on hold. They moved to Iowa to do this hard work, and their stories almost always had a humble spin.

Ronnie Cho was an FO who hailed from Arizona and had convinced his childhood friend Ryan Lynch to move to Des Moines with him.

ME: What made you want to join the Obama campaign?

RONNIE: Hope and Change.

ME: Ha, right. Then how did you convince Ryan to join?

RONNIE: He was broke and lost.

A deputy field organizer, Ryan joked, "I never worked in politics before, but I had a chance to be part of history. When you're twenty-six and all your shit has been in the back of a Honda Civic for over a year, you can be flexible."

Behind the upbeat "What the heck, let me go make a difference!" rhetoric of these selfless, talented people were sometimes dire circumstances: loved ones who couldn't afford higher education, parents who had recently lost their jobs, acquaintances who were overseas in Iraq or Afghanistan. Nobody was working on Team Obama because they thought it would lead to a job at the White House. Obama was the longshot, underdog candidate, and the work his staff was doing was tough and often scary. Ronnie once passed someone with a swastika tattoo while canvassing. He heard the n-word multiple times when he'd knock on doors to get supporter cards. The staff wasn't even being paid much. They were doing this work because they truly believed in our collective ability to make the country a better place.

By the end of the third busy day, Olivia, Megalyn, and I were physically spent and emotionally fulfilled. Our last stop of the trip was to thank staff and volunteers at Obama's Iowa headquarters in Des Moines—an unassuming, one-level office building with faded, thin gray carpeting from the days when it used to be an ice-skating rink. (Today it's a church.) Over the course of seventy-two hours, we had spoken to thousands of college students and hundreds of high school kids.

We said our thank-yous to super-volunteers like sixty-five-year-old Samantha Wright, and took some photos with "Barack Stars" like the energetic seventeen-year-old Romen Borsellino. We hung out with the senator's impressive young staff—Ronnie and Ryan, speechwriter Jon Favreau, and Iowa press secretary Tommy Vietor—before going back to the motel to crash. This place was magic. I was having real conversations with motivated, down-to-earth people who were judged on the content of their character. Megalyn and Olivia needed to fly back to LA the next morning for work, but I wasn't scheduled to be back on set at *House* for another five days.

I couldn't shake the feeling that I should probably do more for people in my life who were in dire circumstances: guys like Brady in Texas. I thought about my grandparents, and the historic sacrifices they made for things much more significant. I considered some of the nonprofits I had the chance to partner with over the years, like ARCH in India, where I spent the summer before eleventh grade. I even thought about the international security graduate certificate program I was enrolled in, wondering if that could help me dabble in public service one day. Inspired by the staff, who were working around the clock for something they believed in so strongly, I wondered, *What excuse do I have not to stay in Iowa a bit longer?*

Before passing out for the night, I asked Teal if it was possible to change my return ticket to LA and extended my stay in Iowa. For four additional days, I did more surrogate events and helped the FOs with canvassing, supporter cards, organizing, phone banking, and late-night data entry. Instead of Colby and his emergency van, I was riding shotgun in various FOs' cars.[6]

On the evening before my new flight home, Paul Tewes called me into his office.

"So, listen," he said with a wide smirk, "we want to hire you. Can you stay here?"

"Hire me for what?"

"Well, we thought you were just an actor who did these stoner movies, but it turns out you're a damn good organizer too," he explained. "Word spreads quickly around here. Every day that you've been here, you've broken the single-day record for supporter cards by a lot. You're dedicated and motivated. You're very good at working with people, and you're incredibly persuasive without being disrespectful. You should stay. I want to hire you. The job pays two thousand dollars a month. I know that's not much, but you're really good at this, and it'll make a big difference."

This was crazy. Flattered as I was, there was no way I could stay in

---

6   Speaking of Colby, it was a few more years before I learned that he wasn't actually an emergency driver at all. He'd never even been inside an eighteen-wheeler. He was just a random young volunteer who happened to look old for his age. The campaign staff didn't want us to back out of the event because we felt unsafe on the icy road, so they made up that backstory to put us at ease. On the East Coast, we call this "hustle." I guess since we didn't die, it was fine.

Des Moines—I was working a hard-earned dream job in Los Angeles. I loved the random week I'd spent on the campaign, but it couldn't last beyond the additioinal days I already put in. "Paul, I'm sorry, but I can't. I'm on a TV show right now, and I go back to work on Thursday morning."

That didn't seem to faze him. "Okay. Just thought you should have a heads-up, because the boss is going to see you tonight and he's planning on asking you to join us full-time. You can be the one to tell him no," he said, still smirking.

Well, shit.

That night, as Tewes had warned, Senator Obama pulled me aside at a small campaign rally I had helped organize. "Kal! I hear you've been breaking some records getting supporter cards."

"Senator, if this is about the kid who asked me to suck his caucus, he *promised* he'll show up on January third. Besides, getting those supporter cards was a huge team effort. The credit goes to all of your amazing staffers. They spent days building the events."

"Aren't they great?" Obama said. "You know, in my daily briefing book there's a list of who's on the road for me, so I see it all. Beyond being a surrogate, you're a talented organizer yourself. My staff all over Iowa has said what a big help you've been to them this week. You're a real asset to the campaign. I want to hire you."

Even with the heads-up Tewes had given me, I was wholly unprepared for this. I thought Obama was just going to soft pitch me the $2,000-a-month job offer. Or maybe he'd forget to ask altogether. But here he was, telling me that he knew about the actual work we were doing and felt that I—some guy who just rolled in for a few days—was actually good at community organizing and could be helpful to his campaign. The way he spoke about this struck a chord. Obama's pitch to me wasn't based on my being a recognizable actor to college kids of a certain age. Or because of Indian American money. He wanted to hire me somewhat independently of any attention I might bring even as a surrogate.

"Senator, I'm really honored. I'm sure this is going to sound silly compared to the hard work everyone here is doing, but I can't leave my job on *House*."

Obama was quick with the rebuttal. "It doesn't sound silly at all, that's a good job. A good show. But aren't all the screenwriters on strike?"

Man, this dude really did know a lot. A few weeks prior, on November 5, 2007, business as usual in Hollywood came to a grinding halt when the Writers Guild of America went on strike in a labor dispute with producers and studios. The strike meant no new scripts for *House*.

"Senator, the writers *are* on strike, but we're still shooting episodes they already wrote," I said.

We looked at each other.

"Well, I hope their dispute gets resolved quickly," he said. "But if it doesn't, and if you run out of scripts, I'd love to have you out here."

I told Senator Obama that I'd compromise. While I couldn't take a formal job, I'd unofficially sign on in a semiregular, voluntary role. I would fly back to Iowa every time I had days off from filming: weekends, midweek, whatever. In a system I worked out with Tewes, I'd work as an organizer and support Obama's youth vote efforts but decline a salary so that I could continue to truthfully be a surrogate as well. Once we did run out of scripts on *House* in a few weeks, I joined the campaign in this unpaid pseudo-staffer role on a full-time basis. Think of it as a Captain Moneybags situation except my new boss was running for president, hired lots of women, and also wasn't obsessed over whether Joseph Gordon-Levitt was "fucking Asian." In exchange, Obama for America would cover the cost of my flights and pay for my luxurious housing at the Quality Inn in downtown Des Moines, effective immediately. It was unofficially official: I was working for the Barack Obama campaign.

CHAPTER THIRTEEN

TWO MINI HACKS IF YOU EVER MOVE INTO THE QUALITY INN IN DOWNTOWN DES MOINES

You may have heard of actors living in hotels for prolonged periods of time. Marilyn Monroe at the luxurious Beverly Hills Hotel. John Travolta at the Pink Beach Club in the Caribbean. I don't know what tips Marilyn or John would offer about their extended stays, but if you should find yourself taking up residence at the Quality Inn in lovely downtown Des Moines (where the clothes hangers are attached to the rod so that you don't steal them), I have two pieces of advice for you:

Tip #1: Insist on a Room with a Mini Fridge. If your employer (the Obama Campaign, for instance) is not in a position to splurge on this type of deluxe accomodation, you'll end up leaving drinks on your window ledge to keep them cold. You'll have to pack the snow around the edges of the cans, and you'll need to set little reminders to bring them inside every now and then, or they'll freeze totally solid. If that happens, you'll convince yourself that a "beer slushy" is even more refreshing than a normal beer. (It's really not.) Get the deluxe room.

Tip #2: Use the Convenience Store Microwave. Let's hypothetically say that after a few sensible beers (and less-sensible shots) with your new campaign coworkers, you get the munchies and buy a delicious refrigerated burrito from the Kum & Go convenience store you guys drunkenly stumbled into. You get back to your room also holding a bag full of lottery tickets and a mesh camo hunting cap with a bright yellow cartoon ear of corn on it that you also drunkenly bought because you thought, *Oh shit, this hat is tite as hell!* and suddenly remember, *Not only do I not have a mini fridge, I don't even have a microwave!* You'll end up turning the thermostat to its highest setting, and you'll place the burrito on top of the heater. This is just sad, you drunk ass. The heater will NOT successfully cook it. You will slowly peel off layers of clothing and end up sweating in your boxers for thirty minutes before realizing the inside of the burrito is still ice-cold. As you attempt to unwrap the cold burrito to see whether any of it can be salvaged, it will spill all over the carpet and you'll spend fifteen minutes picking rice out of your belly button. You will also briefly consider ironing the burrito before talking yourself out of it, "because it's not a panini." You'll fall asleep hungry. Also, you won't win the lottery. The hat is really cool though. Use the microwave at the Kum & Go.

CHAPTER FOURTEEN

RESPECT, EMPOWER, INCLUDE
(The Underdog, Part Two)

*R*espect, *Empower, Include.* Scrawled with markers and paint on butcher paper by our young staff, this phrase was found on banners in each Obama field office. It was a mantra of Paul Tewes, intended to remind each of us of our mission: *Respectfully* talk with everyone, whatever their political views or affiliation. *Empower* people to caucus and vote for the candidate of their choice. *Include* as many people as possible in our movement for change—there is room for everyone. We can't win if we aren't in this together.

With a defined role on the campaign, the depth of my duties increased. One of the people I reported to was Obama's Iowa youth vote director, Andrea C. Stevens, and among some of my new tasks was working with a group of lawyers on issues related to voting rights. While we were spending considerable time and resources educating young people on their right to vote and caucus, other campaigns were trying to persuade them to stay home during the primary.

My first experience with this was at Grinnell College, a beautiful campus about an hour east of Des Moines. I was clad in my Obama

T-shirt, canvassing with a group of students, when a young woman jogging by yelled, "I love Obama! I hope he wins! Wish I was allowed to vote!"

Her parents don't let her vote?

Being the athletic specimen that I am, I jogged after her to find out what was up. "I'm not allowed to vote in Iowa because I grew up in Colorado," she explained.

"Wait a second." I shot back. "The law says that if you're a student in Iowa, you can caucus and vote in Iowa." She slowed her pace and came to a stop as I doubled down. "Who told you that you can't vote here?"

A short break to introduce voter suppression. Have you ever wondered why Election Day is on a Tuesday? (If yes, keep reading. If no, also keep reading.) Election Day is on a Tuesday because in 1845, Congress decided we needed to come up with a standard day that met the needs of the voting populace—aka rich white dudes, as they didn't allow anyone else to vote back then. You'd think that a weekend day like Sunday would make the most sense for the rich white dudes because it was a day off, right?

Ultimately, Congress decided people couldn't vote on Sundays, since it was the Sabbath. (My bad, *God* decided that we couldn't vote on a Sunday.) Monday couldn't be Election Day either, because in 1845 the polls were located in the county seat; in order to get there by Monday, you'd have to start riding your horse and buggy the day before—but the day before Monday is what? Sunday! And we already know God decided we can't do anything on Sunday. So, this ruled out Saturday (since you might have to ride the horse and buggy home on Sunday), Sunday, and Monday.

How about Tuesday? Tuesday seemed to work well so they said, *Let's put a pin in that*. Would Wednesday work too? Nah, Wednesday was a no-go because it was market day for farmers.

Sooooo, Tuesday it was! You could ride your horse and buggy to the polls in the county seat on Monday, vote on Tuesday, and make it back home for market day on Wednesday. This, in a nutshell, is how Tuesday became Election Day. In 1845.

Also in 1845? There was no electricity. No antibiotics. Slavery existed. Life expectancy was thirty-seven. Did I mention only rich white dudes were legally allowed to vote? It wasn't until 1870— *twenty-five years later*—that the Fifteenth Amendment *technically* prevented states from denying the right to vote based on "race, color, or previous condition of servitude."

Women couldn't vote until 1920, though. And as you surely know because you remember your history, most Black folks couldn't really vote until the Voting Rights Act was passed in 1965. That's *one hundred and twenty years* after Tuesday was declared Election Day because of God and horses and buggies and farmers. During those one hundred and twenty years, a whole lot of nefarious stuff went on. (As a brief refresher, google Jim Crow, the poll tax, and voting literacy tests.) In 2013 there was a whole bunch of extra bullshit with regard to a section of the Voting Rights Act in the Supreme Court, which is a separate story that you should also look up.

You might be wondering, *Okay, Kal, but why is Election Day* still *on a Tuesday?* I'll tell you. People in positions of power don't want to lose their power. If Election Day were, say, on a weekend (or maybe even lasted for weeks as it does in states with accessible early voting), it would be a lot easier for single parents, students, and people working multiple jobs to get to the polls. That would mean candidates would have to appeal to the needs of this wider group of people. And if that happened, many of the people currently in power would lose because they don't represent this wider group's needs.

The thing is, the people in power don't want to lose. So, some of them suppress the vote by—among other things—keeping Election Day on a Tuesday. As it's always been. Since 1845. And that's part of the reason America ranks 135 out of 178 nations in voter turnout.[1]

Back at the campaign office, I told Andrea about the strange interaction with the jogger at Grinnell who thought she was ineligible to vote because she heard it on her campus. "I guess some well-meaning political volunteer out there mistakenly told her that college students can't caucus in Iowa?" I asked. It fell to Andrea to pull back the curtain and tell me about the frustrating range of things being done to confuse and discourage young people from participating in the political process.

First, there were robocalls. Some people reported getting official-sounding phone calls telling them, "If you're caucusing for Barack Obama, remember the date of that caucus has changed to January fourth." (It hadn't. There was only one caucus date: January 3.) Another batch featured a caller underscoring Obama's middle name, Hussein, in an attempt to make the senator seem foreign.

Second, there was in-person disinformation. When the Obama campaign embarked on a strategy of encouraging college students to return to campus early from winter break at their parents' homes in order to caucus, it was accused of "systematically trying to manipulate the Iowa caucuses with out-of-state people." From this allegation

---

1   Per the International Institute for Democracy and Electoral Assistance, 2018.

brewed the idea that you should only caucus in Iowa if you "consider yourself Iowan" as a matter of conscience. What a totally ridiculous thing to hear. If I got pulled over after doing four shots of Jäger, my conscience might not consider me drunk, but the cops would definitely arrest me for a DUI because that's what the law says. Considering yourself Iowan was not a real prerequisite for voting—you're Iowan if you live there most of the year, which college students do. No matter how much Jäger they've had on campus.

One of Obama's spokespeople at the time was future White House Press Secretary Jen Psaki, who said, "Barack Obama doesn't believe that we should disenfranchise Iowans who meet all the requirements for caucus participation simply because they're in college. We should be encouraging young people to participate in the political process—not looking for ways to shut them out."

In the early primary states, witnessing this sort of loose-rumored, anonymous voter suppression felt extra shady because I was meeting increasing numbers of young people who were opening up with inspiring and heartbreaking stories of what an Obama victory would mean to them and their loved ones. A young volunteer named Stephen told me that his mom had cancer and no health insurance. He'd had to leave college to help with the bills at home and volunteered after work every day because of Obama's health care plan. A young woman named Sonal had a brother whose student loans were so large that he was unable to make the monthly payments. She wanted to make sure Obama's pledge to double the Pell Grant came to fruition—it would be too late to help her brother, but it would help others like him who were thinking about higher education. And at a campaign stop on a snowy college campus, I was approached by a smiling, heavyset, wheelchair-bound young man named Miguel. After making small talk, Miguel reached into his wallet and pulled out a photo of a fit, handsome marine. "That's me," he said. "When my convoy in Iraq was hit by an IED, I was paralyzed from the waist down. I volunteer for the Obama campaign because both parties voted to authorize that war, and Barack was against it. I never want anyone to go through what I did."

How could anybody try to discourage people like Miguel and Sonal and Stephen from voting? The mistake I made in pondering this question was similar to how I thought about those early stereotypical auditions—by getting caught up in raw emotion. Voter suppression—whether low-level, disorganized, and anonymous (as in the case of Iowa) or codified at a deeper level (as in the case of several recent laws and rulings) is something we can and should fight. It's not new. It's also not usually personal, even though its impact is. Above all else, forms of voter suppression are a symptom of old-school opportunism and power. As far as why anyone would try to discourage young people from participating in the caucus, that was simple: Polling suggested that if college students—like the woman who jogged by me—showed up, they were going to caucus for Obama.

My phone rang two weeks before the caucuses. A well-known, left-leaning Hollywood producer was on the line. "Kal, I've been getting lots of calls from people who are starting to like Obama and considering donating to him. Since you know him, I wanted to bring up a big concern we have. If he ends up winning . . . is Barack going to nominate all Black people to his Cabinet?"

"God, I hope so," I shot back, thinking his question was satirical.

"Seriously, Kal. Will he?"

Oh, this guy was actually worried.

Flashbacks to "so you're not even Latin" flooded my brain. I wanted to go off on this Hollywood liberal, but I could tell it was a pivotal moment in his political life (one that could benefit the guy I was working for if I handled it right), so I dialed back my disappointment and instead told him about meeting Rohan, Brian, and Ronnie. I talked about Jackie and Paulette and Karen. "This campaign is the most diverse place I've ever worked. If the way he's staffed his Iowa team is any indication, Obama's Cabinet will actually look like America. I'm sure he'll nominate the most qualified people, whether they happen to be black or white or brown or yellow or red or *whatever*."

The producer eventually became a supporter.

Respect. Empower. Include. Maybe that's grandiose. Maybe it's even a little saccharine. For Obama to win Iowa and make history, our efforts at expanding the electorate—getting young people and others to attend their first caucus—had to pay off in a majority of Iowa's ninety-nine counties. We were hopeful that the young people with whom we shared intimate, heartbreaking, and hopeful stories would show up on caucus night, but there were no guarantees.

On January 3, 2008, I arrived half an hour early to observe a caucus location at the University of Iowa and couldn't believe what I saw—lines of young people that stretched for blocks. They showed up. Ahead of schedule.

Most of the hundreds of incredible people who caucused at that Iowa City site did so for Obama. Only a handful showed up for the other candidates: Edwards, Clinton, Biden, Richardson, and Kucinich. Obama easily won the precinct I was observing.

These young Americans smelled the "you can't caucus in Iowa even though the law says you can" BS and decided not only to "caucus for Barack" but to spread their stories and experiences via text, email, and social media. This meant their friends were motivated to caucus for him too. "I liked that he didn't talk down to us," said one young woman I chatted with.

I texted and emailed with friends—other organizers—around the state. *What are you hearing? Who won your caucus location? Have you heard from anyone else?* There was nothing to do but wait for the official statewide results, which could really go in anyone's favor. I sped back down I-80 west to Des Moines, where Obama would make a speech, win or lose. My driving companion was a gregarious, fast-talking Minnesotan named Charlie. "You like the band Spoon?" he asked as we pulled out of Iowa City. "Sure," I replied, eager for a distraction from our anxiety. Charlie put on a song titled "The Underdog." Its lyrics were fitting: *You got no time for the messenger / Got no regard for the thing that you don't understand / You got no fear of the underdog / That's why you will not survive.*

While the final polls had tightened in the state, *no one* in the media or in elite political circles was sure if the unlikely underdog—Team Obama—could actually win. It seemed unthinkable that a young, Black, progressive candidate could beat back the Democratic establishment. And we knew that even if Obama *did* pull off an upset in Iowa, we would still have an uphill battle. There was no telling what the rest of the primary season would bring: There were still so many more states to go.

Charlie and I stopped at a small family-owned gas station in Poweshiek County. As we paid for our food, a newscaster spoke on the small, boxy television behind the counter. "We believe that we have results to report. In a truly stunning and historic win, it appears that Illinois senator Barack Obama has won the Iowa caucuses, becoming the first African American in history to do so." Charlie and I teared up, immediately. "Remember the name of this town," he said to me. "Remember that this is the place we were when we found out we made history."

CHAPTER FIFTEEN

I APPLIED FOR MY WHITE HOUSE JOB ONLINE

After the writers' strike ended on February 12, 2008, I split my time between filming in Los Angeles and organizing anywhere the ever-expanding Obama campaign sent me. In the ten months following the Iowa caucuses, I traveled to twenty-six glorious states. My work as a youth vote surrogate expanded to include other tasks like meeting with superdelegates and working with state conventions on electoral vote tallies. I also joined Obama's Arts Policy Committee. During the week leading up to November 4, 2008, the day of the general election, the production team on *House* had managed to schedule me a few days off so I could put in some extra campaign work. I traveled to the swing states of Pennsylvania and New Hampshire to help with Get Out the Vote (GOTV) operations. If Obama lost, I could imagine no crappier feeling than an eleventh-hour realization that—after all this—I hadn't done everything I could have.

Election Day was exciting. I chose to be in Florida, helping students find their polling places and answering last-minute questions from undecided first-time voters on college campuses from Gainesville to Orlando to Tallahassee. The University of Florida was especially lively. On the one hand, their Students for Obama team had built a festive robot to help with GOTV.

On the other hand, the robot and I got rocks thrown at us by some college Republicans. (This was not a first for the campaign; my friend Stephen Brokaw previously had rocks thrown at him outside a campaign office in Ohio.)

From: Kal Penn
Date: Tuesday, November 4, 2008, 4:37 PM
To: Stephen Brokaw
You're now not the only one who's had rocks thrown at him

Obama '08

From: Stephen Brokaw
Date: Tuesday, November 4, 2008, 4:38 PM
To: Kal Penn
WHAT?!

Where?

And welcome to the club!

From: Kal Penn

Date: Tuesday, November 4, 2008, 4:46 PM

To: Stephen Brokaw

University of Florida. Gotta love the Students for McCain.

How's it looking?

Obama '08

By 5 p.m., I and other national surrogates were dialing into radio interviews in Virginia and North Carolina to counter voter suppression tactics in those states. By 7 p.m., we knew that the Hillsborough County, Florida, supervisor of elections hadn't delivered enough ballots to polling locations at the University of South Florida, which was experiencing massive voter turnout. At 9 p.m., I was deployed with a team of youth vote staff and volunteers to remind students to stay in line, that ballots were coming. When we got there, we saw long queues of young people who had already been waiting three hours. They were passing the time by singing and dancing, determined to stay put until those additional ballots arrived so they could cast their vote in this historic election.

An hour later, I was settled into the Florida election night watch party in a hotel ballroom in Tampa, beer in hand. We had definitely done everything we could do. As results from the last states trickled in on the televisions—blue for the ones Obama and Biden won, red for John McCain and Sarah Palin—I received an email from my friend Konrad Ng. As Obama's brother-in-law, Konrad would hold campaign surrogate events with his wife, Obama's sister Maya. We had gotten to know each other over the course of the long campaign, and often traded stories from our time on the road. The email from Konrad simply read:

Date: Tuesday, November 4, 2008, 10:41 PM
I just talked to BO . . . I think we have won this election.

I stood in quiet reflection, drinking my beer and feeling all the feels, waiting for the networks to announce it. Twenty minutes later, the flashing TV screens in the hotel ballroom confirmed what Konrad had told me—Obama was the president-elect. The room erupted in tears and hugs and sighs of relief. I felt a quiet sense of pride, a feeling of end-less possibility. America had elected its first Black president. I felt hope-ful that it might mean I'd fit in more than I had before, that to some small degree the days of people of color being othered might be behind us. As fellow staffers and I refilled our drinks, ready for Obama's victory speech and a hard night of partying ahead, a mass email written by the new president-elect quickly went out to every supporter nationwide:

Kalpen –
I'm about to head to Grant Park to talk to everyone gathered there, but I wanted to write to you first.
We just made history.
And I don't want you to forget how we did it.
You made history every single day during this campaign—every day you knocked on doors, made a donation, or talked to your family, friends, and neighbors about why you believe it's time for change.

I want to thank all of you who gave your time, talent, and passion to this campaign.

We have a lot of work to do to get our country back on track, and
I'll be in touch soon about what comes next.

But I want to be very clear about one thing . . .

All of this happened because of you.

Thank you,

Barack

The days that followed were kind of wonky. My campaign friends
were in withdrawal mode. They started sleeping properly, eating
better, reconnecting with people whose calls they missed, and thinking about what they wanted to do next. Staffers—myself included—
received an email from the presidential transition team with a link to
a website called change.gov, a portal for people to submit applications
for jobs with the incoming administration.

Now that our boss was the president-elect, the stakes had gotten
much higher overnight. Staring at the change.gov email, I thought,
*Is this really possible? Could I actually take my public service interests a
step further than what I'd imagined and work for the next president of the
United States?* The idea seemed so big, so untouchable, that I held it
close to my chest.

The concept of taking a short sabbatical from acting to work in
public service had been in the back of my mind since sometime after
Iowa, when I realized how much I had in common with the campaign
friends I was spending so much time with. It was then that I had started
to ponder the mechanics of how it might work, reasoning that I could
finally finish that International Security graduate certificate I was spo-
radically working toward at Stanford. Once that was complete, maybe

I'd take a year off to work for a nonprofit or think tank. With that often-repeated saying, "We're the ones we've been waiting for" ringing through my head, I'd intended to look into it. At some point.

Staring at this change.gov email, I reflected even further. I had been making campaign promises in more than half the country for well over a year. It didn't seem right to go straight back to acting, expecting that it should be left to someone else to implement those promises. I sort of felt like an actor doing a commercial endorsement. Does Tom Selleck really use the reverse mortgages he pimps out? I doubt it! But did Wilford Brimley actually have *diabeetus*? I mean, yeah, probably?

The thing I wanted to know was: How could I be a Wilford Brimley? And by that I don't just mean, how does a man grow such an aggressive, symmetrical mustache? I also mean, what makes someone qualified to work at the White House in the first place?

There were some personal reasons that made me curious about a life in Washington, DC, too. I was finally enjoying Los Angeles in a way that comes with a television actor's job stability: I had a nicer place to live, was seeing friends regularly, and could afford to take trips home without needing to bid on a flight using Priceline.com. I felt more immersed in a smart, vibrant creative community now that I was acting on *House* every day instead of fighting for auditions. For all this, I was grateful. But something still felt like it was missing. It sometimes felt stifling to be surrounded by people who do what I do for a living and weren't from especially diverse backgrounds—ethnic and racial to be sure, but I'm also talking about diversity in thought, profession, and life experience.

Well into my late twenties, I found LA to be a challenging city to date in too. I didn't like talking about work all the time (*Who's your agent? Did you audition for that project too?*). The newest exercise fads didn't interest me (shoes that look like feet, goat yoga), nor did the latest dietary obsessions (*So, like, there's this new thing called* ghee, *and like, if you put some in your coffee it'll change your life*[1]). In contrast, the guys I dated in places like Chicago or New York seemed more balanced; conversations about books, family, and music were much more my speed.

While filming *Superman Returns*, I became close with screenwriters Mike Dougherty and Dan Harris, as well as Dan's boyfriend, Stephen, who happened to be from Washington, DC, a city that (like LA) is often maligned for being a one-industry town too (so much so that it's often referred to as "Hollywood for ugly people"[2]). During visits to hang out with Stephen and his handsome buddies in Washington, I found a sort of kinship in being around other multitaskers who liked to talk about policy articles and public service.

Add to that the fact that I could be working with the campaign friends I had made during my year on the road for Obama, and a little fire in my brain said, *You might appreciate a personal change of pace, a new career, and a social life in DC for a couple of years.* So, it was with a strong and genuine desire to serve my country, and the smaller hope that a temporary move to a new city might be good for my sanity, that I got it into my head to apply for a job at the White House.

I had heard of other campaign friends applying for jobs on change .gov, but people were pretty tight-lipped about any process beyond that. There was an unspoken culture within the Obama campaign that went something like, "Keep your head down. Do good work. Don't seek attention." It's why you didn't see the same leaks, showboating,

---

1   Ghee can be traced back to India circa 2000 BCE. You should not put it in your coffee.

2   Not my phrase, it's the *people who live in DC* who call it that!

and backbiting in the press as you did from other camps. I didn't want people to perceive me as someone who was leveraging what modest artistic fame he had to get a serious job in the administration by making endless rounds of phone calls—if they were going to hire me, I wanted it to be on merit. So, I too stayed tight-lipped, only briefly mentioning my desire to my manager, Dan Spilo, and a few trusted friends. I decided that the right thing to do was what I assumed most of the thousands of people who worked on the campaign were doing: I followed the directions on how to apply for a job on change.gov. I filled out a form, attached my résumé, and hit Upload. Nobody called.

Two months went by. It bummed me out to know I wasn't qualified for a job in the incoming administration, but I still felt so lucky for the creative career I was passionate about. I was so happy to be back at work filming *House* full-time. Focusing on my acting career again without the juggle of campaign travel was fulfilling. I had missed being on set with Olivia and Peter, pulling long hours. My campaign friends were busy in their own right—some jumping onto the transition team or helping wind things down at headquarters in Chicago. We'd text each other cheesy things like "Yes we did!" with memorable photos from our big rallies and small grassroots events. Peter once grabbed my phone and, upon seeing a photo of a HOPE AND CHANGE campaign poster a friend had texted, pushed out his bottom lip and teased, "I'm Kal Penn and I wish I was running around the country spreading HULLLLLL and change."

On a break on set one day in early January, I saw a missed call from the DC area code. *Holy shit*, I thought, *someone from the transition team is finally calling about my change.gov résumé submission!*

They were not. Instead, I had a voice mail from the Presidential Inaugural Committee, asking if I would speak at Obama's inaugural concert on the steps of the Lincoln Memorial. It would be a patriotic celebration, a way of showcasing how historic his election had been. Performers included those from all walks of American life. Musicians like Bon Jovi, Usher, Beyoncé, and Bruce Springsteen would headline, and between each act, there'd be interstitials where actors would read quotes from previous presidents. On the lineup were Queen Latifah, Tom Hanks, Ashley Judd, and somehow . . . me. It was surreal.

The concert was a free, public event, and every performer was allowed to bring a few guests for preshow food and drinks in the festive, gigantic greenroom tent backstage. I flew out from LA and met my family in Washington. Spilo came too. My mom was wide-eyed and eager to see me onstage. My dad and Pulin were thrilled about the music lineup.

I actually began to worry about just *how* stoked my father was, to be honest. I didn't want his excitement to get the best of him, so before we left our hotel, I pulled him aside and said, "Dad listen, there are going to be a lot of famous people backstage, okay? If there's someone you'd like to meet, pull me aside and tell me so I can figure out if it's appropriate to bother them . . . If it is, then I'll introduce you. Don't go up to people in the greenroom and gawk."

This really offended my father. "You think I don't know this?" he asked indignantly. "I get so annoyed when other people do these things to you! I would never do that to somebody else."

I immediately felt bad. My dad was right—I knew he understood.

We checked in with security and made our way to a tastefully sofaed seating area inside the tent. I set my backpack down on a white wooden end table, and when I turned around, my father was missing.

I quickly scanned the room to locate him and was horrified by what I saw. Dad had somehow made it halfway across the cavernous tent and was standing six inches away from Tiger Woods, enthusiastically taking pictures with his boxy, early-generation digital camera. Flash and everything.

By the time I got to him, Tiger had noticed Dad creeping and was angling his face away from the camera. But Dad continued to aim for the best shot. *Jjjjt!*—his flash went off again. *Jjjjt!* Another flash.

I grabbed the camera and dragged him back. "What the hell, Dad? You JUST said you wouldn't do this!!"

"Do what?" he said, genuinely unaware—deep in his heart—of any wrongdoing.

"You said you'd be respectful of people. I told you there would be celebrities here, and you shouldn't bother them. You agreed with me!"

My dad looked me in the eye as if I was the biggest idiot in the world and exclaimed, "Yes, but this is *Tiger Woods*."

Apparently our verbal contract didn't apply to Tiger. He was in a category all his own. I sat my dad down on the sofa and went over the entire concert lineup. Was there anyone else on this list who would fall under the same category as Tiger Woods?

"Ashley Judd?"

"No."

"Shakira?"

"No."

"Garth Brooks?"

"Who is that?"

"Queen Latifah?"

"No, we already met her. Her mom lives next door to Falgu Auntie." (This is true. I have an auntie who lives next door to Queen Latifah's mom in New Jersey.)

"Tom Hanks?"

"Tom Hanks is here? I want to meet Tom Hanks!"

Luckily, Tom Hanks is the nicest guy you'll ever talk to. I asked him if he'd mind saying hello to my folks, and he was so gracious. My dad got his photo, and things calmed down. With Tiger and Tom out of the way, my parents were able to focus on why we were there: the inaugural concert, which was about to start. They took their seats with my brother and Dan in the audience, and I reported to the performers' hold room—the space where you wait before being sent out onstage.

The hold room for this event was in the civil rights museum that makes up the basement of the Lincoln Memorial. Even with the heavily armed Secret Service assault team stationed in the back, it felt serene, as if you could feel the presence of our nation's complicated history in this one little room. Plaques of quotes from Dr. Martin Luther King Jr. adorned the walls. Footage of African Americans being beaten and hosed for standing up for their rights played on the TV screens that make up the permanent exhibits. Nonviolent civil disobedience. I immediately thought of the trip to Gandhi's Sabarmati ashram with Bapaji, and the dinner table stories Grandma and Grandpa told me. As I stood with the other performers—all of us different colors and creeds—waiting for our cues to take the stage and celebrate the inauguration of America's first Black president, I reflected.

Marveling at how much change had happened in our country, and how much further we had to go, I thought about people I met on the campaign who didn't have health care, who had lost their jobs, were kicked out of the military for their sexual orientation or had faced discrimination for their gender identity. I felt hopeful about our incoming president's leadership, which would take us a bit further down the long path of progress. Moved by the fact that Dad came to America with just twelve dollars and a dream, I wondered, *What must my parents be thinking, sitting out there on the steps of the Lincoln Memorial?*

My mom answered that question when I saw her an hour and a half later: "I never imagined in a million years that my son would be up there doing that. Very few people, especially immigrants, get to share these moments. It was so special. It was the best moment of my life."

After the concert, the Obamas asked all the performers and our families to gather backstage so they could say hello. My parents, brother, and manager stood with me in the rope line next to people like Tiger Woods and Tom Hanks (and Shakira *"No,"* and Garth Brooks, *"Who?"*). It actually felt like we fit in. We *belonged* here. In light of some of my darker experiences in middle school and Hollywood, this was not a feeling I was always used to. Yet here we were, included on a historic, patriotic day.

The president-elect worked his way down the rope line. He was laid-back and every bit his charming self. "We're a long way from Des Moines," I joked. He made it a point to thank my parents, chat with Pulin, and show appreciation to Dan "for letting me borrow Kal for so long during the campaign."

The soon-to-be First Lady followed behind the president-elect by a few minutes. I hadn't yet met Mrs. Obama. She had been dividing her time between the campaign trail and Chicago, where Malia and Sasha were. When she did travel for campaign events, she was the headliner, so they certainly didn't need a surrogate like me. "I can't believe you haven't met Michelle!" staffers would say. "She's the *best*. When you meet her, you'll want *her* to run for president next."

Finally face-to-face there backstage, she was as gracious, impressive, and kindhearted as I'd expected. She thanked my family and my manager, and before leaving, offhandedly said to me, "You've been with us pretty much from the start. I hope you'll continue to stay involved and help us out."

It was a nice thing to say: a friendly bit of benign encouragement that I imagined she said to lots of people she hoped would volunteer at a local community center and vote in midterm elections. As I opened my mouth to say thank you and let her know that I'd surely stay involved, Spilo piped up: "Well, you know Kal applied for a job, right?"

Here's the thing about Dan Spilo. He's been my friend and manager for more than twenty years now. He's phenomenally smart, extraordinarily motivated, extremely loyal, and fights like hell for his clients. He's also sometimes the real-life version of the characters on that HBO show *Entourage* in the most lovable way possible.

Mrs. Obama paused, took in what my Hollywood manager said, and replied, "What do you mean?"

"Yeah, he filled out an application for a job at the White House," Dan continued, "and nobody even called him back."

Jesus.

Mrs. Obama's attention shifted to me. I tried to head this disaster off at the pass by politely nodding at Dan to stop talking so I could explain myself. "Yeahhhhh, I applied for a job," I confessed. "I figured, if I can be helpful, it's something that I'd love to consider."

She seemed more confused than anything else. "What do you mean? Who did you apply with?" she asked.

"Oh, I didn't want to be the guy who bothers people about jobs, so I just put my résumé where the email said to—on change.gov." As soon as the words came out of my mouth, I realized—for the first time—how absurd it all sounded.

Like many other jobs in the world, it turns out that while everyone had to apply for an Obama-Biden White House political appointment via change.gov, the expectation was that we'd also rely heavily on our networks to let the right people know we'd applied. Top-notch senior leadership picked out the talented staffers they worked with on the campaign—field organizers from early primary states, policy wonks who had been on their teams well before the general election, experts they'd consulted with prior to Obama even announcing his run—and found the right White House jobs for the most qualified early supporters. Those who had been with the campaign the longest—before the Iowa caucus, or especially prior to Obama's US Senate days—were top candidates for White House positions because they already knew the president-elect's priorities, tenor, and approach. Early supporters would be assets to a new administration that wanted to hit the ground running with the same ethics and uniformity as the campaign.

I didn't know any of this at the time. I applied on the website just like everybody else, but nobody knew I was interested because I hadn't taken the extra step and told anyone. I thought I was playing by the rules. *They have my résumé. If they think I'm qualified to work in the White House, they'll call.*[3]

In hearing that I—despite having been with the campaign since before the Iowa caucuses—had anonymously uploaded my résumé to the website, without bothering to follow up in any serious way,

---

3   I'm not a *complete* idiot. I did send an email to the head of the transition to let him know I had applied on the website. But I never followed up with him (or anyone else), so no one thought I was serious about it. Okay, I guess that fundamentally changes nothing and I'm still an idiot.

the soon-to-be First Lady seemed almost . . . offended. As someone of exceptional intelligence and honesty, Mrs. Obama has a low
threshold for bullshit. Her expression changed. No longer bemused
or pleasantly surprised, she gave me the look you'd give someone if
they dropped a piece of pizza on the ground and then picked it up
and ate it in front of you.

"You did *what*?" (She was obviously trying to confirm if I was as
naive as I looked.)

"Uh, yeah, I, uh, I didn't want to bother anybody, so I figured
I'd apply on change.gov." At this point, having confirmed that I *was*
actually as naive as I looked, she called her husband over. "Barack!
Come here." The president-elect waved back, signaling that he'd
already chatted with my family, leading Mrs. Obama to repeat with a
bit more urgency, "Barack! Come *here*."

As the president-elect made his way back to where we were standing, Mrs. Obama continued, "Kal, tell him what you just told me."

"Oh, no, I um . . . it's really not . . ."

Mrs. Obama insisted. "Tell him. Tell him what you did."

"Well, sir, I was just, uh, telling her that I applied for a job at the
White House. You know, if there's anything I'd be useful doing . . ."

"You did? Who did you apply with?" Obama asked.

God, that question again.

At this point, Mrs. Obama gave Mr. Obama a disappointed look
that said, *Watch what this dummy is about to say.*

I didn't even want to utter the absurd words. "I uploaded my
résumé to change.gov."

Now it was Obama's turn to react, with a curious, shocked, *I-too-
am-surprised-you're-that-naive* sort of look. Unlike his wife, he seemed
very amused. "Man, you applied on change.gov and didn't tell anyone? Why didn't you just call me?"

I was understanding the reality of a situation like this: If your boss of more than a year—who you're on good terms with—suddenly gets a big promotion and you want to keep working for him, he'd expect you to give him the courtesy of telling him that.

Obama motioned for his personal aide, Reggie Love. "You have Reggie's info, right? You guys have each other's numbers? Reggie's going to give you a call this week and we'll figure out if there's a good fit somewhere," he said. I was embarrassed, relieved, and excited. Either the president-elect was better at being polite than I knew, or Mrs. Obama's reaction was indicative of their belief that as an early organizer and Arts Policy Committee member on the campaign, maybe I *could* actually be good at something in the White House.

Three days later, backstage at the staff inaugural ball where I was to make a speech before David Plouffe and Obama, the newly inaugurated president raised the idea of a job. "Hey man, I was thinking about our conversation. How do you feel about working with Organizing for America?" he asked, referring to the nongovernmental advocacy group being formed to keep grassroots supporters marshalled toward political action. It would have been a great way to stay involved, but not what I had applied for on change.gov. "I want to go all-in," I said to the president. "I want to work directly for you at the White House and help fulfill all those promises we made people."

In retrospect it was perhaps a bold thing to say. I was flattered that he'd even remembered our chat from the rope line at the inaugural concert enough to have given it any thought. Reggie passed my number along to Chris Lu, the new head of White House Cabinet Affairs, and he reached out to me a few days later. "The boss is excited about the prospect of you joining the staff. It's good you two spoke," he said. "In the Office of Public Engagement—OPE—on the out-reach team, we're trying to fill three jobs: We need to find someone to handle outreach to young people, outreach to Asian Americans and Pacific Islanders, and outreach to the arts community. OPE is one of the offices senior advisor Valerie Jarrett is going to oversee. Tina Tchen is heading it up, and apparently you really impressed her at the DNC back in August, so she wants you on her team."

I hadn't initially planned on attending the 2008 DNC (Democratic National Convention). I thought my time would be better spent on the road campaigning through the summer. But when my former Iowa boss, Paul Tewes, recruited me to be something called a floor whip, I couldn't really say no. "The campaign needs a few trusted volunteers to work the floor of the convention," he said at the time. "One whip will oversee two delegations. Duties include standing, handing out signs with quippy slogans on them timed to convention speakers so that everything looks good on TV, and blocking journal-ists and other roamers from coming too close to the delegates and disrupting their work."

The other part of the floor-whip job was to keep an eye out for anyone who might potentially hamper a smooth convention. The pri-mary had been contentious, and the worry was that disgruntled del-egates of other candidates might orchestrate some sort of takeover on the (televised) convention floor—causing a potential embarrass-ment to the nominee (Barack *Hussein* Obama). Each day I was given a sweet walkie-talkie with an earpiece, and a bright yellow vest to go over my clothes. I was expected to be thoughtful and engaging with the delegates, to quietly spot and report potential trouble, and to be unapologetically tough in dealing with any outliers. Overall, I gath-ered that floor whips were sort of like political bouncers. Tewes had assigned me to the Illinois and Hawaii delegations—Obama's home states, and therefore sort of a big deal.

What Chris Lu was telling me now was that Tina, the president's incoming director of Public Engagement, had been one of those Illinois delegates and that I'd impressed her with my work that week. "So, the President's Liaison to Asian Americans and Pacific Islanders, Young Americans, and the Arts Community," he continued, "those are three separate jobs, but we only have the salary to pay for one staffer. Between your campaign experience, your arts background, your graduate program, and your teaching position at UPenn, you have expertise in all three areas, so we thought it might actually be perfect. How do you feel about that?"

"Three jobs?! Yes! Of course!" I didn't miss a beat. "I'd be honored to."

There was only one little problem: I already had a job. A publicly known job with a contract, on the TV show *House* (which I was enjoying). When I initially applied on change.gov, I hadn't thought through what would happen if I was actually offered a White House job. So, as I provisionally accepted the offer from Chris, I knew this wasn't going to be a straightforward process. I couldn't just ghost on my TV gig.

Even though it was basically Spilo's fault that I had this job offer, he suddenly had concerns. "Are you sure you want to do this? You're on a hit television show you've worked your whole life to get on. Why don't you just wait until next season in case the show gets canceled?" But I couldn't do that. *House* ran through the following May; it was mid-January and the White House job started immediately.

Besides, *House* was in its fifth season; it wasn't going to get dropped anytime soon. I knew it and he knew it. So, I asked my manager and agent (not Barbara Cameron, she had retired) to see if they could get me out of my contract.

The answer came back fast: It was a hard no as far as the network was concerned. I asked them to check once more, and after a week of additional lobbying, I had gotten nowhere: "The network and the producers say they won't let you off the show."

I really didn't want to call Chris Lu back and tell him I couldn't take a job in the White House because my agent said I had to keep playing a fake doctor on TV, so I took matters into my own hands. Motivated by old Hollywood stories of gentlemen putting on smoking jackets and handling their disagreements one-on-one over a glass of scotch (which I finally knew how to drink thanks to John Cho), I made an appointment to see our show creator, David Shore, at his office next door to our soundstages on the Fox lot.

David is kind and approachable, the sort of boss who makes you feel comfortable enough to speak candidly. "David," I said, "I know my agent has reached out to you directly a few times to see if I could get out of my contract to go work at the White House. I enjoy being on *House* and am so grateful for this experience, but serving our country is such a unique opportunity—a once-in-a-lifetime chance to help change the world. It's the kind of thing I think I'll regret not doing. Under the circumstances, I thought it was right to come to you myself."

David looked at me quizzically and said, "This is the first I'm hearing of this."

"What do you mean?"

"Yeah, no one looped me in. You actually got a job in the White House?"

I should have seen it coming. Agents make a commission off an actor's work. No work, no commission. Either my agent never asked, or the request was squashed at the network before it ever made its way to David. "Are you unhappy on the show?" he asked.

"No, not at all. I'm *very* happy," I replied, truthfully. "Honestly, I know a lot of people will think I'm crazy for doing this. I finally have a lucrative job in television, on a show I enjoy. It's just, thirty years from now, am I going to look back and say that I didn't serve my country when I had an opportunity? Am I just a flashy Tom Selleck, or will I be proud that I had the balls to be a Wilford Brimley? I hope," I continued, "I'm going to be able to say that even though I lost a lot of money and momentum by pausing an acting career that I'm passionate about, I'm glad I took a chance to help make the world a better place, even if it *was* a crazy move."

David took that all in. "Well, look, I don't know if you know *my* story. I was a lawyer in Toronto. I always wanted to be a screenwriter, and everyone told me I was crazy. They said I had a great gig going as a partner in a law firm, and that I would be throwing it all away if I were to try to go the Hollywood route. I finally decided I was going to pack up, move to LA, and become a screenwriter anyway. So, bottom line, who am I to tell you that going to work at the White House is crazy? Happy to help you do it—I just need a couple weeks to figure out how we're going to write your character off."

I was so grateful. David was the best.

Just over a week later, he called me back into his office: "Two things. First, your agent called to tell me that you're not *really* going to leave the show for the White House and that I shouldn't take it seriously. That's incorrect, right?"

"Right."

"I thought so. Second, here's the deal: We're going to accelerate your departure from the show. In the next episode, Kutner is going to kill himself."

"Woah, what?" This was a gut-check moment. It was all fun and games until you realize that your character and the salary that comes with playing him are going to die.

"We've actually been looking for a catalyst for Dr. House to be institutionalized. There needs to be a problem he can't solve and we're exploring some mental health stuff anyway, so it works. BUT . . . You can't start your job at the White House until after that episode airs in April. It'll tip people off that something in the script has changed if you start before then, and if anything leaks, it destroys that plotline. So, you can't move to DC just yet."

I took a deep breath and thought about it for just a split second. Not being able to publicly acknowledge that I was leaving the show meant that I couldn't formally accept the White House's offer until April 6—the date my last episode would air. Could I take their word that the government job would still be there? It felt a bit like when a gambler puts it all on black. Deep down, I knew what I wanted. As David and I sat there face-to-face, two gentlemen definitely not drinking scotch, I looked him in the eye and confidently said, "Thank you."

I had a quick phone interview from Los Angeles before flying to Washington, DC, for a more formal sit-down with senior advisor Valerie Jarrett ("VJ" for short), and her deputy Michael Strautmanis on April 13. To prepare, I had asked our *House* screenwriter Eli Attie for advice. When he was one of Al Gore's speechwriters, Eli had an office in the White House, so he gave me some helpful background like, "Ask for the title Special Assistant to the President, it's the most junior of the senior-level positions; it means you'll have a higher salary and more direct decision-making authority."

I asked for the senior title and the salary—and failed at securing either. Still, what I was offered was pretty great. I would be an associate director of the White House Office of Public Engagement. As Chris mentioned, that meant I'd also be the President's Liaison to Young Americans, the Arts Community, and Asian Americans and Pacific Islanders. I was all in. As the interview wrapped up, I needed to settle any jitters I had about the reasons for my employment once and for all. "Valerie," I began, "can you assure me I'm not being hired just because I'm a recognizable actor?"

VJ looked me in the eye and said, "I can assure you"—she smiled politely—"that you're being hired *in spite* of it."

I was deeply proud of the hard work we put in with Team Obama: all the late campaign nights, learning the craft of politics from scratch—I was relieved to know for sure that my private-sector career wasn't the reason for my public-sector hire. My path to government wasn't part of a grand strategy; if anything, it came out of a lack thereof. I knew that taking a leave of absence from Hollywood would be a risk, and it might be hard to get hired again if I stayed out of the acting game for a couple of years. It didn't matter; taking a sabbatical to go work for the Obama White House felt right.

Sometimes it takes dedicated work, uploading a résumé onto a website, naively waiting by the phone for a call that never comes, and getting hazed by Michelle Obama in the realities of job hunting to push you along. Whatever the path, now that I was one of the ones we were waiting for, it was time to get to work. But first, I had to tell my parents.

I called them as soon as it was official, knowing how excited they'd be to learn that after moving to America and toiling so hard, their son had been hired to work for the first Black president of the United States.

On the other end of the line was my father, laughing maniacally.

"Dad, are you there?" I said, confident that he misheard something.

"Yeah," he said, trying to catch his breath between giggles.

"What's so funny?" I asked.

"I just can't believe"—he was interrupted by his own full, deep laughter—"that after ten years of working so hard, you finally have a stable acting career, and you're calling to tell me that you're going to throw it all away to work in the government—" He burst out laughing again. "What do you want me to say? We told you not to become an actor and you did it anyway. Whatever our advice is, you'll do what you know is the right thing for yourself."

CHAPTER SIXTEEN

A LETTER TO A THIRTY-ONE-YEAR-OLD ME

*I*n our tenth-grade English class, we wrote two letters: one to our former selves, to teach us to embrace change and growth, and another to our future selves, to teach us how to set goals. Recently, as I thought back to my time in the White House, I realized how many of the things I learned there would have been good to know before going in. What if I could write a letter to my thirty-one-year-old self and give him some advice before his first day at 1600 Pennsylvania Avenue? What words of wisdom could I impart so that he would be prepared to serve the country with honor and distinction?

Dear Baby Kal,

Can I just say that you look great? I feel like people didn't tell me that enough. So, I'll tell me now: You look great. No need to thank me; I'm you. But either way, I'm welcome.

I know you feel a fascinating combo of excitement and pressure, and you don't want to screw this whole thing up. You haven't worked in politics before and, already, a lot of people are paying attention to your decision to take this sabbatical from acting in weird ways.

You know all those super-original headlines like, "From White Castle to the White House!" and "From Dr. House to the White House!" that every publication thinks are unique? Yeah, you won't stop seeing them anytime soon, so view it with amusement and shake it off like you will those adorable protestors who'll excitedly show up at some of your Obama reelect events in a few years—it's all a sign that you made it, son! Congratulations!

(Above: Such clever slogans!)

Remember, the only person you need to prove anything to is the guy who hired you, and he's the president of the United States. So, tune out all the distractions, ignore the bullshit, and do the hard work you came here to do. With some practical tips from me, your future self, you're going to do great.

Settling In

The West Wing is super small (you'll see). As far back as 1799, most staffers have had offices in adjacent buildings within the White House grounds. Yours is in the Eisenhower Executive Office Building, or EEOB for short. Giant, ornate, and seven levels tall, the EEOB spans a full block and originally housed the Navy, War, and State Departments. The vice president has a ceremonial office on the second floor, the National Security Council is above that, and—huge perk—there's a bowling alley in the basement that you can reserve on occasion.

A short walkway separates the EEOB and the West Wing. You'll be shuttling back and forth between the two buildings several times a day. Before things get hectic, take some time to get acclimated to your new office and don't be afraid to personalize the space. Quarters are tight—there are six of you to a room, and you're going to be working long hours. Thankfully, your coworkers will be some of the most dedicated, intelligent people you'll ever meet—they'll also help make your little corner of EEOB 112A feel like a second home.

Tip A: Invest in a Mini Fridge

We both know you have a tendency to get hangry, so let's talk about the culinary situation at the White House. You're not in Hollywood anymore. There's no catering, and there are no production assistants, so no one is ordering you a vegan burrito with fair-trade, organic, shade-grown coffee at 10 a.m. Also, 10 a.m. is super late in Washington; you'll be at work by seven thirty most mornings. Make yourself some oatmeal before you leave home.

Lunch is easily brought or bought, but since your workdays will usually end between 8:30 and 11 p.m., you'll need to plan ahead for dinner. As a midlevel staffer, you're not allowed to access the nice White House Mess—that's reserved for senior officials and, despite Eli Attie's advice, you are not a Special Assistant to the President. Unlike what you saw on *The West Wing*, forget about ordering delivery. Sure, the cooks at G Street Food seem nice, but the Secret Service won't allow it because foreign or domestic adversaries working at nearby restaurants could decide to poison your meal when they see where it's going.

Also, bad news: The area around the White House becomes a gastronomic dead zone after about 6:00 p.m. So, you'll have to do what normal people across this great nation do every day: be economical and healthy and pack a dinner from home. DC is an expensive city. Save your pennies.

Since a homemade salad or tacos won't keep on your desk for twelve hours, invest in a mini fridge. Go to the Target in Columbia Heights on a Saturday. The fridge is a bit bulky, so ask your intern James to help you bring it back on the Metro, through Lafayette Park, and into the northwest gate. He's going to be comically bad at lifting things and you're going to want to yell at him a little, but this is not Hollywood and you're not an actor so you can't throw tantrums to get your way. *Be nice.*

And don't be intimidated by the Secret Service guys on the White

House roof with sniper rifles: Yes, you're two dudes walking through Lafayette Park with a big box trying way too hard not to look suspicious, but you have your blue badge and they know what's up. They have to eat too; they understand the need for the fridge.

One final food tip: In emergency situations only, you can head down to the basement and pick up a vending machine sandwich. It's in a small nook down the hall from the bowling alley. Bring $2.25 in exact change. The cheese sandwich is the most edible option and consists of two slices of (allegedly) yellow cheese on (supposedly) white bread with (purportedly) mustard-colored mayo. For me, your future self—don't eat too much of this stuff. Your friends in Hollywood would be horrified if they found out you consumed white carbs. And please let our thirty-one-year-old metabolism know I miss you and I'm sorry I took you for granted.

Tip B: How to Hang Things on Your Office Wall

Look at that bare wall. If this is a second home, it needs to look like one. Put up some photos!

Moved as you were in the civil rights museum during the inaugural concert, you'll want to be reminded of Grandpa's legacy of public service each day as you begin your own. So, you'll consider bringing in that framed photo of Gandhi that Grandpa had at his house—the one you remember from your childhood summer visits—to hang on your office wall. It's an important family heirloom safely stored in a New Jersey attic, and I know you're nervous about it. Relax, the White House is the safest place in the world. (See: snipers on roof, no-poison food.) Nobody is going to steal the photo.

Heads-up, when you do bring it into the office, a coworker will politely inform you: "You aren't allowed to nail anything to the walls, Kal. You're going to have to call GSA." The GSA is the General Services Administration—one of the entities that helps support the basic functioning of federal agencies. They enforce the rules about the rules. As a public servant, you have to obey those—they have been set up to ensure good government.

You'll think to yourself: *Okay, no problem, I guess I'll just call GSA to get permission to hang the Gandhi photo and be good.* Not so fast. You have to follow a few *simple* steps. I'm writing them out here for your reference:

Step One: Fill out a Work Order form, which is easily found on the office intranet. Print it out, sign it, and go downstairs to the room where Work Order requests are filed.

Step Two: The door will be locked. Come back later in the afternoon.

Step Three: The door will still be locked. Someone in the hallway will casually mention that the woman who processes those forms has worked in government for decades and has accordingly accrued a lot of time off. She usually comes in around ten thirty, takes an unnecessarily long lunch, and leaves work by three thirty.

Step Four: Wait a full day. Don't worry pal, that picture is going to look great on your wall.

Step Five: The next day, schedule your meetings around Five-Hour-Workday Government Lady, and you'll finally be able to complete step one: dropping off the form. It's now in a basket on her desk. Great job! Don't bother asking anything like, "When will they let me hang it?" because she'll only tell you, "They'll be in touch."

Step Six: At some point, you'll get an email asking when you can be available for a call (Step Seven, below) to talk with someone about the Work Order request (Step One) you have put in (Step Five) for the photo you want to hang. You can complete Step Six by replying via email to schedule the phone call (Step Seven) for the next day. Hello Gandhi!

Step Seven: The phone call. The following day, somebody will call you to confirm the details you have already listed on the (Step One) form: How big is the photo? How heavy do you think it might be? The Step Seven human will eventually ask to schedule a time and date when (Step Eight!) he can come to your office. He'll be booked for a few days, so go ahead and save yourself some time by scheduling an appointment for the following week.

Step Eight: When half a fortnight passes, a nice man wearing an exceptionally large tool belt will show up and complete the final step—he'll hammer a nail into your wall. Then he will leave. Oh, you thought he'd go ahead and hang the picture up too? Silly, silly, Baby Kal. He is Captain of the Nails. He only shows up to hammer one into the wall. It's your responsibility to hang the picture up yourself. Welcome to the federal government, buddy.

Now look, I know these rules are meant to be followed, so you can choose to do all of that bureaucratic time-wasting nonsense with the forms . . . *or* . . . make things more efficient. Keep this between us and take a peek behind your office door. You'll see a stray nail in the corner—leftover from when some past staffer took down a picture. Wait until everyone has left for the night and yank it out. Use the back of your stapler to bang it into the wall next to your desk, and hang that photo, homie! After all, your grandparents marched with Gandhi because they were idealistic. They weren't rule followers.

Getting Down to Business

You're not here to spend your time buying fridges and hanging pictures. It's time to get to work. And even that follows a process in the Executive Branch.

Tip C: Work Email Is Not like Personal Email

Sure, you've had email before. But you've never had White House email. It's important to keep in mind that all of your work email is considered a presidential record and will be archived for potential public release one day through something called the Presidential Records Act (PRA). Messages will fall under two general categories: those from within the Executive Branch and those from outside. Let's start with outside first. As a federal employee, your email address isn't that hard to figure out. You work for the Office of Public Engagement, and because a lot of good people pin their hopes and dreams on what's happening at the White House, your in-box will be inundated daily. You'll feel an obligation to respond to all the messages. Don't try to do this or you'll never get any proactive work done. Learn to triage and set up filters to sort the necessary emails from the nonessential.

When it comes to constituents whose organizations you're working with, be sure to read between the lines of people's email signatures. The more items somebody includes at the bottom of their email, the more accolades they announce, the more superlatives they advertise, the *less* legit they usually are. Sometimes this will be obvious; other times, the best sign that you're dealing with a crazy person is how many pieces of flair they gifted themselves at the end of their message.

Here's an example of a type of email you'll get soon. You should take this one seriously:

From: Nicole River
Date: Thursday, July 23, 2009 5:25 PM
To: Kalpen Modi
Subject: DREAM Act

Mr. Modi:
Congratulations on your appointment as President Obama's right-hand man for issues related to Young Americans! My name is Nicole River, and I run a nonprofit called Campus Forward. I left word for you earlier today. We'd previously been working with Paul Monteiro in your office. We'd love to have the opportunity to brief you on the work our 3 million members are doing nationwide around the DREAM Act and share with the president our vision for immigration reform. Looking forward to hearing from you.

Sincerely,
Nicole
President, Campus Forward

Nicole seems like a good person. She is eager to help. Her note was professional, and she's outlined the reach of her organization. You can easily google the great work she and her team do. They have a strong history and track record of working in politics. And heck, look at that signature line: "President, Campus Forward." Concise. Not self-congratulatory. She'll be effective to work with.

Now let's look at a different type of email. Pay special attention to the signature:

From: Jonathan Middleton
Date: Thursday, July 23, 2009 5:25 PM
To: Kalpen Modi
Subject: URGENT! MR. MODI I HAVE LEFT SEVERAL VOICE MAILS URGENT REGAR . . .

DEAR MR. KALPEN MODI:
IT IS VERY URGENT FOR PRESIDENT OBAMA TO ACT IMME-DIATELY TO HELP YOUNG PEOPLE. I RUN AN ORGANIZA-TION BASED HERE IN VIRGINIA. WE HAVE ALWAYS MET WITH EACH PRESIDENT SINCE KENNEDY AND HAVE NOT HEARD ONE PEEP FROM THIS OBMAMA ADMINISTRA-TION. I HAVE LEFT SEVERAL URGENT VOICE MAILS AND HAVE NOT GOTTEN ANY CALLS BACK. THIS IS NO WAY TO ENGAGE FOR THE OFFICE OF PUBLIC EGNAGNEMENT. TIME IS TICKING MR KALPEN MODI. HAVE A HEART FOR ARE YOUTH

Sincerely,
Jonathan Middleton
—

Jonathan Middleton

Founder and President, Virginia Community Activists for Change that has 450+ members and impacted the lives of more than 3,000 youth to be community leaders in 45 counties

International Speaker, Boys and Girls Club (5 chapters!!)

Advisor, Young Leaders Association of Richmond (1998–present)

www.jonathanmiddletonrocks.com

Follow on Twitter @realjmiddletonrocks

*Motivational leadership for young people

    *TTOP Speakers Bureau

    *Teamwork and advisory council for parents

    *Founder of Summit for Virginia/Maryland Youth (SVMY) Conference (12 states in attendance!!!)

WINNER: Southeastern Leadership Conference of the Greater Virginia Leaders of Tomorrow (SLCGVLT)

WINNER: Greater-DC Area Chamber of Public Service Impact Award

"Life isn't about waiting for the hurricane to pass. It's about learning to dance when it drizzles." —Unknown

Even if you hadn't read the body of Jonathan's ridiculous email, the fact that the signature is longer than the rambling note itself tells you all you need to know. Emails from legit people will be confident and crisp. They don't need to prove themselves with the girth of their email signature. (Yes, that's a euphemism. I can make dick jokes again, but you shouldn't. Not a great look for a White House staffer.)

Speaking of euphemisms and dick jokes, let's discuss internal White House emails. You'll often be looped into large-group email chains, many of which will require quick responses or dedicated decision-making throughout the day. Others are just for your situational awareness. One day, the National Security Council (NSC) will email you and eighty other staffers a memo with a list of talking points about an upcoming visit to the United States by a delegation of government officials from the Philippines. It'll be your first NSC loop-in.

I want you to know that almost everything in government is an acronym, as you see in the last paragraph. When a name is introduced, it will be written out fully, with the acronym in parentheses—"The President of the United States (POTUS) is convening a meeting of the National Security Council (NSC) next week." Subsequently, only the acronym is used—"The POTUS NSC meeting is at 4:30."

The Filipino memo from the NSC will include several pages of talking points, but you'll be super obsessed with item fourteen:

"One of the main terror groups in the Philippines is the Moro Islamic Liberation Front (MILF)." Your hopes are confirmed by the next few bullets:

- MILF is considered highly dangerous.

- MILF has a long history of recruiting young men.

- Many young men who join MILF come to regret their choice, as the novelty of life with MILF wears off.

Listen. You can only laugh to *yourself* about a terror group named MILF. Don't make the same mistake I made. <u>Do not</u> Reply All to the email. Don't write, "Whoa, their main terror group are the MILFs? Amazing!" If you do this, the chain will go silent for thirty minutes before an older NSC career person will also Reply All with the message, "Looks like Kal Penn is in the building."

Oh sure, your friends will laugh in the hallway and secretly high-five at your joke, but they will not have your back in any official capacity on this serious internal email chain. On the plus side, it's the only time you'll ever screw up in this manner, so I'm saving you the hassle. Don't reply to the MILF email. Just smirk quietly at your desk. If you need to share it with someone, use the phone so there isn't a permanent PRA-mandated record of your deliciously immature joke.

Tip D: Nobody Is Crazy

Try not to use the word *crazy* in describing anybody, especially the constituents. Just as in Hollywood, nobody in the political world is actually *crazy*. People can have *colorful personalities*. They can be *eccentric*. They may even have *unconventional views*.

You can say something like, "Wow, Anthony from that think tank sent me a *passionate* email about the president's foreign policy strategy," or "Anthony from that nonprofit has such a *peculiar* take on leadership!" People in DC will know that you actually mean Anthony is one hundred percent completely *batshit crazy*.

In the rarest of situations only, you *might* actually need to use the word *crazy*. At these times, close your office door, lower your voice to a bare whisper when you reach the offending word, and affect the same kind of apologetic tone that white ladies use when they say things like, "Linda, it's just terrible. She has cancer." And "Oh, Bethany,

I'm sure she'd love to go on a date with him but he's gay." Like that, you can say, "Anthony is straight-up crazy."

But in general, try to avoid the word altogether.

Tip E: White House Snail Mail Is NOT like Fan Mail!

Passionate emails with girthy signatures can be annoying. Colorful snail mail . . . now that's just fun! In your old life, your publicist weeded out the weirdest notes your fans sent you. Now, the Secret Service handles this task, except you're not getting any letters about your spread in *People* magazine's "Sexiest Men Alive" issue, and they're filtering for anthrax, not for crazy.[1] So, get used to receiving random items in the mail, including:

- trash (yes, actual, physical garbage)

- tiny bits of paper with weird nonsensical slogans scribbled on them, including gems like: "Because of the triumph of the spider in metaphysics" and "Nocturnal challenges await the waited"

- random, unmarked CDs (obviously, don't try to play them or insert them into any computers)

- Post-it Notes about conspiracy theories stapled to articles

- Post-it Notes about conspiracy theories not stapled to articles

---

1   It's fine to use it here.

- long manifestos claiming to be from the *real* president

- rants from people claiming to be intergalactic commanders

- a weirdly stapled packet of color photos, including pics of someone's great-grandfather and directions to his house along with the handwritten caption: "This is my house. Here are the directions. You can come over and I will cook you yummy Indian food."

- really sweet notes from former ambassadors with absolutely incredible names.

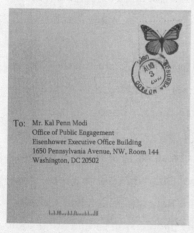

It doesn't feel this way, but you're getting a window into America: a place with shadow presidents, would-be intergalactic commanders, and (Ambassador) Dick Swett. Appreciate these notes. You'll miss them when you go back to acting, and your fan mail is being screened for content instead of poison.

Tip F: Be Attentive, and Be Careful What You Agree To

One day, you'll need a haircut. You'll google "Barber, Dupont Circle DC." Raucous Rodolpho will have an opening right away.

"Kal! Penn!" he will shout, staring at you in the mirror, eyes wide. "Wow man, it's really you! How's Obama?"

DC is a smaller city than most people realize, and word about political hirings and firings spreads quickly. Even among the non-political crowd—in bakeries, barbershops, and bookstores—people follow what's happening with a microscopic intensity not found elsewhere in America. Raucous Rodolpho will have heard about your job at the White House. "I'm askin' cuz I'm not just a barber, man, I own a tapas bar too, you need to come check it out, man! And hey! You should bring Obama!"

Nobody is immune to awkward barber small talk, but the Obama factor really turns it up a notch. You're no stranger to this, having watched similar situations accelerate quickly during your time on the campaign. Remember when people would tell you—not ask you—that you should bring Obama to all sorts of random places— restaurants, schools, sweet sixteens? That will ramp up even more now that he's president, starting with Raucous Rodolpho. "How big is your office, man? HEY. How many people? You should bring your whole office to my tapas bar, man! AYYYY, free tapas-bar goodness for everybody! We open at eleven a.m. every day. Michelle can come too!"

Always politely decline these kinds of invitations right off the bat. Good-natured as they are, they're also impractical and against the rules. We can't speak for any shadiness before or after our administration, but during Obama world orientation, each White House aide will be shuffled into an auditorium and put through a no-nonsense ethics briefing:

☑ *Keep all work and personal emails separate.*

☑ *For your protection, always hide your security badge after you exit the complex.*

☑ *Don't accept free anything.*

That last one is a biggie: The president has made it clear—no White House aide should be perceived to be endorsing a private business, accepting gifts, or leveraging their position at the White House. Even the mere optics of any special benefits is not okay with the boss. The president and senior staff had to turn down expensive watches gifted to them by the king of Saudi Arabia, and you'll need to decline the free tapas-bar invite.

You'll explain the situation to Raucous Rodolpho, who instead will double down: "Look, man. I'm a small-business owner from a minority background. I got this barber shop, and I got my tapas bar. It would be such an absolute honor to have you guys there. If you can't accept anything for free, I'll charge you. And you can leave a big tip! I just want you to come, and I guarantee . . . you'll all have a great time."

"I'll tell you what, man," you'll say, eager to change the subject, "why don't you give me your card. If we're planning a staff holiday party or an out-of-office event that needs a bar, I'll definitely give you a shout." Raucous Rodolpho will light up. He'll hand you his business card, which you'll slip into your back pocket. Don't encourage his excitement further. Keep things professional.

That night, you'll empty your pockets onto your nightstand: keys, some change, and Raucous Rodolfo's tapas-bar card. You'll look at it for the first time: a glossy black background with a long, thin drawing of a barber pole running down the center. Why is there a naked woman swinging on that barber pole? Just underneath her exposed cartoon breasts you'll find the name of the tapas bar emblazoned in shiny block letters. This is where you agreed to potentially have the White House Office of Public Engagement holiday party: RODOLFO'S LADIES: TOPLESS BAR.

Topless, not tapas. Be attentive. And be careful what you agree to.

Tip G: Be the Best Gatekeeper You Can Be

You shouldn't hang around with sketchy characters. That's good life advice in general. As it applies to your government job, you'll be putting together meetings and briefings for POTUS that include community leaders from outside the White House world. That can turn into a bit of a process.

You have to collect their Social Security number and send it to the Secret Service for a background check. Then, their online and offline profiles are analyzed by the research team to make sure there's nothing offensive, incendiary, or otherwise potentially distracting from the work everyone is doing for the Office of the President of the United States. That research department will be led by an amazing woman named Liz Jarvis-Shean. Be good to Liz. She's a saint. She also has a couple of bottles of really nice scotch on a shelf, which she'll share with you on especially late nights at the office.

In a couple of years, you'll be planning a young leaders' round-table for the president during a visit to Davenport, Iowa. You're going to remember that energetic kid named Romen Borsellino, who put together Senator Obama's first-ever high school surrogate event during the campaign. You'll want to tap him to help with this meeting.

So, you'll send Romen's name and vitals to Liz for vetting, and she will email you a couple of days later:

From: Liz Jarvis-Shean

To: Kalpen Modi

Subject: Romen Borsellino

In the middle of vetting for your Davenport event. Can you please have Romen Borsellino delete the tweet pasted below?

← **Tweet**

Romen Borsellino
@RomenBorsellino

@NihalShrinath I heard you got cum on your thesis

1:45 PM · Apr 24, 2012 · Twitter Web Client

You'll stare dumbfounded at your computer screen, trying to come up with the words to reply, when the phone at your desk will ring. It's going to be Liz, and besides the cum thesis problem, she'll bring up something Romen has on his Facebook wall that needs to be taken down too. She'll email it to you:

When she sends you this photo, you're going to laugh your face off. Then you'll send Romen a cryptic message, asking if he can talk "about something important." You'll catch him on a drive from Des Moines to Davenport, and he'll be nervous, wondering what you're calling about. My advice? Play this up. Do not let on that you think any of this is funny. Make him sweat a little. For example:

ME: I just got part of your vetting report back. There are a few problems. I need you to take down a Facebook photo . . . the one with the dildo.

Silence

ME: Hello?

ROMEN: Yeah.

ME: You have to take down the photo you have on your Facebook wall. The one with the dildo.

Silence

ME: Can you hear me? On your Facebook page, there's a photo of you with a giant dil—

ROMEN: —Yeah. Will do.

ME: There's also a tweet. About somebody getting cum on his thesis.

ROMEN: Oh, God . . . just so you know, that means cum laude. My friend Nihal got cum laude on his thesis. It was a congratulatory tweet.

(He's trying to negotiate with us?!)

ROMEN: So, can I leave that one up?

ME: If a journalist asks, can you and Nihal prove that he got cum laude on his thesis, and that it happened right before you posted that tweet?

ROMEN: Yes.

ME: Okay, so I guess you can leave that one up.[2]

Keep things professional. Try not to laugh. Politely thank him and end the call. Having successfully "cleaned up his digital footprint,"[3] Romen will be cleared to attend the meeting. It'll be a few more years before you find out that he had the dildo in his dorm because he was a student health educator who used it to teach students how to properly apply a condom. Or so he claims.

Anyway, congratulations. With Liz's team taking the lead, you've successfully avoided a Fox News headline like *MUSLIM "PRESIDENT" HUSSEIN-OBAMA MEETS WITH DILDO-MANUFACTURING, CUM-TWEETING TERRORIST.*

---

2   It's still up.
3   A fancy, political way of saying "deleting dick pics."

Don't let them make your boss the butt of a dildo joke. See what I did there? Future you has still got it.

Working in DC can be frustrating sometimes, even with my tips. And it can almost make you sympathetic to people who malign the government, who treat it as a big, bad, faraway entity that taxes them too much, does too little, and should get out of the way.

But you have a choice: You can dwell on the negative, letting it get to you until there's nothing left of your soul. Or you can focus instead on the vast majority of people who entered public service—career staff and political appointees alike—because they (like you) are proud of our country and want to help it succeed. You are a patriotic American who took a solemn oath to protect and defend the Constitution of the United States of America. Choose the latter. Keep your head down and do good work. Don't eat the vending machine sandwiches if you can avoid them.

Remember that it's the non-sexy-sounding, non-headline-making work on outreach around environmental rules, bureaucracy that impacts human rights issues, or improving people's ability to access education and health care where government can shine. That's the stuff that happens when you believe in what you're doing. You got this!

Kisses,
Kal

PS—If President Obama asks your advice on whether he should wear a blue or a tan suit to his August press briefing, for the love of God don't say, "Tan seems kinda fun."

CHAPTER SEVENTEEN

YOU DOWN WITH OPE?

The real power in the US government rests with the White House Office of Public Engagement (OPE), where I worked. Okay, I acknowledge that maybe the president has a *role to play* in running the government. I get that he has the nuclear codes and yes, he is the final word on every bit of policy . . . Okay, fine, *I'm agreeing with you*, the president of the United States is an important job with huge responsibilities. I guess what I'm actually trying to say is that a lot of the day-to-day, nuts-and-bolts work of running the country is done by junior and midlevel aides in offices like mine.

Oh, before this book you'd never heard of the Office of Public Engagement? You're not down with OPE? Well, you will be in a moment. OPE wasn't as well known as the communications or press offices. We weren't the social media, policy, or digital strategy teams, even though people often thought we did that work. We were the outreach team, the proverbial front door to the White House: a place that executed one of Obama's central campaign themes—that every community has a voice and that every American should have a seat at the table. Nobody should fall through the cracks.

If you wanted your voice heard in a previous White House, you'd usually need to follow tradition and hire elite, well-paid lobbyists. If you didn't have the money, you may not have reached the right places. To Obama, that was crazy,[1] so he restructured the boring-sounding Office of Public Liaison and turned it into OPE, making it more accessible in the process.

At OPE, we proactively established direct relationships with community leaders and advocacy organizations. We invited them to the White House to listen to their concerns and build support for policy changes. Each OPE staffer was in charge of several issue-group and demographic-group portfolios: Jewish Americans, African Americans, Energy and Environment, Athletics and Fitness, Rural Americans, Irish Americans—you name it, someone was there to open that proverbial front door from the inside. The president would lean on us when it came to these groups, and the outside groups in turn leaned on us when it came to sharing their respective communities' priorities with the president.

Need to know about Obama's stance on LGBT issues? Call his LGBT point person, Brian Bond. Immigration or Latinx issues? Email my office mate Stephanie Valencia. Disability policy? Hit up Kareem Dale. Bringing Osama bin Laden to justice? Ask bin Laden himself . . . OH WAIT.

Some issues (like national security) affect everybody pretty much the same, while others disproportionately impact certain communities—like LGBT folks when it comes to workplace discrimination, or young Americans when it comes to student loans—so a multifaceted dialogue was important to have.

---

1   Okay to use here too!

Of course, people don't just care about issues related to their identities; they care about a wide range of things. In prior administrations, the traditional approach to politics often merely included specific communities when it came time to check some sort of box— "May is Asian American Heritage Month, let's make sure there's an Asian American event." While that sort of thing is important in a country whose textbooks still don't integrate the full range of American communities' contributions, Obama wanted to make sure that Muslim Americans were at the table for conversations about the Affordable Care Act, Jewish Americans were at the table for meetings about clean energy, the LGBT community was at the table for sessions on student loans. You get the point. He wanted the intersectionality and patriotism of the campaign to be part of his White House and governance.

My job as an associate director of the Office of Public Engagement was to serve as President Obama's point person to the three communities Chris Lu had outlined in our first phone call: (1) the Arts Community, (2) Asian American and Pacific Islander (AAPI) Communities, and (3) Young Americans. Those were huge portfolios: hundreds of arts organizations spanning multiple disciplines, more than thirty-five different AAPI subgroups,[2] and young people in all fifty states and the territories.

---

2   The AAPI community is a very large umbrella encompassing groups as culturally, financially, and economically disparate as wealthy Japanese American doctors, Hmong farmers, and Native Hawaiians; when I was President Obama's representative to the Council on Native Hawaiian Advancement Conference in 2009, I became the first Executive Branch representative to ever visit the Papakōlea Homestead, in what was a very emotional afternoon for all (a homestead is like a reservation, except unlike Native Americans and Alaska Natives, Native Hawaiians still don't have federal recognition, largely because of the US Senate).

* * *

I hit the ground running on day one. My boss, Tina Tchen, handed me a large binder and explained that one of my first duties was to over-see an executive order (EO) the president wanted to create and sign, reestablishing and updating the Clinton-era White House Initiative on Asian Americans and Pacific Islanders (WHIAAPI), henceforth to be known as "Whappy" cuz that sounds a little more fun. Among its other functions, the Whappy EO would help address health and economic disparities unique to Asian American and Pacific Islander communities.

"Read this tonight," Tina said about the binder. "You have a 10 a.m. conference call tomorrow with reps from twenty-four of the federal agencies. A decision needs to be made about whether the Department of Hot Dogs (DHD) should be part of the EO or whether POTUS would find it wasteful."

[There is obviously no Department of Hot Dogs—or is there? (There isn't.) Out of respect to a confidential intragovernmental review process, instead of naming the actual federal agency in ques-tion, I'm calling it the Department of Hot Dogs, or DHD, for fun because everyone knows hot dogs are delicious. If OPE was <u>actually</u> involved in deliberations about hot dogs, there would first be an office-wide meeting to discuss the various groups we represented and which type of hot dog would be most inclusive given our spe-cific goals—definitely no pork since that would exclude the Muslim and Jewish communities. Devout Hindus don't eat beef. By the time you're down to chicken or turkey dogs you might as well just get the soy ones, but at that point nobody wants them anymore and that's why there's no such thing as the Department of Hot Dogs in real life.]

I read Tina's binder overnight and dialed in to the call the next morning, ready to take vigorous notes to share with my new boss. By 10:15, my fingers got tired of writing in my notepad. By 10:20, I thought my hand was going to fall off. By 10:22, I realized I was an idiot and started typing the notes on my computer instead. By 10:40, the conversation was so deep into the weeds of policy nerdom that my notes wouldn't have made much sense outside of a think tank; it made me feel good that I (a government employee) being paid by you (the taxpayer) did in fact understand *everything* that was happening.

By 10:50, the call started to wrap up.

A voice said, "Good talk, everyone. So, is DHD going to be included in the EO? What's the decision?"

I hit the Return button on my computer, typed **Decision:** and waited.

A couple of seconds went by. Another voice on the call said, "Come on folks. I have to leave for an eleven o'clock meeting. What's the decision?"

My cursor blinked. A few more seconds of silence. *Man, these people were making it so juicy! What would they decide?!*

A third voice spoke up, this one more authoritative and intimidating.

AUTHORITATIVE AND INTIMIDATING PERSON: Well, who's on from the White House?

I took myself off mute.

"This is Kal."

AUTHORITATIVE AND INTIMIDATING PERSON: Okay, Kal. So, what's the decision?

The world stood still.

I thought to myself, *Surely there's an actual* adult *from the White House on the phone to make this decision about whether an entire federal agency should be included in President Obama's executive order, right?*

Without missing a beat, what I said instead came out confidently.
"The president would find it wasteful to include DHD in the process,
so we'll eliminate them from the EO. Thanks for the great conversation. Looking forward to next week's call, everyone."

Twenty-four voices immediately said thanks amid a cacophony
of loud dings as they each hopped off the conference line.

I had made my first decision on behalf of the president of the
United States, and I had done it on genuine instinct. *Was it the right
one?* I sprinted out of my office, down the first-floor hallway of the
EEOB, across the little footpath on West Executive Avenue, and up
three flights of stairs, taking two steps at a time to the top floor of the
West Wing where Tina's office was located. Her door was open, and
her assistant waved me in.

Tina was at her desk typing something very fast. "I just—" I
said, panting and out of breath. "I just *hhhhhh* got off that conference call and *hhhhhhhh* I said DHD *can't* be part of the president's
executive order *HHHHHH*." Consummate multitasker that she was,
Tina never stopped typing and never broke eye contact with her
computer screen. "Great," she threw out casually. "That's why we
hired you."

I guess I was probably expecting either (worst case) a stern repri-
mand for making the wrong decision or (best case) an emphatic pat
on the back for being a genius. I got neither—and as I recognized in
the moment, that's obviously how it should have happened. Making a weighty decision like that was just my job. I knew what I was
doing and was trusted for it. "You know," Tina smirked, finally looking at me, "next time instead of *running* here, you can just send me
an email."

*　　　*　　　*

Having shaken off my rookie insecurities, I spent four more months spearheading a dedicated team of staffers across the Executive Branch—from lawyers to senior advisors to junior staffers—to get the EO through the interagency review process. By October we had worked out all the details. The document was ready for President Obama's signature. In a stroke of good timing for an AAPI Executive Order, the date of the signing ceremony happened to coincide with Diwali—the Hindu festival of lights celebrating the triumph of good over evil.

Diwali is celebrated by a billion people spread out around the world. When I was growing up, we'd celebrate Diwali with bright *diyas*, delicious food, family, friends, *rangoli*, and lights. Boxes of sweets were exchanged. My parents would huddle over the telephone for hours, going through a thick notebook full of pencil-written phone numbers, wishing others well. Our phone rang for at least two weeks with greetings of *Sal Mubarak!*—Happy New Year.

Previous administrations had hosted Diwali events, but never in the White House residence, and *never* with the president himself in attendance. This year would change all that—during the signing ceremony, President Obama would personally observe Diwali by lighting a *diya* in the East Room. It was going to be a big deal.

Since the event had gone from being something important to something truly historic, I felt some *extra* pressure to make sure it all came together well. The press had taken so much interest in my leaving *House* for a job in DC, I could already see their headline if something went wrong: *Without Harold, Kumar Screws Up White House Signing Ceremony and Diwali Event.*

I couldn't risk it. While I didn't have a Harold, I did have my talented intern, James.

On the Saturday before the event, James and I worked our asses off and triple-checked everything we had spent the last several months doing. We pored over the list of invited guests and their vetting reports to make sure there were no weird glitches. (I mean, you wouldn't want the Salahis to get turned away at the door.) We went over the last draft of the president's speech with the exacting speechwriting team to ensure that the boss's remarks would lay the groundwork to achieve the goals OPE and Whappy were going to be executing.

By Sunday, I was spent. I came into the office running on empty and my exhaustion was showing. Fueled by the reasoning that I had no public meetings, I hadn't bothered to shave for a few days and was rocking a stubbly hipster beard. I also hadn't been to the dry cleaner that week, so my suit looked like I'd been rolling around in it. I was kind of a mess.

I wanted to rehearse the movements of the coming Wednesday's signing ceremony to avoid any hiccups: That day would begin in my office. Then I'd shuttle back and forth to the East Wing before briefing the president in the Oval Office and walking with him to the East Room. *After I briefed him in the Oval, was it a right or a left turn down the hallway?* James and I spent some time that Sunday morning walking the entire route just to make sure I knew. As we returned down the colonnade and back toward my office from the East Wing, I was absorbed in my BlackBerry, reading an email about last-minute changes from the speechwriting department. James suddenly tugged on my shirt-sleeve. *"UMMMMM,"* he whispered frantically, *"I think that's Barack Obamaaaaaaaa."*

I looked up from my BlackBerry. POTUS was dressed casually, leaving the Oval and walking down the colonnade toward us. Still three days away, I didn't think the Whappy signing ceremony would be on his radar, since he was busy doing much smaller things like saving the economy and trying to give twenty million people access to health insurance. So, when he stopped to say hello and ask what we were working on, I gave him a quick, broad description of the EO: "It was one of your campaign promises. It reestablishes the White House Initiative on Asian Americans and Pacific Islanders, which, among other things, will reduce barriers to education, jobs, and health care."

"I know," he said with what seemed like an introspective smile. "I'm glad we're finally doing that. It's the right thing to do."

We wrapped up our work an hour later, and I spent the second half of Sunday taking care of all the personal hygiene I had slacked on— got a haircut from someone other than Raucous Rodolpho, had my suit pressed, got a refill on my face lotion, the whole works. Wednesday would be my first time briefing the president in the Oval Office. White House photographer Pete Souza would be there, documenting it as he did every meeting and event. Though I was buried in the work itself, I was well aware that my parents and future kids would see these photos. Forty years on, I didn't want to have to explain why Grandpa looked like a grizzled prospector. So, I shaved and groomed and made sure I looked good for Pete's camera.

On Wednesday, I printed several copies of the president's briefing memo before checking myself in front of a mirror one last time. I headed down to the Oval Office with Tina and our team, feeling good. As we walked in, POTUS approached, arm outstretched for the handshake–bro hugs he's known for.

"Heyyyyyyy," he said, eyeing me with a hint of friendly ridicule, "look who decided to shave today!"

In his remarks during the signing ceremony, Obama talked about the unique history of Asian American and Pacific Islander communities.

He shouted out prominent people we had invited, like Wat Misaka, the first nonwhite NBA player.[3] He gave props to the 442nd Regimental Combat Team, comprised of second-generation Japanese Americans who proudly fought in World War II, despite many of their families being thrown in internment camps. The executive directors of dozens of nonprofits were in attendance, from anti–domestic violence organizations to criminal justice reform groups. In the very room where LBJ signed the Civil Rights Act in 1964, the president was formally recognizing the unique contributions that all communities make to the American project.

With his remarks finished and while a Hindu priest recited a prayer, the president walked to his left to light the Diwali *diya*, symbolizing the victory of light over darkness. Centered on the wall behind the president and the pandit, just above the *diya*, hangs artist Gilbert Stuart's famous Lansdowne portrait of George Washington. The painting was saved by Dolley Madison when the British burned down the White House in 1814, nearly a century before they beat and jailed my grandfather for standing up for his human rights. From the back of this room, I watched as Obama became the first president of the United States to personally celebrate Diwali, honoring the dignity and contributions of South Asian Americans right alongside everyone else. Middle School Me smiled.

Six months later, it became clear why work on these kinds of executive orders was a priority. On April 20, 2010, the oil and gas company British Petroleum's Deepwater Horizon rig in the Gulf of Mexico started to spill what would ultimately be two hundred million gallons of crude

---

3   New York Knicks, 1947, in case you're wondering.

oil into the ocean over the course of eighty-seven days. It was the biggest oil spill in US history. Sixteen thousand miles of coastline were affected, along with the livelihoods of thousands of families.

A sizable percentage of American fishermen in the Gulf happen to be of Vietnamese descent, and many don't speak English as their first language—potentially complicating an already dire situation. Overnight, I and other OPE staffers handling outreach to constituencies affected by the spill began to receive emailed reports from the White House Situation Room. These updates would arrive every few hours, outlining everything from areas impacted to environmental and economic damage. It was a critical tool that guided our outreach efforts toward the people who needed it.

On the ground, there were rumors that BP might try to get these Vietnamese American fishermen to sign complicated legal documents with measly settlements, knowing that they couldn't understand the labyrinthine language. They would need help navigating this and other aspects of post-disaster life.

While there are great nonprofit organizations serving AAPI communities in the region, they weren't equipped to deal with challenges of this magnitude. They needed support in the form of federal government liaisons, translators, and interpreters—not to tell people whether to sign things like settlement documents (that was obviously a choice for their families to make independently), but to assure that everyone had the same equal access to understanding what was going on in the first place. Thanks to the executive order, there was now a mechanism in place tying assistance across federal agencies and community groups; the Obama Administration was able to send staff from OPE and Whappy to help.

When he campaigned on bolstering government in a way that assures none of our fellow Americans fall through the cracks, Obama

obviously couldn't have predicted the oil spill or BP's gross negli-
gence. And yet, our ability to respond to those types of disasters is
exactly what he knew the richest and most powerful country in the
world was capable of.

I've thought about this experience often in the years since, especially as our politics has grown more cynical and fatalist. The Americans we were able to help in the Gulf lived mostly in Louisiana,
Alabama, and Mississippi: places where Obama is *despised*. These red
states didn't vote to elect him, and they wouldn't be voting to reelect
him. That didn't matter to the president. Our job was to be there for
them, no matter what their political affiliation.

The Sunday afternoon when my intern and I stood alone with
the president in the middle of the colonnade, there were no journal-
ists around who might print sound bites of his words. No donors
nearby who might hear what he said and feel motivated to write a big
check. The president simply meant what he said as he thought about
the Americans his executive order would help: "I'm glad we're finally
doing that. It's the right thing to do."

CHAPTER EIGHTEEN

NASCAR AND CHILL

Why is NASCAR considered a sport? I mean, just look at it: A bunch of cars drive around a circle for a few hours, crashing every now and again while drunk fans hoot and holler at the carnage. Dodgeball is more of a sport than NASCAR. Or bowling.

As a northeastern elite, my interaction with NASCAR was minimal until 2010. That's when, in the midst of my multifaceted DC social life—the kind I had hoped for in moving from the uniformity of Los Angeles—I met a very handsome, quiet guy at a bar. Our first date was a few days later at Townhouse Tavern on R Street, a dive by Dupont Circle. Josh is from a small, rural town in Mississippi. He has a distinctively southern accent and the kind of relaxed, laid-back personality that any high-strung northeasterner like me envies. I was looking forward to getting to know him, and had a good feeling going into the evening.

A couple of minutes after sitting down, as soon as his first drink came, Josh nonchalantly pulled a well-worn koozie out of his back pocket and slid his beer into it. *Did this dude seriously bring his own koozie with him?* I thought to myself. I was incredulous—I had never seen a human unironically bring a koozie anywhere before, let alone to a bar, let alone to a *date* at a bar.

The only other time I had even seen a koozie outside of a souvenir shop was at my buddy Michael O'Neil's house. O'Neil has a collection of more than a hundred koozies. When you go to his place for a party, you are offered your choice of beer with your choice of koozie. When I was writing this book, he sent me a koozie emblazoned with the words "If you are reading this, I'm not writing my book."

To me, a koozie is either 1) a souvenir or 2) an awesome party favor from a quirky friend. A koozie is not something you bring in your back pocket to a date. This was definitely *not* going to work out. It was time to make small talk while I finished my beer and bounced as quickly as possible.

"Do you always bring your own koozie to a bar?"

"Yyyyyep."

"Cool, cool. Does it actually keep your beer cold?"

Josh took a sip and slowly shook his head. "Keeps mah hand warm."

What a line. This dude was *smooth*. He didn't pull that understated one-liner to make a move; this was just who he was. Once the koozie deliberations were over, we talked about other things: family, hobbies, food. Maybe I could look past his obsession with beer insulation for another beverage or three?

As appealing as Mississippi Josh *seemed* given his koozie-using nonchalance and my moderate beer-buzz, I had to be sure. A midweek second date would be the perfect gauge. I like weeknight dates because you can get to know a person and still make it home at a respectable hour for work the next day. (Also, if the dude turns out to be a weirdo, you have a totally reasonable way out. *Oh, is it already eight p.m.? I have to get going, I have CrossFit at five a.m. tomorrow and then I gotta brief the president about this thing I can't talk about. It was nice to meet you!*)

For date number two, I arrived back at Townhouse Tavern before Josh and grabbed a seat upstairs. I was more nervous than I expected to be, which made me realize I probably liked him more than I thought I did. Looking to take the edge off, I ordered a vodka soda. That's what Hollywood agents and celebrity personal trainers tell their clients to drink *if you are going to drink anything AT ALL, Kal. Do you really want to be fat?* An agent once took an Amstel Light out of my hand at a work event and replaced it with a vodka soda, reprimanding, "You're shooting a movie in two weeks!" Amstel Light has like ninety-five calories. That's how much they don't want you to be fat.

Josh showed up, ordered his beer, and pulled his koozie out of his back pocket, sliding his bottle into it. He eyed my tasteless, colorless vanity drink. "Not feeling a beer tonight?"

Overthinking every move, I nervously blurted out, "Oh, I was just getting warmed up. I'll have a beer next!"

He nodded. Awkward silence.

My next drink was a beer. The bartender put the bottle down in front of me and Josh smoothly reached into his back pocket and pulled out *a second koozie.* He handed it to me; I accepted. I wrapped it around my dumb beer and said, "Thanks for the handwarmer." We had a third date.

Josh showed up at my door for date number three with his understated smile, an eighteen-pack of Coors Light, and two koozies. Points won. My TV was already set to *SpongeBob SquarePants* because I'm a romantic. As he sat down, I went into the kitchen to put the drinks in the fridge.

When I got back, there was a NASCAR prerace show on my television. At first I thought he had made some kind of mistake, or that the show he actually wanted to watch was about to start, but no. This dude had arrived, sat down, turned off my *SpongeBob SquarePants*, and turned on NASCAR, without even flinching. Points *immediately* rescinded.

What the heck was he doing? NASCAR? This was not part of the plan. If Josh had suggested watching NASCAR together, I would have pretended to have gotten called into work for something very top secret and important.[1] I stared at Josh with a deer-in-the-headlights look, but he didn't see it because he was already way, way into what was happening on the TV. I was stuck, so I did the only thing a nice guy could do in a situation like that: I tried to be a good sport and not DIE OF BOREDOM watching a NASCAR prerace show with some dude I had really only met twice.

Why is there even such a thing as NASCAR prerace? Watching my Yankees on the YES Network or getting some pregame stats before the Knicks hit the court made sense to me. What the heck is there to say about drivers in fast cars who are about to make left turns all day? Josh remained totally transfixed as a commentator exclaimed, *"Hoo-wee, don't forget that trouble Denny Hamlin had last week gettin' loose comin' outta turn four."*

What did these words mean? With the subtitles on, I'd have still

---

1   I did not have a top-secret security clearance.

been lost. On-screen, one commentator with ridiculously amazing hair and a Jon-Stewart-doing-his-impression-of-Lindsey-Graham flamboyance talked about whether driver so-and-so had an advantage on today's track as opposed to last week's track because today's track was much longer. Huh. I didn't know the tracks were different lengths. I guess that was kind of interesting, but not enough to keep my focus. The commentators turned things over to an excited man in a brightly colored suit with black square glasses and a ginger beard.

His name was Rutledge Wood. As I sat with Josh, halfway through a still-perfectly-cold-because-of-the-koozie beer, I found myself temporarily drawn in by the badassness of the guy on TV. *Rutledge. Wood. That's a pretty cool name, actually. And he's articulate. Maybe this guy can make sense of what I'm see— Is that a talking doll?*

The screen cut from Rutledge to . . . a puppet named Danny Hammerdropper: light brown mustache, dressed in a hat with the number 88 on it, holding a microphone. In a high-pitched puppety southern drawl, he yelled, "Dale Junior ah love youuuuu!"[2] I looked back at Josh, who was still watching intently as if all of this was perfectly normal. Sure, Josh was handsome, smart, relaxed, and had amazing eyes. But it was all too much. I knew right then this would *really* never work out. I just had to get through the next few hours and that would be that.

The race began. Half an hour in, a sort of madness crept in. *My limited downtime is important to me. How did I get myself into this situation? What if these races go on for hours and hours, like golf? I don't think I'll be able to stand watching cars go around for—* BOOM!! A car

---

2 I found out later that Dale Junior was a super popular driver who drove the number 88 car, and the puppet was a superfan.

with a duck logo violently crashed into a car with a beer logo. The lights around the track suddenly flashed bright yellow as the duck logo car erupted into massive flames. Holy shit! No human could ever survive such an inferno. The driver, clearly deceased, was no longer in control of the vehicle, and the flaming duck car sped off the track and spun out on some grass before smashing into a wall. "OH MY GOD! HOW DID THAT HAPPEN?! DID HE HAVE A FAMILY?!"

Josh took a sip of his beer and mumbled, "It's jussalittle ohlfaar."

"A WHAT?!"

"Jussalittle ohlfaar."

"WHAT'S AN OHLFAAR?!"

Josh casually took another sip of his beer and enunciated: "It's. Just. A Litt-tull. OIL. FIE-errrr."

Just a little oil fire? I looked back at the TV as the dead driver casually pulled himself out of the burning duck car and walked away as if nothing happened. Wow. The crowd loved it—and I had to admit, I kinda did too.

We had more dates.

I asked lots more questions about NASCAR during those subsequent hangouts.

"Why does the guy on the lifeguard stand wave different flags?"

"It's called a starter's stand—that's the start/finish line. Different colors mean different things: green for go, yellow for caution, checkered when the race is over."

"Why are they all racing in a row, like why don't the drivers just try to pass each other?"

"They do try to pass each other! That's the whole point! When you're going two hundred miles an hour in close quarters, it's hard!"

"If that's the case, why don't people just watch the last ten minutes to see who wins instead of sitting through hours of this?"

"Because the last ten minutes is . . . not the whole race. What kind of question is that? Would you only watch the last ten minutes of a basketball game, because that's when you see who wins?"

Josh also schooled me on some of the more sensational aspects of the sport, like drivers having beef with each other. It turned out that NASCAR World was full of intrigue. It could also be a little confusing. Some rich people own multiple cars and have contracts with multiple drivers. Drivers who are signed to the same owner form teams, even though they compete individually. Team members have loyalty to each other, so sometimes drivers on the same team help each other out, and sometimes they don't.

In March of 2013, Denny Hamlin and his former teammate Joey Logano were neck and neck for the lead in a race in Bristol, Virginia. At a key moment, Denny tapped Joey's car, sending him spinning into a wall. After the race, an enraged Joey headed over to Denny—a little fight ensued with guys from both teams pushing each other. Later that month, Joey hit Denny's car and it too ran into a wall, giving Denny a compression fracture in his back. Can you believe the drama? It's like *Real Housewives of New Jersey* meets the NFL.

What's cool is that NASCAR isn't just spectacle. For Josh's family—and families throughout the country—NASCAR is way more than a means of entertainment through cars, talking puppets, and idiosyncratic rivalries. It's a way to spend time together. He told me about how many childhoods had been defined by the trek that moms, dads, and kids would make to see a race, often requiring hours of travel. And not just nuclear families: A day at the track could be spent with cousins, grandparents, aunts, and uncles. Friends and neighbors were included. Cars, trucks, and vans were packed with grills and food. They'd set up entire areas outside the track to tail-gate, complete with cornhole games, beer and soda coolers, hot dogs and hamburgers. On special overnight trips, they'd also get to tailgate *inside* the track. Josh explained that many NASCAR tracks allow families to park their trucks and RVs in the middle of the track itself—the *infield*. You set up your tent or trailer and grill and drink beer as the cars race by. Imagine going on a camping trip as a kid, but you also get to watch fast cars whizzing *around* you? Wild.

Growing up, my parents would take my brother and me camping a few times a year, usually in the early fall or late spring. It was an economical choice for a family that wasn't wealthy enough to take frequent trips to fancy places for leisure, and it was a great way for us to spend time together while getting to enjoy some of the coolest nature spots. Camping became a tradition that I loved. My folks would pack up the station wagon, a process they had down to a science: one sturdy yellow tent, one large blue cooler full of drinks and snacks, two smaller red-and-white coolers full of food my mom had cooked and frozen, charcoal, and some lighter fluid for the grill. Several suitcases in the back, three suitcases strapped to the roof, and off we went. Family time!

We'd head to campgrounds all over the Northeast: some close to the Delaware River, others up through the Adirondack Mountains. Sometimes it was the four of us; other times we'd go with my cousins. One time, a suitcase that wasn't attached securely enough to the roof flew off onto the highway.

"Was that our bag?" Dad said, looking in the rearview mirror as it disappeared behind us.

From the shoulder of the New Jersey Turnpike, we watched that suitcase get run over again and again. It was thrilling, in a way, waiting to see if my Snoopy shirt would join the few stray items of clothing that might blow over to the shoulder to be salvaged.

On another camping trip with Hansa Auntie, Dhiren Uncle, and my cousins Shami and Sagar, a couple of beautiful birds perched themselves on a branch above our picnic table. Eight-year-old me thought it was so nice to see these little birds watching us make our sandwiches; meanwhile, Hansa Auntie was beyond convinced that the birds were about to poop. *We only have enough sandwiches for today's lunch, kids!* She tried to shoo the birds away. The next thing we knew, a mean, MEAN blue jay swooped down and viciously began pecking Hansa Auntie's head. As she ducked and swatted, she called to us: *"Kids, protect the food!"*

Birds were supposed to be as cute and docile as they were in Disney cartoons. They weren't supposed to try and kill Hansa Auntie. I cried. Should I run away and hide in the tent? Would the bloodthirsty blue jay find me inside the car? WAS ANYPLACE SAFE?! Luckily, my cousins saved our lunch and Hansa Auntie chased the bird off. I finished my PB&J with one eye on the trees.

On at least one occasion we were joined by family friends who had returned from a trip to India, where the kids had picked up a few bad words in Hindi. These were eagerly shared among the children. "Did you know that the word for stupid is *sally*, like the girl's name?" a fellow eleven-year-old would say. "And the word for penis is *lund*! If someone's name was *Sally Lund* that means her name is Stupid Penis!"

My Sally Lund and I loved our Northeast camping adventures. As

I learned about Josh's NASCAR camping trips and he learned about mine, I thought, maybe he and I weren't so different after all.

The more time we spent together, the more comfortable Josh and I got. I told him about winning the parking lottery and sharing the Panoch. About getting bullied and playing the Tin Man. I even gave him the backstory on my wishful childhood obsession—yet unfulfilled—of scouring every gift shop I came across with the hope of seeing a keychain, a shotglass, a license plate—anything—with my name on it. Sometime around date six or seven, my nerdiness took over, and I started to read about the science of NASCAR. It turns out that drivers have to understand more than just the *basics* behind objects in motion in order to do well in competition. They have to familiarize themselves with vehicle weight, the temperature of the rubber tires, and computational fluid dynamics. They need some proficiency in physics and engineering for the same reason that NASA astronauts do: so they don't die. Why didn't they teach all this in high school physics class? I also learned that NASCAR drivers *are* athletic.

When I first saw NASCAR on television, I thought, *They drive cars. I drive cars. How hard could that be?* A lot harder than meets the eye, it turns out. The cars are moving so fast that you have to be in total and complete control of your body. Even the slightest wrong movement of a steering wheel and you could be toast. Besides that, temperatures in those stock cars can top 130 degrees Fahrenheit, so you have to be able to withstand tremendous amounts of heat and keep your head about you. And it's not just the drivers, either. Pit crews go through rigorous training the same way other athletes do.

Those tires and gear are heavy, and they need to be able to move them in and out in a matter of seconds, with immense technical specificity. You need to be strong and agile, just like a football player. Take that, bowling.

I was getting into it. I was discovering an exciting new world with Josh as my guide. He eagerly explained all the things that he already knew, steering me in the directions of my natural curiosity (NASA comparisons! Soap opera dramatics between drivers!). And my interest just grew and grew. By the time Josh and I graduated from casually dating to formally being together, I was following a few of the drivers on Twitter, and I was even bantering back and forth with other fans.

For my birthday that year, Josh handed me a neatly wrapped square box. "You didn't have to get me anything," I said in the obligatory manner, "but I appreciate it." Inside was a sturdy white-and-blue mug with an astronaut on it. Just below the astronaut, in big block letters across the side of the mug: Kalpen. It was easily the most thoughtful gift anyone had ever gotten me. Josh had remembered the story about my childhood obsession, knew I'd never find a mug with my name on it at a gift shop, and had one specially made. What a keeper.

That same week I attended my first in-person race at Richmond Raceway, a two-hour drive south of Washington, DC. Josh and I were joined by two Republican friends and one lefty vegan. The five of us rode in my American-made hybrid car, and we tailgated in the infield. Our version of NASCAR, and tailgating, is subject to rare bipartisan agreement—koozies from the Reagan/Bush '84 campaign peacefully coexisted with my OBAMA COLORADO bumper sticker.

We scored some "pit passes," which allow access next to the track, and met drivers like Carl Edwards and Joey Logano—great guys who introduced us to their engineers, press peeps, crew chiefs, and families. Everyone was so easygoing. Carl even put up with my extended interrogations about the physics of it all. Just before the drivers started their engines, out of the corner of my eye, just a few feet from where we were standing, I saw the puppet—Danny Hammerdropper—in the flesh (well, fabric).

The day was special to me—Josh was the real fan here, and I was taking my crash course in racing, playing catch-up. I enjoyed every minute. A NASCAR race is aural, visual, and olfactory: not just the crazy-loud cars that you feel in your chest as they speed by, but hearing technical conversations about fuel allotments, smelling fresh rubber while you watch a car pit.[3]

Josh and I were having so much fun that I wanted to take

---

3 For the uninitiated, *pitting* is when they change the tires and refuel the car in like five seconds, and you make a dad joke like, "How come they can't do that when I take my car to the shop?"

our relationship to the next level—I wanted to go camping in the infield, at one of the biggest races, like the Daytona 500 or Talladega. I reached out to a wonderful woman named Gladys Cheng at NASCAR marketing for guidance, letting her know how much of a superfan I had become. I quickly got an email back that I had never, ever expected: an invitation to be a presenter at the NASCAR Awards in Las Vegas.

I guess I had never expected it because, like you before reading the last sentence, I had no idea that the NASCAR Awards were a thing. Josh and I rented tuxes and flew out to Vegas for the weekend. Hammerdropper wasn't in attendance this time, but we did get to hang out with a bunch of drivers and team owners, including some of our new friends (Rutledge, Logano, Edwards, and his incredible wife, Katherine). Onstage, I got to introduce Jeff Gordon.[4] The highlight of the event was a special tribute to a NASCAR driver from back in the day. His name was Tiny *Lund*.[5]

Sadly, most relationships come to an end eventually. We had had some good times together, but like many other fans, I got tired of some of its quirks, like the constant rule changes; my work schedule also made it tough to get to races. NASCAR in person is where my love blossomed. Watching it on television just didn't feel the same . . . Although, if I'm being honest, while flipping through channels on a Sunday if I happen to catch part of a race, I find myself rooting for Logano, Bubba Wallace, or Ryan Blaney.

While my relationship with NASCAR may not have sustained,

---

4   If you're not a NASCAR fan and you're wondering why Jeff Gordon's name sounds familiar to you, it's probably because of the Nelly song "E.I.": "I drive fastly, call me Jeff Gord-onnn, in the black SS with the naviga-tionnnnn / . . . Andele andele, mami E.I. E.I. Uh-ohhhhhh." NASCAR's awesomeness is everywhere!

5   I'm not making this up!

my relationship with Mississippi koozie Josh turned out better. All
in all, I walked away from my NASCAR phase with three permanent things: a fiancé, an unironic appreciation for beer koozies,
and a recognition that stock car racing is, in fact, an honest-to-
goodness sport.[6] For the uninitiated, if you're able to hit up a race
in person, I still highly recommend it. Go for the day with friends,
or camp out in the infield for a weekend. It's a great time. And
when you see flames erupt, act cool: It's probably *jussalittle ohlfaar.*

---

6   Yes, we'll probably do koozies for the wedding reception.

CHAPTER NINETEEN

HAVE A HEART

There was no such thing as a typical day in the Office of Public Engagement. It's sort of like how no two subway rides are alike. Some mornings the Duke Ellington School jazz musicians you expect to see on the Red Line platform are replaced by an old, weathered Chinese man playing a *jinghu*, and let me tell you that dude is a real bummer if you're hungover. Working as the president's liaison to different constituency groups was kind of like having a real-life version of the giant magnet that Peter Griffin and Homer Simpson talk about in the crossover episode of *Family Guy*. When the White House turned it on, it could bring everything in its vicinity together. In politics, Peter Griffin's giant magnet is called *convening power*—if OPE invited people to a meeting, they'd usually show up.

★   ★   ★

Beyond the MILF memo, my time in government included meetings with health care advocates, conversations with aviation industry representatives, and summits with climate change activists. Our portfolio areas sometimes overlapped, like when President Obama hosted Chinese president Hu Jintao. As the Asian American and Pacific Islander liaison, I was to oversee a portion of the State Arrival Ceremony on the South Lawn. As the arts liaison, I had the honor of helping facilitate the official gift that Obama would give his guest.

For the latter, Tina suggested POTUS commission a painting by Chicago-based Chinese American artists the Zhou Brothers. Each week, I'd join a series of conference calls between the State Department, artists, and the national security team. Huddled around a packed conference table in the Situation Room, my small portion of the meetings—led by my friend Ben Rhodes (then a deputy national security advisor)—was to update the entire team on the progress of the gift. "The color red is auspicious to the Chinese, so expect there to be lots of red tones," I'd say. "Eight and six are considered lucky numbers. The artists are going to paint on a canvas that's eighty-six inches wide and sixty-eight inches high."

What I enjoyed most about these meetings was that they allowed me to hear what people I admired had to say. The highlight was usually Samantha Power, (then the National Security Council Senior Director for Multilateral Affairs and Human Rights), who in the case of Obama's gift coyly vented what I assumed were issues stemming from her own portfolio, "A painting eighty-six inches wide, wow. Eighty-six. Eighty-six . . . Eighty-six Uighurs who could be freed if we raised the issue with President Hu . . ."

The Zhou Brothers' painting was being sent from Chicago and

was set to arrive at the White House the same evening as the Chinese charter carrying President Hu's gift for Obama from Beijing. (We were told this would be a bronze statue of President Lincoln, created by Chinese artist Yuan Xikun.) Ice and snow led to delays in travel. Both gifts were finally cleared into the complex around 3 a.m. Standing with Secret Service agents at a door adjacent to the South Portico when the truck finally pulled up, the frigid air slapped my face awake.

"We're going to take the crates to screen further. Do you want to wait until that's done to see everything out of the boxes?" an agent asked.

"No, I'm good now that it's all here. I know what our painting looks like, and I've seen statues of Lincoln before." I hailed a cab home and went to bed.

The morning after the gift exchange, word around the office was that President Obama had prominently displayed the Lincoln statue on a pedestal outside the Oval, so that it was visible to the visiting delegation. I was looped into a quippy email chain of AAPI staffers: "Kal, have you seen the bust of Lincoln?"

I had quickly peeked at it from the back, in passing, but hadn't gotten too close a glance yet. My friend Gary Lee wrote, "What's with Lincoln's *eyes*?" With mild concern that there may have been some damage to the statue during the unboxing that I missed, I surreptitiously walked by the Oval to get a closer look. No obvious signs that the statue had been dropped. I leaned in. Lincoln's eyes looked . . . how do I say this correctly, his eyes looked . . . like they belonged less to President Lincoln and more to . . . President Hu? "Holy shit, they gave Lincoln *Asian eyes*."

Power move, President Hu. Power. Move.

*   *   *

Aside from dealing with statues and giant magnets, there were touching issues that were brought to our attention, sometimes more discreetly. One morning I received a joint letter from forty-three members of the House and six senators, asking that—as the president's liaison to the Asian American and Pacific Islander communities—I encourage POTUS to take action on the issue of two Sikh Americans who were being denied the ability to serve in the military.

Army rules dictated that turbans and beards were prohibited, effectively preventing Sikhs from serving for decades, but when Tejdeep Singh Rattan and Kamaljeet Singh Kalsi enlisted, they were assured by their recruiters that their articles of faith would not be a hindrance to service. Both men trusted the process and completed four years of schooling, which the army paid for. When they showed up for active duty, however, they were promptly told to remove their turbans and cut their beards and hair. If they refused, they couldn't serve and would have to pay back the army for the cost of school.

The letter urged that I raise this issue with President Obama, who should act swiftly to grant exemptions to these two men so they could proudly serve with their articles of faith intact. It seemed like a no-brainer. I took the letter next door to VJ's deputy, Michael Straut-manis. I stood across from Straut in his ornate EEOB corner office (decked out with Chicago sports memorabilia and a portable mini-golf setup) trying to read his face as he read.

"You mean to tell me," he said calmly as he closed his thick oak office door, "that these brothers are trying to serve our country and we're preventing them from doing that? That's some fucking bullshit."

Strautmanis quickly looped in our coworker Matt Flavin, the president's director of Veterans and Wounded Warrior Policy. Flavin agreed, it was totally un-American to be denying these men the right to serve. The problem was that on matters like this, the army was considered an independent agency. As commander in chief, Obama did not have the authority to unilaterally grant individual exemptions to this rule. Flavin would have to raise the issue with the army in a way that made it clear the president *would strongly urge them* to grant the exemption, but we had to take care to avoid saying that we somehow mandated it. I was hopeful that this would just be a formality—was the US Army actually going to say no to a request from the president?

Perhaps the bigger complicating factor was the issue of Don't Ask, Don't Tell (DADT), the policy that prohibited gays and lesbians from serving openly in the military.

More than thirty-two thousand servicemembers were discharged under DADT and its predecessor policies. In the midst of our protracted battle to repeal it through legislative action, if word got out that we were pressuring the army into granting exemptions for two Sikh captains who couldn't serve because of their turbans (but not the tens of thousands of LGBT service members who couldn't serve because of their orientation), it could turn into a real problem.

The fundamental differences between the two policies were pretty clear: Sikhs were prohibited from serving because of a 1984 rule-change made by then army chief of staff John A. Wickham Jr. (not a law passed by Congress), whereas Don't Ask, Don't Tell was a law passed by Congress (not a rule made by the army chief of staff). The mechanism to repeal each terrible policy was therefore fundamentally different. LGBT advocates had nevertheless already railed against Obama for refusing to pause DADT by executive order, and we knew we had to tread lightly or risk losing both gays *and* Sikhs in the military.

As Flavin worked the ins and outs of lobbying the army, I could offer only broad pledges of support to advocates of the Sikh community that we were "doing everything we can" to help (and we were). Don't Ask, Don't Tell was ultimately repealed by Congress. The army eventually granted Captains Rattan and Kalsi their exemptions, and I had the privilege of meeting them at a reception in celebration of Asian American and Pacific Islander Heritage Month that year.

Ninety-nine percent of my White House job had nothing to do with Hollywood. In fact, I went out of my way to avoid the mere perception that I was in any way different from other staffers. One afternoon, a coworker named Ken Williams-Bennett brought his excited kids into the complex. His son told me he was a big fan and asked for a photo. I was usually polite in declining these types of requests, but I must have been having an especially hectic day. "I'm not really here for that," I told him curtly as I walked away. A few years ago, I was at the MTV Video Music Awards and ran into Chance the Rapper. I told him I was a massive fan, and he quickly let me know that he was the kid who I iced out of a photo at the White House. I still feel bad about that one.

Besides the Chance fiasco, there were only a small handful of times when there was any overlap between my White House job and my old life as an actor. Sometimes OPE would support the Social Secretary (Social) and Secret Service (USSS) for what was known as "gate duty." It's exactly what it sounds like. When we had gate duty, we'd stand with Social and USSS at the White House gates and help check names off of guest lists for various signing ceremonies and events that were being held in the complex. The Obama Administration was notoriously short-staffed given the scope of things we were trying to get done—and while OPE was focused on outreach (not event planning), since we did help put together the lists of attendees for official meetings and events, it stood to reason that we would also pitch in from start to finish to make sure everything went smoothly. One time, Chris Rock saw me staffing the northwest gate of the White House when he was coming in for the National Medals of Arts and Humanities ceremony. I could tell by his shocked look that he thought I left the television show *House* to literally work the front gate of the White House checking names off a list. Even if that had been my whole job, working the gate is an honorable gig, Chris Rock!

A more substantive intersection of my life in Hollywood and my years at the White House came at a darker time, immediately following the earthquake that decimated Haiti on Tuesday, January 12, 2010. More than three hundred thousand people had died. Another three hundred thousand were injured. Countless more had lost their homes, their livelihoods, everything. With few close nearby allies, America had to help Haiti, and the Obama Administration led the international response.

Within hours of the disaster, the president directed the entire staff to do everything we could to assist. Valerie Jarrett and Tina Tchen called several emergency staff meetings to offer regular updates from the National Security Council. The Situation Room began to email hourly reports similar to those we received after the BP oil spill. Given Haiti's limited capacity and infrastructure, it would be critical for Americans to contribute money to the recovery effort rather than donating supplies that couldn't physically be sent to the island.

President Obama had spoken with Presidents Bush and Clinton, deputizing them to take the lead on fundraising efforts on behalf of the American people. In a few days, the three presidents would jointly announce the Clinton Bush Haiti Fund. Valerie and Tina asked the staff for any and all ideas we might have on how best to get the word out about it. There was something rolling around in my head, an idea that I knew I was in a unique position to bring up.

I hesitated for a second. I had been trained to be inconspicuous and do good work as a dedicated staffer, extra mindful that any transgressions could be perceived as arrogance. For this reason, I didn't generally offer up ideas outside the mandate of my narrow portfolios: young Americans, AAPIs, and the arts. But the timing around the January 12 earthquake was full of especially unique circumstances.

* * *

The Golden Globe Awards were set to take place five days later, on January 17. I had been to the Golden Globes and Emmy Awards with my *House* cast and had firsthand experience with how awards-show publicity worked. The show would draw millions of viewers. If we sent some talking points to each of the nominees, I knew that most of those actors, directors, and writers would want to help by repeating them in red-carpet interviews. That would connect generous audiences at home with the best information on how to donate to those in need once the president announced the Clinton Bush Haiti Fund. I was confident that the idea was an efficient way to raise both awareness and cash quickly.

Valerie and Tina agreed. I was encouraged to run with it.

I assembled a plan that mirrored our other Public Engagement protocols. The reach and impact would be huge but the first task itself was pretty simple: Put together a contact list of Golden Globe nominees' and their representatives—who serve as their gatekeepers—and invite them all to a conference call to run through key talking points. This was the email I sent out:

From: "Modi, Kalpen S." <Kalpen_S._Modi@who.eop.gov>
Date: Fri, 15 Jan 2010 14:32:25–0500
To: <kmodi@who.eop.gov>
Subject: White House Conference Call on Haiti

On behalf of the White House Office of Public Engagement, I wanted to extend an invitation to you and your clients to participate in a telephone briefing on the current response to the disaster in Haiti.

Since you may be asked questions on Haiti or on how to help, we are holding an off-the-record briefing to provide you with the most up-to-date information.

White House Briefing on Haiti
TODAY, Friday, January 15, 2010
3:30PM PST / 6:30PM EST
CALL: (800) 36███████
PASSCODE: Haiti Update *provide in lieu of passcode*

If you can't make it, please let us know who will take your place.
Thanks,
Kalpen Modi
Associate Director, White House Office of Public Engagement

As I expected, people were overwhelmingly receptive. Everyone wanted to help. Well, *almost* everyone. There was one particular whopper of a response, from a publicist working with a well-liked Golden Globe nominee, that goes down as the most ridiculous email I've ever gotten. Because of the sheer absurdity of it, I've chosen to publish it here, in the spirit of humankind learning from the worst among us:

From: ███████████████████████████
Date: Friday, January 15, 2010 3:11 PM
To: Modi, Kalpen S.
Subject: Re: White House Conference Call on Haiti

I know this is going to sound absolutely SUPERFICIAL to someone that works in DC, but I suspect I got this because of ███

███ and with the Golden Globes being this Sunday and all hands are on deck dealing with dresses, shoes, hair, makeup, etc., we're not going to be able to fit this in today. If there's an email with information I'm happy to distribute that.

I couldn't believe it. Imagine: hundreds of thousands of people have been hurt or killed in an earthquake. You have an opportunity to use your privilege to help the survivors. So, what kind of human responds with concerns about that Sunday's "dresses, shoes, hair, makeup, etc."? To me, the most appalling part about it is that they recognized it was "superficial"—and thought it was a good idea to go ahead and press Send anyway.

Holding my tongue, I replied to the email with the details the publicist asked for, and then got back to focusing on the job at hand. I couldn't dwell on that bad apple, because right then, Valerie asked for help in dealing with a new issue involving another actor.

"Kal," she said, "we got word that ███ is trying to take his private jet to Haiti. POTUS needs you to call him to let him know he can't do this. The island doesn't have enough fuel right now, so planes that are landing can't take off again, and they take up space on the tarmac. We need to make sure we can land real aid planes as quickly as possible."

Jesus. As if shoes and makeup weren't bad enough, now an actor was trying to fly down to Haiti to be a hero, and it was my job to stop him. I called my buddy Tommy Vietor, who had recently been promoted to National Security Council spokesman (and was being deployed to Port-au-Prince himself), for more background on the actor. "Yeah, this situation is shitty," he confirmed. "He actually seems like a good guy. He's trying to bring three nurses with him and has volunteered in the country previously, so I'm sure he's desperate to help everyone he knows there. Basically, since the Haitians control their own airspace and landing, we can't prevent him from going. But it looks like he might try to pay them off in order to land his jet. It's true that he'll take up space on the tarmac, and those larger aid planes won't be able to land."

My job seemed simple enough: I'd have to call this actor and tell him not to go. If he was committed to saving lives, he needed to know that this was absolutely going to do the opposite—he'd be making things worse, not better. I dialed his agent. I made it clear to the assistant who answered that I was calling from the White House, on behalf of the president of the United States.

She put me on hold.

Fun fact: Hollywood is the only industry in which people would put us on hold when we called on behalf of the president or the White House. You could get through to pretty much anybody at all, in any profession in the whole world . . . except people in Hollywood. This always embarrassed me.

"Hi, sorry," the assistant said, getting back on the line. "What is this regarding again?" To my Hollywood friends reading this, please promise me: When President Ocasio-Cortez's staffer calls you, don't put her on hold. I repeated where I was calling from and said specifically that it was about one of their acting clients who was trying to make a trip to Haiti in his private jet. "Oh, okay. Please hold."

As I was holding on line one for this actor's mega-agent, I saw another call coming through on line two: *another* 310 area code, *another* person from Los Angeles. I put line one on hold and clicked over to answer line two. This time, it was a Hollywood producer who sounded like Alicia Silverstone's character Cher from the movie *Clue-*

less. She had gotten the conference call invitation email and wanted to pitch me something brilliant:

> *Hiiiii! SO. I have an idea? Like for Haiti? Okay. SO. It's called: Heels for Haiti. And like, we were thinking you know, how like, these women? These poor, POOR women, right. They, like, have nothing? And we, like, have all these high heels and like, you wear them once and then you're never going to wear them again but they're still good heels. WE SHOULD SEND THEM TO HAITI!*

Great idea! Except, oh man, by the time the heels get there, they'll be out of season. I needed to get this delusional time-waster off the phone, so I could get back to—what was I doing?—oh yeah, waiting on hold for the agent whose client might try to bribe a foreign government to land his private jet. What a day. I hastily told the Heels for Haiti producer to email me a proposal, politely hung up, and resumed waiting on line one.

After another five minutes on hold, the mega-agent himself finally got on the phone and flat-out refused to give me the actor's phone number. I reiterated that the White House was imploring his talented client to please not go to Haiti, that the president was instead calling on him to help with critical, lifesaving fundraising. As directly and respectfully as I could, I told him straight up, "That flight will cause big problems for aid workers and the victims they are saving. People could die. Please, we just need him to know."

Hearing this, the agent laughed at me as if we were discussing someone's frivolous hobby. "Oh, that's just how ███████ is! He's going to do what he wants to do."

I looked out my two-foot-thick bullet-and-bomb resistant office window, staring at the Washington Monument in the distance, feeling angry and sick. My mind was racing. *These are exactly the times when you're not supposed to let your passion or emotions get the best of you because it'll derail the rest of the work you need to do.* I thanked the mega-agent for his consideration and politely hung up.

I glanced at my in-box. Underneath a grim Situation Room update was a new email, subject heading, "Heels for Haiti!" Jesus Christ, she had actually emailed a full proposal.

Often, when writing responses from the White House, I'd compose a draft in the heat of the moment and then—because of the Presidential Records Act (PRA)—remember what I wanted my contribution to history to be and I'd revise it. So, I might have started by typing exactly what I wanted to say: "Please, do not send your $1,200 Diane von Furstenberg heels to a natural disaster zone, you fucking lunatic." Then, knowing that such a response would be put on PRA and one day make me look bad, *and* because I was a dedicated staffer whose guidance might actually save lives, I'd graduate to writing, "Hi! Thank you for your thoughtful suggestion! I can tell that you are passionate about making a unique contribution to this important cause on behalf of the American people. Right now, the most helpful thing is financial donations. Regarding the heels, perhaps you might consider organizing a fundraiser auction benefiting the Clinton Bush Haiti Fund."

These bizarre incidents make for great stories, but they were, thankfully, real outliers. Most people (Hollywood or not) were generous in their eagerness to help—and in ways that were more meaningful than donating used pumps to people who didn't have food.

Some examples: George Clooney's Haiti telethon raised $61 million. Olivia Wilde had been working outside Port-au-Prince since long before the quake and stepped up big-time by raising money and awareness. Sean Penn had a strong connection there, too, and after the earthquake, he expanded his efforts via J/P HRO, his organization on the ground. The outpouring of generosity from the entertainment community was heartening. Lots of celebrities used our talking points to guide the public to the right places to donate and help, and those good people all over the country opened their hearts and bank accounts. Everyone was doing their part.

Our round-the-clock week finally came to a close late Friday night. On Saturday morning, as planned, Presidents Bush and Clinton would be joining President Obama to formally launch the Clinton Bush Haiti Fund from the Rose Garden. I wrote a final memo at Tina and Valerie's request, detailing our entertainment messaging and outreach, then walked over to Tina's office in the West Wing to make absolutely sure they had what they needed for the next morning's senior-level meeting with the former presidents.

"We're ready. Just go home and get some sleep," Tina said. "And you don't need to come in tomorrow." This is one of the many reasons we all loved Tina. Her expectations were high and she could be tough, but she also cared deeply about her staff. "Thank you," she said as I turned to leave. "POTUS really appreciates this, the extra push is huge. Get some rest!"

That was all I needed to hear. I was exhausted. Since the news of the earthquake, we had all worked nonstop for almost a week. So, I badged out, went straight home, changed out of my suit, and . . . went out to get hammered with other overworked staffers who wanted to blow off some steam. (Don't tell Tina.)

After too many picklebacks and Jell-O shots at the old Adams Morgan dive Millie & Al's, I made a pit stop at 7-Eleven to invest in the universal, peer-reviewed hangover cure: Gatorade, ibuprofen, and a frozen pizza of questionable vintage.[1] I finally crashed into bed at around three thirty. Three hours later, I woke up to use the bathroom and noticed that the red light on my work BlackBerry was blinking. I checked my email while stumbling to the toilet.

From: "Jarrett, Valerie." vj@who.eop.gov
Date: Sat, 16 Jan 2010 06:21:14–0500
To: "Modi, Kalpen."
Subject: This morning

Can you pls meet us in the Cabinet Room at 7:30am to brief 42, 43, and POTUS on Haiti outreach at Golden Globes?[2]

Oh, FUCK. I threw down my BlackBerry and jumped in the shower. I wasn't drunk anymore but wasn't hungover yet—I was in-between. The In-Between is the *worst*. In the In-Between, you feel both completely invincible and totally screwed. You *hope* you've avoided the debilitating crapulence of your actions, but you know

---

1   Oh, you do this too? Hello, friend.
2   42 is President Bill Clinton, the 42nd president of the United States. 43 is President George W. Bush. 44 is President Obama.

there's still residual alcohol left inside you. You're either totally fine—heroic even!—or you are about to vomit.

Now, imagine feeling that way and knowing you need to brief three presidents. Terrified, I darted out of the shower, threw on my suit, and bolted out the door. The weather was surprisingly mild for a January weekend. I ran a block. No cabs. Jesus. One more block. No cabs. Seriously? Damn it, DC.

The S1 bus wasn't running, and this was a pre-Uber world—I couldn't just whip out my phone and get a car. I *had* to get down to the White House, so I did the only thing that made sense: I ran. In a full suit and dress shoes, I sprinted all the way to the northwest gate of the complex. (I don't recommend going for a panicked run if there's a chance you might hurl.)

As I bounded up the driveway at seven forty-five, the impassive marine sentry stationed outside opened the door for me. In the lobby, I found ROTUS—the president's nickname for the West Wing receptionist, or Receptionist of the United States—at her desk. The first ROTUS of the administration was Darienne Page, a friend who—at that moment—looked at me like . . . well, like I was totally insane.[3] I stood there out of breath, glistening with alcohol-infused sweat. "I'm here to see Valerie in the Cabinet Room." Consistently calm, ROTUS stared at me wide-eyed. "Are you sure?" I pulled out my BlackBerry to show her the email. She was still skeptical, which makes sense, and I think it was with a decent amount of hesitation about my future that she pointed down the hall and said, "They should still be in there."

---

3 The last ROTUS of the administration was my former intern Leah Katz-Hernandez. Both are remarkable women, and—shameless plug—you should look them up. This video is an inspirational start: https://www.youtube.com/watch?v=7ubUhTRzREM.

A flock of security personnel parted to let me through. I made a left turn and walked down the hall to a room where one current and two former presidents were sitting. I hastily wiped my face with a napkin stuffed in my pocket, knocked, put on a professional smile, and went in. Two friends inside—Ben Rhodes and Tommy Vietor—immediately recognized my in-between state and smirked. Invincible!

"You *just* missed the presidents," Valerie said. "Have a seat. You can brief Doug and Andy." Doug Band and Andy Card, respectively Clinton's and Bush's chiefs of staff, seemed to know I had been called in last-minute, so there were no hard feelings for my tardiness. (Whew.) I took everyone through the White House outreach plan "to magnify the ways in which our outside partners would help with earned media during the Golden Globes the following day."

Yes, it was a relatively easy thing to brief somebody on but let me tell you, under the circumstances, I *crushed* that briefing. As I learned on my second day at the White House (after running to Tina's office post–Whappy conference call to tell her about the Department of Hot Dogs decision), I knew not to expect a pat on the back for doing my job well. Still, if I'm being honest—considering the 7-Eleven food I was struggling to keep down—I was thankful that I seamlessly executed. Nobody except my friends could tell I was In-Between. I was proud of how far I'd come. I'd gone from not ever having worked in politics before to briefing two presidential chiefs of staff on something of substance without breaking a sweat. (Proverbially. I guess I was still lightly perspiring from running a 5K in businesswear.)

We finished up our meeting and waited for our bosses next to the entrance to the Oval Office. Someone had placed a tray of cookies on a table, but I didn't think it was smart to test the fortitude of my stomach by having one.

As we stood side by side, all of us serving people who were either currently running the world or had run it before, we talked about normal things: how people's kids were doing, the fact that it was cardio day for me (done and done), that I might pick up my favorite Chinese food at Great Wall on Fourteenth Street for dinner. It was a reminder of the paradox of the West Wing: that you can stand in the same space where so much history has been made and still debate the ideal spot to get ma-la cold noodles.

The casual banter broke as the presidents started walking out of the Oval, on the way to deliver their sobering announcements. President Obama walked out first—and he didn't even look at those cookies. Talk about self-discipline. President Clinton exited next. He stopped to take a peek at the cookies, but he didn't pick one up. "My doctor says these are bad for my heart," he mentioned to President Bush, who exited last.

President Bush saw the cookies and took one. Then he took *another* one. He smiled ear to ear, looked off in the distance, and said, "Some people say I don't even have a heart."

Standing in the Rose Garden watching the announcement, I felt my BlackBerry vibrate. An email chain with Rhodes and Vietor, who were standing an arm's length away from me. "Hey, didn't you do a movie with George Bush?" Tommy wrote. I had, sort of. Actor James Adomian played President Bush in *Harold & Kumar Escape from Guantanamo Bay.* In a now-iconic scene, Harold and Kumar hang out and smoke weed with him in his Crawford, Texas, ranch. Standing there in my in-between state, feeling proud of my small contribution to this moment, and getting ribbed by my friends a few feet away, I thought about how to respond. This announcement by three presidents was a somber one. I also had a quick flashback to my MILF email and knew I should be cautious in whatever I wrote back. Stifling a laugh, and craving Advil and water, I simply typed, "I can't believe you put that on PRA."

CHAPTER TWENTY

#SEXYFACE

I first met Barack HUSSEIN Obama in 2007; we doctored his birth certificate in a secret meeting at a socialist madrasa in Indonesia when . . . Wait, this isn't my speech. Who's operating the teleprompter, Sarah Palin?

—A rejected section from my proposed opening remarks
at the 2012 Democratic National Convention.

In all, I had the honor of serving in the Obama Administration for just over two years—a year longer than I initially planned. While the shorter-term victories had been meaningful, I hadn't wanted to leave until we finished with some of the bigger items I had the privilege of working on: passage of the Affordable Care Act, repeal of Don't Ask, Don't Tell, an attempt at the DREAM Act, doubling the Pell Grant. I felt a sense of grounded humility in knowing there were people whose lives would be better off because of small but consequential decisions our team was part of making. In all, working in government reinforced the reality that when citizens are more involved, good things can happen. When you work at a place like the White House, you realize early on that none of it is actually about you. You take an oath to protect and defend the Constitution, and have the honor of serving the public.

When it was finally time to leave Washington and transition back to my acting career, when I took that photo of Gandhi off my office wall[1] and packed it with the American flag I kept on my desk, I felt more hopeful than ever about our collective ability to impact the democratic process. If more people got involved, paid attention, spoke up, and partnered on the issues they cared about, we could push the country so far forward.

I felt lucky too for things in my personal life. Josh had decided to join me for the move back to Los Angeles, and as we settled down on the West Coast, the transition was made even better by my two new jobs. First, a recurring role on season seven of one of my favorite sitcoms, *How I Met Your Mother*. Then, a holding deal with CBS Television that culminated with a role on the short-lived comedy *We Are Men* with Tony Shalhoub, Jerry O'Connell, and Chris Smith.

That there was positivity in the move back to LA is not to say there weren't frustrations or missteps. One of my first film auditions after the White House was supposed to be for a movie in which Denzel Washington plays an airline pilot. For about a week, Spilo excitedly updated me on when I might be called to read for the project. "They're interested in you!" he'd say. "They're calling in a few days with more information."

When nothing materialized a couple of weeks later, I called Dan and learned that one of the producers ultimately felt they couldn't hire me because they already had a performer of color in the cast.

"They don't want to waste your time by asking you to come in, since they already know they won't cast you."

Curious about my competition, I poked Dan for more info.

"Who else did they cast?"

"Well, Denzel," he said.

"Wait, you're saying that they told you I can't be in the movie

---

1   And left the nails for the next person, don't worry.

because they already have a person of color and that person of color is *Denzel Washington*?!"

"Something like that, yup."

"But we aren't even on the same level!"

"Oh, trust me, I know."

I got hot-tempered.

"Give me the casting director's phone number."

"Why?"

"Because I want to call them and tell them that if the *real* first Black president of the United States didn't have a problem hiring a *real* brown guy at the *real* White House, maybe a fake airline wouldn't have an issue hiring real black and brown guys to work together in a movie!"

Dan shrugged it off with a polite laugh. "Welcome back to Hollywood, Kal."

You'd think that with experiences ranging from instances of frustration to microaggressions to straight-up overt racism, I'd be well versed in the nuances of how bigotry and power work. Sadly, that hasn't always been the case.

I was scrolling through Twitter one afternoon on the *We Are Men* set when I came across an op-ed from then–New York City mayor Michael Bloomberg. In the piece, Bloomberg (who I felt disarmed by upon reading that he was friendly with Obama) at first seemed reasonable to me in outlining the merits of what he described as an anti-crime initiative that allowed cops to target violent suspects, called Stop-and-Frisk. I would quickly learn that Stop-and-Frisk was actually an abhorrent racial profiling policy.

Brashly convinced by the case Bloomberg was making at the

time, I retweeted the article along with misguided follow-up rants. I even grew arrogant and defensive when people tried to point out I was horribly, unquestionably wrong. I dug a deeper and deeper hole of idiocy until my phone rang off the hook. Advocates in Washington, DC, who I'd worked with were confused, and furious. "What are you tweeting?" one of them texted. "You're advocating for racial profiling. You don't seriously believe any of this stuff, unless something recently changed. We need to talk, immediately."

That wake-up call came too late. I handled what should have been a series of apologies completely the wrong way because I *still* didn't fundamentally understand what the Stop-and-Frisk policy that I had tweeted in support of actually was. By the time I did learn—thanks to the countless friends and followers who reached out and spoke to me slowly like a third-grader who needs to be taught the rules of tic-tac-toe—I had hurt a lot of people. In the process, I'd given voice to right-wing zealots who scoured the internet for unlikely allies. To this day, I remain deeply sorry.

The entire situation made me think, if someone like me—who has actively worked on progressive causes and passionately talks about his own experiences dealing with discrimination—can get so easily baited by a dangerous combination of internalized, anti-Black racism and gaslighting, what about those even less informed? How was it possible that I was so blind to these wrongs and so ignorant of the need to coalition-build and stand up for our Black brothers and sisters? Those of us who have experienced one form of racism can often be blind to the ways in which we perpetuate it.

I swore I'd use my platform to check my own privilege and help make things right. In a process that continues today, I began to dialogue with and support organizations that do necessary racial justice work (starting with groups like South Asian Americans Leading

Together and early iterations of what is now the Black Lives Matter movement), helping out where I could. The whole thing was inexcusable. A hurtful experience for many people, and though the phrase makes me cringe, a teachable moment in the end.

After about six months back in Los Angeles, I got an unexpected email from my former White House coworker Buffy Wicks. Buffy had left OPE to become director of the reelection campaign's grassroots strategy known as Operation Vote. "Got a minute for a call?" she asked. On the phone I learned that the Obama/Biden 2012 team was asking me to serve as one of thirty-five national cochairs for the reelection campaign (aka the reelect). The position would be part-time and pro bono. I said yes immediately.

The other cochairs were bona fide A-listers in their worlds. I had briefly met a few of them, like Senator Dick Durbin ("I'm a fan of your show *House*"), then attorney general of California Kamala Harris ("I'm here in Des Moines to knock on doors because we want to make sure everybody caucuses for Barack!"), and Massachusetts governor Deval Patrick ("Whoa Kal, Josh is really hot. Don't fuck it up"[2]). I hadn't met most of the others, like CEO of PSP Partners Penny Pritzker and retired navy admiral John Nathman—both clearly a big deal in their own worlds. Regardless of any previous interactions, the fact that I was in the company of such serious and accomplished humans gave me momentary impostor syndrome. It's like having John, Paul, George, Ringo, and . . . Kirby. At least that was the sensation.

The truth is, as cochairs, we each brought a complementary skill

---

2   Actual quote.

set to the reelect, and I was deeply honored that Obama and Biden felt I belonged there too. After my previous campaign and government roles, it felt good to know that my expertise on policy and outreach strategy was valued as much as my private-sector arts experience. I was years past the point of Iowa State campaign director Paul Tewes being temporarily worried that a Google search of my name might reveal images of me humping, smoking, jizzing, and a few other –ings that could have made me a political liability.

I had already agreed to resume my 2008 role and help out as a surrogate on the reelection campaign, traveling the country and speaking at various events on behalf of the president in between my acting and producing gigs. Once I accepted the national cochairship, there were a few additional requests of my time. In early August, I was preparing to give opening remarks ahead of POTUS at a low-dollar fundraiser being held at the Bridgeport Art Center in downtown Chicago. The large, bright windows and high roof of the event space resembled an idyllic old barn. That's where I caught up with Obama's senior advisor David Plouffe and campaign chairman Jim Messina backstage. Plouffe is a young dad who has likable-nerd qualities—very smart, with a deeply inspiring work ethic and drive. Messina I'd describe as something of a "likable cutthroat"—always kind to me, no-nonsense, and straight to the point. In the middle of our conversation underneath the rustic wood-beamed ceiling, the two looked at each other and Jim decisively said, "Hey, will you speak at the DNC?"

I was fired up for our four-hundred-person summer fundraiser speech. Nationally televised remarks in front of millions of people just wasn't on my radar. "The Democratic National Convention? *That* DNC?"

I immediately thought back to the 2008 convention, standing for hours in jeans and comfortable sneakers with the bright yellow vest and an earpiece, floor whipping my delegations into such good shape that it led to my White House job.

What Plouffe and Messina were asking in this hot Chicago barn in 2012 was whether I actually wanted to be ON the stage this time. David grinned, assuming the role of the good cop in this good-cop/good-cop situation: "It'll be fun. We think you'd have a lot to say."

I enthusiastically accepted.

The parameters for my DNC remarks were simple: It should be no more than four minutes in length and encourage young people to vote. Besides that, I could pretty much say whatever I wanted. Even before I began formally writing, I had a good idea what I might want to talk about.

As a presidential aide, I had celebrated with fellow staffers and outside advocates during the big legislative victories like the Affordable Care Act. I had mourned when Congress refused to work with the president to pass bold and meaningful environmental legislation and blocked the closure of the prison at Guantánamo Bay. Through those highs and lows, I had the privilege of seeing what the world was like from the perspective of the boundless advocates we worked with every day, and the frustrating government bureaucrats whose checks and balances often stood in the way. In other words, the nature of our jobs as White House staffers meant we could see more of what was happening inside and outside of government—simultaneously—than most people around the country.

The point now was that I had an opportunity to speak to cynics *and* shout out successes. I could elevate the great work young people all over the country were still doing in partnership with the administration. I wanted my DNC speech to encapsulate their tough-fought victories. I wanted to connect real faces to the things Obama was trying to get done—from human rights to education to the economy. I figured maybe sharing the stories of people whose lives were impacted by politics could help cut through boring-sounding political jargon and make a strong case that young voters should come out for Obama again in 2012.

I thought about meeting my buddy Walker Burttschell—a marine who spent seven years advocating for the repeal of Don't Ask, Don't Tell after he was kicked out of the military for being gay. Among his advocacy work was a 250-mile march from Norfolk, Virginia, to Washington, DC, to ask Senator Jim Webb to support the repeal. I considered the experiences of my friend Jose Antonio Vargas, an undocumented immigrant and tireless justice activist who was brought to the United States as a twelve-year-old from the Philippines. He pushed so hard for the DREAM Act, and his story was not uncommon.[3]

When I lived in Detroit for a few months while shooting *A Very Harold & Kumar Christmas*, I had an acquaintance whose parents brought him to America from Russia as a child. It wasn't until he went to the DMV to get his driver's license that he found out what his parents never told him: He was undocumented. The summer before my speech, he was arrested and thrown in detention by ICE. He obviously wasn't a violent criminal. In fact, at the time of his arrest, he was working as an educator, teaching English to inner-city kids. (Yeah, let that one sink in; we tried to deport someone who was teaching English to other Americans.)

I also thought about my friend and White House coworker Ash-

---

3   Except for winning a Pulitzer.

ley Baia. When Ashley was a child, her mother contracted cancer and lost her job. Watching her mom struggle to pay bills, Ashley decided she'd help the family save money by convincing her mother that her favorite food was mustard and relish sandwiches. It was the simple and pure action of a young girl who understood enough about the cost of her meals to want to help put more food on the table of her struggling family.

And with a giant grin across my face, I remembered a particularly debaucherous night on a USO tour that I did to South Korea. My college buddy DLC joined me on that trip, and one night after wrapping up our duties visiting with American troops at our military bases, we stopped for a couple of drinks at some nearby bars. A gay bar we stumbled into was technically off limits to American military because Don't Ask, Don't Tell was still in effect, so it surprised us to see a small group of soldiers proudly enjoying their beers and shots inside. "Only one of us is gay," one of them explained. "When the rest of us found out about him, it wasn't even a question that we'd never report him to our higher-ups. We're a unit. We'd take a bullet for each other. We protect American freedom. We're not going to get him kicked out. The only thing that's changed is that we now hit up both gay and straight bars on our days off, so that all of us have a shot at getting laid."[4]

I wanted to shout out all these passionate people in my speech. As I got my outlines together, I realized I had the emotional arc of the stories down well, but man, it had been a while since I'd written some-

---

4 When President Obama signed the repeal of Don't Ask, Don't Tell, we made sure that soldier was invited to the ceremony.

thing *fun*. During my two years in government, as a by-product of the risk-averse White House Communications team, the Public Engagement liaisons had pretty much been told to "be boring." The thinking was that junior and midlevel government staffers aren't supposed to be interesting, let alone funny. When we blogged on the White House website or spoke in front of audiences, we were supposed to convey the information in a straightforward way, avoid stepping on land mines, and quickly get out of the room. Break those rules, and we'd risk *being* the story instead of *conveying* it. When this staff policy was introduced, I thought it was so totally ridiculous that I printed out an image of a backbone and stuck it on our office wall. "Someone in this building needs to find where theirs is," I said to three of my officemates before asking, "Why is everything we do reactive? Why is it based in fear?"

Stephanie Valencia, Obama's Latinx and Immigration liaison, took me on a walk and explained how the currency of political capital in DC is saved and spent. Greg Nelson (Energy and Environment liaison) and Jenny Yeager Kaplan (deputy director of the White House Council on Women and Girls) patiently helped me understand where the Communications team's advice was likely coming from. They all agreed—it wasn't ideal for the president's Youth liaison to have to make things purposely boring, and it would definitely hurt my ability to do my job (no college student wants to join a conference call where bureuacrats read talking points). But it just wasn't worth the risk that a reporter might pick up the wrong story on the wrong day and derail something big that the president was working on because I described the American Opportunity Tax Credit as "tite as hell."[5]

Prepping for my speech by looking through old notes made me

---

5   I did not describe it this way. But I might have if they let me.

cringe. "Hi. I'm Kalpen Modi. In fiscal year 2013–14, President Obama's budget plan increases infrastructure investments by a percentage of . . ." Ugh. *Damn it, Kal, be funnier!* (Yelling at yourself to be funnier isn't a good recipe for being funnier.)

I wanted my speech to be as uplifting, heartfelt, and hilarious as possible without crossing a line. Given the chance to write like a human being again, I was worried I couldn't do it. Fortunately, I still had a network of funny friends outside of DC. I sent early drafts of my DNC remarks to Jon Hurwitz and Hayden Schlossberg, the creators of the *Harold & Kumar* franchise. They helped me with some punch-ups and reassured me that my own sense of humor was not actually gone.

I spent a few weeks perfecting my remarks. I finished my final draft and sent it to the campaign's research and political team for fact-checking and approval. Turns out that, aside from my "doctoring Obama's birth certificate at a socialist madrasa in Indonesia" bit, they didn't have major changes. So, speech in hand, I rehearsed and rehearsed, over and over, until I was totally prepared. I was confident that I knew this thing inside out. And then, at the eleventh hour, with drafts done, checked out, and memorized, I added just a handful of words to the opening.

This tiny revision had nothing to do with me, or the White House, or the president. It wasn't because anyone said there was something wrong with the speech. No ma'am. It happened because of something our wonderful friends across the aisle—who get in the way of ideas like universal health care, sensible gun regulation, and funding for science—did. I'm talking about America's cockblockers-to-progress: the Republicans. *Dun dun dunnnnnnn.*

In 2012, the Republican National Convention took place in Tampa, a week *before* the DNC. If you watched the RNC and remember anything about it, it's probably the bonkers speech by Clint Eastwood to an empty chair.

To refresh your memory, a large photo of Mr. Eastwood wearing a cowboy hat and carrying guns appeared on the jumbotron. The crowd went *nuts*. This threesome—Clint freaking Eastwood + guns + a cowboy hat—was too much to keep the right-wing audience calm. Even people who might be expected to show a bit more restraint—like vice presidential candidate Paul Ryan and his wife—went absolutely tumescent with excitement.

As soon as Mr. Eastwood came out on stage, everyone noticed that there was an empty chair placed next to his podium. I jumped up from my couch in the living room, where a few friends and I had gathered for beers, burgers, and other similar food that elite coastal liberals eat. "Oh no!" I said. "Some poor stagehand is gonna get fired for leaving that empty chair up there!"

After three and a half painfully rudderless minutes of a rambling introduction, Eastwood gestured to the empty chair and said, "Uh . . . so I've got . . . uhhhm . . . I've got Mr. Obama sitting here . . ."

Sorry, what? Did Clint Eastwood have an empty chair placed on stage *purposely*? Also, did Clint Eastwood just turn to this empty chair he purposely brought onstage and pretend there was an INVISIBLE BARACK OBAMA *sitting* in it?

The crowd loved it. They thought it was the second most amazing thing they'd ever seen. (The first is *Duck Dynasty*.) Then, after gesturing to Invisible Obama, Eastwood started *talking* to him. "So, Mr. President, how do you handle promises that you made . . ." Mr. Eastwood paused as if the imaginary Barack Obama was replying to him.

Speeches are traditionally monologues; Eastwood's was a dialogue with an invisible president sitting in a quite-visible, quite-empty chair. He went for seven whole additional minutes. It was insane. And of course, the crowd ate it up like Willie Robertson would attack a bowl full of ranch dressing.[6]

On the substance of it, Clint Eastwood's speech got my competitive juices flowing. I know that Mr. Eastwood is a legend, but hey, he's an actor, I'm an actor. *Their* actor ranted at an empty chair. I had to bring that up, right? So, at the last minute, I included a quick, subtle jab that I knew would play well in the arena, the campaign okayed it, and we were good to go.

A week later, after a speech by Rahm Emanuel and before Craig Robinson and Maya Soetoro-Ng took the stage, I delivered the following remarks at the DNC:

Kal Penn
Democratic National Convention
Charlotte, North Carolina
Sept. 4, 2012

I am honored to accept your nomination for president of the United States!

Wait, this isn't my speech. Prompter Guy, can we pull up my speech?

While we're waiting: a special message for those of you at home who have recently turned eighteen. Good news. I can now legally . . . register you to vote.

I've worked on a lot of fun movies, but my favorite job was having a boss who gave the order to take out bin Laden—and

---

6   Willie Robertson from *Duck Dynasty* spoke at the 2016 Republican National Convention. They really do love that show!

who's cool with all of us getting gay-married. Thank you, Invisible-Man-in-the-Chair, for that, and for giving my friends access to affordable health insurance and doubling funding for the Pell Grant.

I started volunteering for Barack Obama in 2007. But nothing compares to what I saw behind the scenes at the White House, when I had the honor to serve for two years as President Obama's Liaison to Young Americans. I saw how hard he fights for us.

One of the most special days was a Saturday in 2010. The Senate repealed Don't Ask, Don't Tell, so anyone can serve the country they love, regardless of whom they love. But that same day, the DREAM Act was blocked. That bill would give immigrant children—who've never pledged allegiance to any flag but ours—the chance to earn their citizenship. Simple. Important.

I was in a small office on the second floor of the West Wing with eight other staffers. We'd worked our hearts out and cared deeply about what this would mean for other young people. There wasn't a dry eye in the room—tears of joy for the history that was made, but also tears of sadness because some American dreams would still be deferred.

Five minutes later, President Obama walked in, sleeves rolled up. He said to us, "This is not over. *We're* gonna keep fighting. I'm gonna keep fighting. I need *young people* to keep fighting." That's why we're here!

A few months later, President Obama fought to keep taxes from going up on middle-class families. Our Republican friends said, "Sure you can do that." But one of the things they were willing to trade is a little item called the college tax credit, which today is saving students up to $10,000 over four years of school.

Now, President Obama paid off his own student loans not too long ago. He remembers what it is like. He said making it easier to go to college and get technical training is exactly how we grow our economy, create jobs, and out-compete the world. So, he stood firm. And that tuition tax credit is still here. But, if we don't register, if we don't vote, it won't be.

I volunteered in Iowa in 2007 because, like you, I had friends serving in Iraq, friends who were looking for jobs, others who couldn't go to the doctor because they couldn't afford it. I felt that had to change. So, I knocked on doors. I registered voters.

And I'm volunteering again now because my friend Matt got a job at a Detroit car company that still exists, and Lauren can get the prescription she needs. I'm volunteering because Josiah is back from Iraq, Chris is finishing college on the GI Bill, and three weeks ago, my buddy Kevin's boyfriend was able to watch him graduate from Marine Corps training. That's change! And we can't turn back now.

So, before I close—and as I wonder which Twitter hashtags you'll start using when I'm done talking—hashtag SexyFace—I ask all you young people to join me. You don't even have to put pants on! Go to commit.barackobama.com and register right there. And the oldies out there, you can do it too.

Let's keep fighting for a president who's never stopped fighting for us! Go online. Find your local campaign office.

Call your friends. Call some strangers. Volunteer. That's how
we're going to win this thing.

I really enjoyed listening to Rahm's speech. But he's a
mayor now, so he can't use four-letter words.

But I'm no mayor. So, I've got one for you:

VOTE.

Within seconds, #SexyFace was trending on Twitter. I had a hunch
that it might go viral—that's why I put it in there. To my amusement,
the trending continued throughout the night as people started co-
opting it to tweet their favorite hot pics of Zac Efron and Justin Bieber,
two legitimately sexy-faced artists in their own right. I enjoyed scrolling through and seeing a nice balance of politics and smiling faces, but
maaan, did it piss off some die-hard politicos who were cranky that
anyone would use the hashtag for something other than tweets about
voter turnout. (Of course, this amused me even more.)

How dare you, Jared Oban? America *never* needs an excuse to
tweet Zac Efron pics! My phone started blowing up with texts from
Obama White House buddies, campaign folks, and other friends
from across the country: They liked the speech! The *Los Angeles Times*

even called it a "generational takedown of the Republicans" because it stood in such stark, energetic contrast to the old-timey nonsense they had put up on a pedestal during the RNC. Woohoo, mission accomplished! When I jumped off my couch and yelled at my television a week prior, I realized one goal of my speech was to swing back at regressive rhetoric by uplifting younger, more diverse voices.

← **Tweet**

Los Angeles Times ✔
@latimes

Kal Penn, aka #sexyface, gives Democratic response to Eastwood lat.ms/NPNkTC

8:33 PM · Sep 4, 2012 · Hootsuite

27 Retweets   **11** Likes

♡   ⇄   ♡   ⬆

I was glad that a speech defending the progress America had made under Obama was well received, because it was about more than just that campaign, or that election, or even about the age-old fight of Democrats vs. Republicans. Politics is personal—on a selfish level, it was about me, and my desire to get married one day. And it was about my friends—and yours—who were finally getting access to better jobs and health care, and serving openly in the military regardless of their sexuality. It was about people we may never get to meet, and doing things to make their lives better, not just cockblocking stuff *other* people had done or wanted.

There's no denying that being asked to give that speech and having it go well felt like a special moment for me. My parents, who watched with Josh from a special seating area in the arena, were proud. In the big picture, the convention and the campaign were about making America a fairer place to live. While my primary motivation for delivering a kickass speech lay squarely in my belief that Barack Obama and Joe Biden deserved a second term, I felt like my professional journey had come full circle.

Unlike all the silly "White Castle to the White House" headlines, my government coworkers didn't see it as a hindrance that I came from the world of entertainment. Being in DC thankfully hadn't made me lose my voice as an artist. I've always believed in the power of thinking creatively and discussing serious topics at the same time—in many ways, that was the essence of an administration that prioritized the input of a younger generation. If nothing else, at least after this I had one more credit on my Google search results: #SexyFace.

CHAPTER TWENTY-ONE

HOW TO DO BUSINESS WITH GANGSTAZ

A few years ago I was offered a small part in a tiny independent Indian film shooting outside Mumbai. The dark, dramatic script offered me the opportunity to play the type of brooding role I hadn't done before, so I welcomed the challenge. It wasn't going to be the kind of payday people often think of. For two months of work, I'd make $11,000, before taxes. On that pretax eleven grand, I would need to pay a ten percent commission to my agent, another ten percent to my manager, and five percent to my lawyer.

Compared to Hollywood (universally known as the capital of morality), what you should know about Bollywood is that Indians tend to abide by their own set of contradictory standards in business. *Yes* can mean no, *No* can mean no, and the *infamous Indian head wobble* can mean "yes I understand," which can also mean . . . *no*. If you're unfamiliar with these rules, I assure you they are both infuriating and impressive—you might want to pull your hair out and high-five someone at the same time. Doing business in India is a bit like playing mind games with the world's best poker player.

I am terrible at poker.

After you accept an offer for an independent film, it's standard practice for the producers to quickly wire-transfer your salary into a third-party escrow account that is released to you according to the filming schedule. After I accepted, a week went by. Then another. Three weeks before I was set to leave for the shoot, instead of a confirmation of the escrow transfer, I received an emailed first-class ticket on British Airways from LAX to Mumbai. This seemed so fancy!

I called Spilo. "Dude. Can you ask them to give me the money they spent on that ticket instead? I can buy myself an economy seat and pocket the rest!"

My manager laughed. "I think the airline might be a partner of the production. Companies can write off certain expenses, and they have financiers who cover others, so unfortunately, you can't take the ticket cost as cash. But their $11,000 wire transfer will come through soon; it has to show up before you get on the plane."

Fair enough. I had work to do. In the weeks before the flight, I prepped for the project: doing Skype rehearsals with the director, creating my character's backstory, and breaking down beats in the script. Three days before I was set to leave, an update from my team: "Just a heads-up—the salary escrow hasn't arrived. The producers said there were two bank holidays back-to-back in India, so it didn't get out in time. They're begging us to let you get on the plane on Monday anyway. We obviously can't do that."

This wasn't good. Leaving from LA on Monday would get me to India on Wednesday for rehearsal. We were to start shooting on Thursday. "If I wait for the money to come," I told Spilo, "I'll lose that valuable rehearsal day with my director and cast." My manager was insistent: "Kal, you'd also lose any leverage in getting paid if these guys turn out to be shady. You can't get on that plane."

I got on the plane. This project was never about money; it was about pushing myself creatively. I really didn't want to lose the only rehearsal day I had before we started production. I decided to trust my new bosses. With no more bank holidays holding things up, the money would surely arrive by the time I landed in India. I put my bag in the overhead bin and settled in for a long flight.

This first-class cabin, man oh man, I had never seen anything like it! The British Airways flight attendants had posh English accents like on *The Crown* and constantly came around to ask the passengers if we needed anything. They'd also apologize for *everything*.

"May I take your coat, sir?"

"Oh, sure, thanks."

"So sorry I didn't come to take it earlier."

This is how rich people roll?

A woman appeared by my side as I buckled my seat belt. "Can I get you a drink, sir?" She handed me a six-page menu of fancy, unfamiliar beverage options.

"I'll have a glass of water, please."

"Would you like—"

"—no ice, please."[1]

Eight seconds later, she returned. "Here's your water, sir, and apologies for taking so long." I considered asking her to stop apologizing but didn't want to be disrespectful to rich-people culture. (Also . . . I kinda didn't mind it?)

I had had the opportunity to fly business class—and on the rare

---

1 Immigrant Indians and their children rarely ask for ice. You get more drink that way.

occasion first class—on long-haul international flights for previous jobs (like *The Namesake* and *Superman Returns*), but always on more budget-friendly airlines.[2] Those cabins were nowhere near as fancy as this. Aside from the awkwardness of the over-the-top service, this whole situation was objectively pretty awesome. The seat was complete with a side lamp and a big TV. If you pushed a few buttons, it would flatten into a bed, which of course the flight attendants also apologized for. "Sir, I'm so sorry I didn't ask you sooner. Would you like a rest? Shall I push the buttons for you?"

The food situation was the bomb, and they served it on glass plates with silverware, not in a plastic TV dinner container with a peel-off cover. They even had fancy champagne. Goodbye glass of no-ice water!

Halfway through the flight, the woman in front of me turned around to tell me she was a big fan of *House*.

"Holy moly, you're *Diana Ross*!"

How had I not noticed that she'd been sitting in front of me the whole time?!

"Thank you, Ms. Ross!" I said. "I'm such a big fan of yours too!" If you're unfamiliar, Diana Ross is an icon. Motown. R&B. Soul. AND, she played Dorothy in the 1978 film adaptation of *The Wiz*. "You know," I said, trying to connect deeper, "I played the Tin Man in our eighth-grade production." Diana Ross looked past my drama club approach with a smile. She was really polite and friendly, and I loved chatting with her while the flight attendants distributed fancy chocolates that I couldn't eat because I'm allergic to tree nuts.

If my grandfather were still alive, he would've first reprimanded

---

2   If I can even use such an absurd phrase to describe something that's still so one percent.

me for drinking alcohol but then would've started shedding tears of joy at the sight of British people serving his Indian grandson and a Black American woman, and not the other way around. We made it, Grandpa! *Brushes shoulders off*

I landed in Mumbai not wanting to deplane.

I was greeted at the immigration checkpoint by a nice Indian lady in her midforties. "Passport, please."

"Of course, here you go."

"Oh! You are Mr. Kal Penn? Theeee ACTOR?!"

"Yes, I am. Nice to meet you."

Her smile faded. A serious look of concern and disappointment took over. "You've put on weight."

What the fuck?

Where were those polite British people who were paid to be nice to me? Bring them back!

I exited the airport to find what felt like the full population of all one billion Indians crowded around the arrivals door. I called up one of the producers, who was waiting for me in the crowd. *"Bol,"* he answered in an intimidating voice, using the Hindi word for *speak*. "Hey dude, it's Kal Penn. I'm at the airport, just trying to figure out where to meet you."

"Mr. Kaaaal Pain," he said, "I'm *just here*."

"Sweet, which one are you?"

"Have you come out from the door? When you come out from the door, I'll *just be there*."

I looked at the mob of people waiting, and they all looked the same to me, *and before you tell me I'm being racist,* you should know that each person was a five-foot-seven-inch-tall brown man in a beige short-sleeve, button-down shirt with a half-inch-thick black mustache. Half of them had silver cell phones sticking out of their front pockets.

"You see me? I'm *just here.*"

"Sorry, which one are you? I'm standing right in front of the arrivals door."

"Do you see the sign for the Costa Coffee?"

"Yes."

"I'm just there."

After several "just here"s and "just there"s, I found the producer. On the bumpy ride to the hotel, he made every effort to reassure me that the escrow of the $11,000 was done. "I have personally myself confirmed it. It has been received in Los Angeles. You don't worry." He also nonchalantly mentioned that in addition to being a movie producer, he was some sort of construction magnate. In the New Jersey of my late-'80s childhood, urban legend had it that a construction magnate was often code for a gangster, usually someone in the mafia. Was the urben legend the same in India too?[3]

I checked into the hotel before rehearsal and called my agent to say I arrived safely. What hadn't arrived, she promptly informed me, was the $11,000. Why would Gangster Producer lie about this? I confronted him after the first rehearsal.

"Just a simple miscommunication," he said. He showed me a piece of paper confirming a wire transfer for $11,000 from the Bank of India to my agent's escrow account in Los Angeles. "See? It's there. It has been *sent.* Just not *received.* These things can take up to a week to process. You don't worry."

Filming started the following day, so I decided to table any con-

---

3   I heard yes!

cerns about delinquent payments for a few days. It was time to focus on the work I had traveled there for. I dove into my craft. Even though Gangster Producer was sketchy, the exact opposite was true of the cast and crew I was working with. They had all worked together several times before and didn't hesitate to make me feel like a member of the family. My fellow actors wasted no time inviting me to dinner and making every effort to ensure that I was comfortable. The shoot was going great. When I checked back in with my agent a week later, the money *still* hadn't arrived.

I called Gangster Producer. This time, he admitted there was an error in the processing. "So, send it right now without the error."

"See. Tomorrow is a bank holiday, so it will take some time. You don't worry."

As the weeks went on, a few of the Bollywood actors on the project got wind of what was happening and pulled me aside. "Kal, you're too nice. At this rate, you're never going to get paid. This is India. The guy is lying to you," one told me.

"He showed me a new bank transfer confirmation!" I protested.

"That was most definitely fake. It's a trick. They show you these fake documents and then don't pay the salary. Don't be so naive!"

"Are you guys telling me this dude went through the trouble of forging multiple fake bank escrow documents?!"

"Yes."

"Okay, that's actually pretty impressive."

"It is," one of them agreed. "Some of these documents are very well faked. Excellent craftsmanship. In any case, if you want to be paid, you quietly don't turn up to work one day. That's how we operate here. Don't show up, then they'll pay you."

I may be a terrible poker player, but I understood the strategy.

The following week, I told anyone who would listen that I would not be coming to work unless I got my salary: Gangster Producer, the director, the crew, the other producers, the production manager. "I don't intend to work tomorrow unless I am paid!" Everyone nodded casually and said they understood. It was as if I was stating the obvious: Tacos are tasty. This shirt is green. Kal won't come to work anymore unless he gets paid. Surely the *threat* of not turning up to work would do the trick, right?

The money never came, and I kept going to work like a chump. *Another* week and a half went by. Was I the idiot who cried wolf?

With two days remaining before the film was set to wrap, I pulled Gangster Producer aside. "Look. I just wanted to let you know that I'm *really* not coming to work tomorrow unless I get paid." He gave me the infamous Indian head wobble and said, "You don't worry."

At seven thirty the next morning, the telephone in my room rang as it did every day when my ride showed up. "Sir, your car is downstairs." I took a deep breath, finally ready to play their game. "Please let the driver know he is free to leave. I'm not going to work today, thank you."

I hung up.

Five minutes later the phone rang again. It was Gangster Producer. "Mr. Kaaal Painn. I understand we have a PROB-lummm?"

"*Nahi, kuch problem nahi hai.* There's no problem. As you know, I just haven't been paid yet, so I can't come to work unless that money hits the escrow account."

Gangster Producer feigned disbelief. "Oh, Kaaal! How can you do this? How will I wire the money in just one day's time?!"

The thing about me? People think I'm nice. And I *am* nice. But I'm also from New Jersey. And in the unfortunate event that you mess with me the way Gangster Producer did, my inner Jersey comes out. Don't make me Jersey. You wouldn't like me when I'm Jersey.

I lashed out, berating Gangster Producer, reminding him that he had weeks and weeks to wire the money, and so far had only come up with weeks and weeks of excuses. First it was a bank holiday, after that a wire issue, then there was another bank holiday. Only an idiot would not be able to get it together. "But Kaaal . . . if you don't come to work today then I won't be able to finish the film!"

"I KNOW, ASSHOLE! THAT'S THE POINT!"

Silence.

Neither of us spoke for what was probably ten seconds but felt like hours. Did I cross the line? Should I not have called him an asshole? He broke the silence, his tone no longer pleading. He was calm and confident, like real gangsters in gangster movies.

"I see. You do one thing. Just remain in your room. In two hours' time, my boy will come. You don't worry."

"Why do you keep saying 'You don't worry'? Stop saying that! Also, why do I need to stay in my room and who is this 'boy' who's coming in two hours?"

"Please. Mr. Kaaal Painn. You remain there."

Click.

My heart raced. *This is how you get murdered, Kal. Remember the book* Maximum City? *This is the part where you yell at a gangster on the phone because he hasn't paid you, and he sends one of his goons to slit your stupid throat. Why did I let my inner New Jersey come out and offend? This project was about pushing myself creatively! Couldn't I have quietly not shown up to work and waited for the wire transfer to go through like the Bollywood actors said?!* Remain in your room.

Should I remain in my room?

I remained in my room.

Indians are never on time for anything, ever. Anywhere. On the planet. So, it surprised me that there was a knock at my door *exactly* two hours after I hung up the phone. *This must be the "boy" he was send-*

ing over. I hesitantly looked through the peephole and saw only the very top of someone's head. *Oh, he has literally sent a small child so short that his hair is barely visible in the peephole. Maybe I won't get stabbed.* I trepidatiously opened the door to ask the child what this was all about.

Surprise! In front of me stood a four-foot-eleven-inch-tall *fifty-something-year-old man*. On his faded yellow T-shirt was a giant white drawing of a panda with the caption "I love Giraffe." This was *beyond* surreal. This teeny panda giraffe uncle was holding an excessively wrinkled brown paper bag that he motioned for me to take. I peered inside. It was full of American twenty- and fifty-dollar bills.

"COUNTIT," he said.

I emptied the cash on the table. Bills spilled out, and I counted $5,500. The phone rang.

"Everything okay?" It was Gangster Producer. "Car is downstairs."

"Hang on a minute, man. This is only *half* of what you owe me."

"Correct. You have two days of filming remaining, so second half you'll receive tomorrow. Car is downstairs."

Unbelievable. Even after sending Teeny Panda Giraffe Uncle to deliver half my salary in cash in a brown paper bag, this dude was trying to negotiate again. I suppose by his weird logic he wanted an assurance that I would show up at work the next day too. I locked the $5,500 away in the in-room safe and went downstairs, wondering, *What if the bills are fake?* I reasoned that there was no point in stressing about it because "there's no way that money is going to still be there when I get home tonight anyway."

When I got to the set, people were going about their business as if I hadn't just held up production and arrived a few hours late. They all knew how the game worked.

The rest of the day was enjoyable without having the business aspect of things hanging over my head. When I got home that night, I was surprised to see that the money was still in the safe. I hadn't slept that well since I'd arrived.

The following morning the situation repeated itself: The producers sent the car at seven thirty. I said I wasn't going. Teeny Panda Giraffe Uncle came to my room with the second payment of $5,500 in a wrinkled brown paper bag, this time wearing a disappointingly normal beige shirt like the dudes at the airport. I went to work for my last day and finished the film.

Back at the hotel that night I was restless. *These people know that you have eleven thousand in cash with you. They're supposed to take you to the airport tomorrow evening. What if they send Teeny Panda Giraffe Uncle back, this time to steal the money? Or steal your kidney? Or slit your throat? Or steal your kidney, slit your throat, and THEN steal the money?*

I plotted an escape from the hotel.

First step: I crept down to the empty lobby in the middle of the night and settled my bill with the front desk. That way I'd have the best chance of noticing if someone was watching me. But I didn't officially check out, so I could mislead everyone into thinking I was still in my room. In the morning, I could disappear without any fanfare. If anyone did ask, I would say I was going to run an errand or visit family. I had this thing all figured out.

At 11 a.m., six hours before I was supposed to be picked up, I took the $11,000 out of the safe and counted it again. It was all still there. I put my laptop, passport, and the cash in my backpack, and walked down fourteen flights of stairs. I slipped out a side door, feeling ten percent like Jason Bourne and ninety percent like Kevin McCallister sneaking out of the Plaza in *Home Alone 2*. *Merry Christmas, ya filthy animal.*

Through an alley and around the corner from the hotel, I hailed a rickshaw. In passable Hindi, with my luggage and my backpack full of dead presidents, I told the driver to take me to the international airport, *fast*. I checked in early and cleared security, hopeful that Gangster Producer's reach didn't extend this far.

I boarded the plane and breathed a sigh of relief. I was in the clear! Away from Gangster Producer, Teeny Panda Giraffe Uncle— even the immigration auntie who called me fat. I was ready to get apologized to by British people on the return flight to LA.

As the plane approached LAX, customs forms were distributed. ("So sorry, sir, we should have handed these out sooner.")

I've filled out these forms many times. They're straightforward: No, I'm not bringing any snails or other wildlife with me. No, I haven't been in close proximity to livestock. But when I came across question thirteen, my stomach dropped: Are you carrying currency or monetary instruments over $10,000 U.S. or foreign equivalent: ☐ Yes ☐ No

I have $11,000 with me! I have to check the Yes box. What does that mean?! I turned the form over as instructed. "The transportation of currency or monetary instruments, regardless of the amount, is legal. However, if you bring in to or take out of the United States more than $10,000, you are required by law to file a report on FinCEN 105 with U.S. Customs and Border Protection." That's fine, right? This is my legal pay. That I earned.

I felt so shady. Was it legal to be *paid* in cash like this, or just to *carry* the cash? What if the bills that Teeny Panda Giraffe Uncle gave me *were* actually fake? These dudes already forged bank escrow documents. Now I was going to be transporting these fake bills through customs into the United States. This was not good.

I declared the $11,000 on the customs form and waited in line, sweating the whole time. My turn came. I was assigned to a twenty-four-year-old customs officer named Parker who immediately lost his damn mind. "I'm a *huge* movie fan, especially comedies, bro! *Espe-*

cially comedies. Hahahaha, whaaaat!?! How is Kal Penn in my line right now? This is so crazy! You don't have any weed with you, right? Hahaha, that would be *sick* if I got to bust Kumar for weed."

I love my fans unconditionally, but I must have looked super annoyed. Officer Parker took a deep breath, acting like the last thirty-eight seconds hadn't happened. "So, what brings you here today, sir. You have something to declare?"

I had to be completely transparent. I told Officer Parker the entire story of the $11,000 in cash I was carrying: about the wire transfers and escrow, Gangster Producer's lies, the forged documents, the bank holiday excuses ("I mean how many bank holidays does India have?"), and Teeny Panda Giraffe Uncle dropping off the two bags of $5,500, "which I hope is not counterfeit cash."

At each juncture in the story, Officer Parker looked more crestfallen. By the end, he seemed fully depressed. His eyes were brimming with a quiet disappointment as he let out a long, delicate sigh. "Kal Penn only makes $11,000 for a movie?"

"This project was about the art!" I shot back.

"Apparently."

Officer Parker awkwardly took the bills into a back room and verified that they were, thankfully, real. As he handed the stack of cash back to me, he whispered, "You guys should make another one of those movies. Maybe *Harold & Kumar Smuggle a Tiny Amount of Money into America*," and burst out laughing to himself once more.

CHAPTER TWENTY-TWO

(pea) COCK BLOCKED

I'm standing in a lofty writers' room on the third floor of a modern glass building at the edge of the Universal Studios lot, completely fulfilled. I'm making a comedy for NBC, one of America's most iconic television networks, the one I used to watch *Family Ties, Seinfeld, Diff'rent Strokes*, and *NewsRadio* on. This comedy is mine, I cocreated it, I'm acting in it, I'm executive producing it. As if I needed one, I get a reminder every morning about how blessed I am and how far I've come when I pull onto the lot and slide into my own parking spot with my name on it right next to my own trailer. I smile so widely with such deep happiness and gratitude that I let out a little laugh. Every morning.

At the end of each day, my smile is even bigger. It reflects the creativity of the talented cast and writing team I've spent all day with. It still feels surreal to have been able to hire what we're told is the most diverse writers' room and cast in network television history. And because of this diversity, I find that I never have to justify myself or set up a cultural reference point. I never have to overexplain that actually no, this joke I pitched has no ethnic or racial signifiers. In this group of talented artists, I just get to *be*.

When I leave in the evenings, I don't head out the way I came in. I always back out of my parking spot and go a few hundred feet past our soundstage, so I can drive through *Back to the Future*'s Courthouse Square. This home of the famous clock tower that powered Marty and Doc through space-time happens to be just past our building, so I make the pilgrimage each night, taking Middle School Me along. I roll down the windows and the warm California air runs across my face, drying my still-wet skin, a result of the makeup wipes that close out each shooting day. I usually drive a full loop and a half around Hill Valley, through the square once, then past the sign that says LYON ESTATES before disappearing through a parking lot bordering facades of a Brooklyn street, and onto Lankershim Boulevard and the 101 Freeway. I live each day with the excitement of what it means to be part of this world. Television is magic. I am fulfilled by my reality beyond measure.

Designated Survivor (the political conspiracy drama on Netflix in which I played a press secretary) was going into its third and final season when I began to work on a pitch for a long-simmering idea for my own sitcom. The basics were this: A down-and-out guy who is trying to get his life in order ends up teaching a US citizenship class to pay his rent; I wanted it to be forward-looking, aspirational, and patriotic. I was somewhat influenced by my childhood love of shows like *Head of the Class* and *The Fresh Prince of Bel-Air*. Rather than being overly edgy or cynical (as lots of great comedy can be), those shows always had a way of making the audience feel good by the time they turned off their televisions at night. It wasn't just the episodes that I loved, it was the experience of watching them—gathering around the TV with the whole family on a specific night of the week, at a particular time; going to school the next morning and repeating some of the funniest lines with my friends, knowing that they too had watched the episode with their families at the very same time.

I wanted to re-create that feeling—uniting audiences into laughing in a way that celebrates the best of who we are—in a way that actually reflects America's diversity. I had dabbled with pitching and selling a few pilots in the years before. The process was something I really enjoyed, but none of the projects I created ever made it past the script stage.

The closest I came was probably the year after my White House sabbatical ended. I had sold a concept for a comedy about young staffers at the United Nations. The humor was a blend of intelligent and stupid, and when it came time for notes, the network seemed to always get stuck on the silliest jokes, like one I borrowed from marines on a USO tour I was on years ago: In a scene in which an African ambassador is on the treadmill at the UN gym, the camera pans over to notice his T-shirt, emblazoned with the slogan "I was all up in Djibouti." (That's the whole joke and I love it.) "It's funny," the network said during that week's notes session, "but we don't think most of the audience will know what Djibouti is or how to pronounce it. Can you change the name of the country to, like, France or something?"

"What do you mean? 'I was all up in your France' doesn't make any sense."

"Just make it a joke about a country people know."

In the end, they didn't move beyond the script stage of development, giving me the polite yet frustrating, "It's great but doesn't fit with our other scripts. We're passing on this." (That's the network equivalent of *It's not you, it's me*. Except that, in this case, it's actually them.)

This time around, I made it a point to talk about the tone of what I wanted much earlier in the process. This time, it would be intelligent and dumb, and the right buyer would need to be okay with that balance before we moved forward with a script. Streaming platforms, cable, paid television—while there were plenty of edgy places to consider, it was the idea of making a diverse patriotic comedy for a traditional television network that I was excited about most.

After my experiences in *Harold & Kumar* (which conventional Hollywood thinking initially said would never do well because of its two Asian American leads), I was excited by the idea that now, maybe you could change hearts and minds across the country without hiding behind a television paywall. Mine would be a proudly silly, proudly American comedy without being preachy or laying a message on too thick. My goal wasn't to beat people over the head; I wanted to get them to laugh from their bellies.

My representatives at United Talent Agency (UTA) and Spilo set up meetings with a wide range of really great writers for me to consider developing it with. Some (like Bill Lawrence, who created *Scrubs* and cocreated *Ted Lasso*) seemed to understand the vision of what I wanted to do with my citizenship class idea very well. Others didn't get it quite so much. One of the highlights was pitching to *Big Bang Theory* (and a hundred other shows) creator Chuck Lorre. When Chuck kindly told me and Spilo that the idea as we described wasn't exactly one that he found compelling, I assumed that was it—meeting over, I should quickly leave this busy icon's office. To my surprise, he invited us to stay and spent the next hour basically giving me a master class in television development. What a profoundly generous dude! With all he had on his plate, and despite not connecting with my idea, the fact that Chuck friggin' Lorre took the time to essentially mentor me on how to get a show on the air and make it last was not something I saw coming. It immediately elevated him to the level of the really great, encouraging people I've had the chance to work with in my career.[1] Chuck's advice was helpful in deciding what I somehow already knew in the back of my mind—my show shouldn't be the kind of multicamera sitcom with a laugh track that he does so well; it needed to be a more intimate single-camera comedy to get my desired tone right.

I found my cocreator and writing partner in a *Brooklyn Nine-Nine* and *Parks and Rec* scribe who I incidentally met a decade and a half ago. Enter Matt Murray.

In the mid-2000s, shortly after finishing *The Namesake*, I had moved from LA to a tiny West Village apartment in Manhattan. Around the same time, three of my LA buddies—the Lonely Island geniuses Jorma Taccone (one of my first friends at UCLA), Andy Samberg (who had gone to NYU with my high school buddy Jonah Goldstein), and Akiva Schaffer (who had attended UC Santa Cruz with our close mutual friend Matthew Bettinelli-Olpin)—moved in a few blocks away to start their breakthrough gigs on *Saturday Night Live*.

Matt Murray was also an *SNL* writer. I can't recall on which of the alcohol-fueled nights I first met him, but I remember enjoying his company as someone super funny, supremely genuine, and oddly

---

1 He joined the ranks of Sonia Nikore and David Shore.

soft-spoken for a dude who could write specifically weird comedy bits like a sketch where Will Ferrell is born as a fully grown man.

Back in the day, we hung out a few times before subsequently losing touch. As we reconnected during our meeting, I learned that Matt was under contract with Universal Television. His good friend and fellow *SNL* alum Mike Schur had just re-upped a deal with Universal for nine figures following the success of a hit comedy he created, *The Good Place*. Matt and Mike often partnered on projects, and I was flattered to be considered in their comedic company. Clearly these guys had the kind of business background and clout that mattered. But what sealed the deal for me was ultimately the creative: Murray and Schur understood and vibed with the tone of the uplifting citizenship class concept so completely that by the end of our conversation, we were already pitching each other on how to make it better. "There's a woman I knew," Matt said, "a crossing guard at my kid's school. She was a lawyer and chief of staff to the First Lady of her home country before coming to America. She saved up tons of money. She doesn't need to work. She's a crossing guard now because she really enjoys it. Would be fun to have a character who has like thirty jobs. Not because she has a tough financial situation, but because she wants to get the most out of life." Matt and Mike and I clearly had great chemistry. I was excited to move forward with them.

We brainstormed the project, taking the initial concept and improving upon it. Inspired (if that's the right word) by a hockey player who famously tried to get out of a DUI by bribing the cops with the promise of a billion dollars (he was *that* hammered), Matt suggested we make my character a recently fired city councilman from Queens, who gets kicked out of the apartment he shared with his girlfriend for a similar drunken indiscretion. Moving in with his sister, his only path to redemption (and money) is to teach a course in which he helps a diverse group of people navigate the US citizenship process. I wanted to have some fun in naming the characters and give a subtle hat tip to some things I'd experienced in the past.

Over the years, when I'd play a character with an Indian name, some South Asians would inevitably complain, "Why is his name Prajeeb? How come he can't just be named Seth or something?" But when I played someone with a name that wasn't traditionally Indian (like my character in *Designated Survivor*, who was literally named Seth) others would grumble, "Why does his name have to be Seth, why can't it be something like Prajeeb?" People have understandably emotional reactions to this stuff; the power of seeing our own names on-screen (or on the flipside, the privilege that comes from "passing") is undeniable; strong feelings are a result of the fact that while immense progress has been made, it's still something of a novelty to see a brown person on television at all. But conversations about those opinions are not ones that anyone wins. So, I figured why not dig a little deeper and turn that experience into a fun, nuanced story behind my character's name?

After his parents immigrated to the United States, the silly back-story goes, they fell in love with American television, especially *Diff'rent Strokes*. When they saw that *Diff'rent Strokes* housekeeper Mrs. Garrett was also Mrs. Garrett, the housemother on *The Facts of Life*, they thought, *Look at this woman! She is the hardest working person in America! We will name our son after her. We will call him Garrett*. After Garrett was born, his parents felt they perhaps needed to bequeath to their next child a name with far fewer expectations, so they went with the frivolous Mallory from *Family Ties*. In our pilot episode, of course, Garrett is the lazy one who's down and out, while his younger sister, Mallory, is a successful, hardworking doctor. Matt and I finished writing a pitch and went out with the "Untitled Kal Penn Project," with Mike Schur, David Miner, and Dan Spilo executive producing alongside us.

There was quick and enthusiastic reception from NBC. Given Schur's relationship with them (*The Good Place* was going into its final season), we figured that developing the "Untitled Kal Penn Project" there gave us the best shot of having it end up on the air. Most importantly, they committed to us that they would invest in the show if they picked it up. "Comedy is hard. It takes time to find its audience. Sometimes multiple seasons. We're the best at what we do because we know how to invest in comedy and sell the ones we put on the air." Creatively, the NBC executives seemed to be especially proud to develop our unifying feel-good comedy at a time when the nightly news featured mostly the opposite. We turned in a pilot script, and they actually allowed us to shoot it. We called it *Sunnyside* because it sounded as uplifting as our story and it's also a wonderfully diverse part of New York City. Another option was *Flushing*, but that's a really terrible title for a show.

This was new territory for me as a producer and creator! Things moved fast. I needed to hire an assistant to help juggle my different obligations. I didn't have to search far: Romen Borsellino (of cum laude thesis and Obama dildo vetting fame) had moved to LA to pursue a career in entertainment. I brought him on quickly. I couldn't believe it but the unbeatable casting director Allison Jones—who did *Family Ties* and *Fresh Prince*—agreed to cast *Sunnyside*. (Allison is *the* comedy go-to in the casting world, and only takes on projects she believes in, truly the highest compliment for any comedy creator.) We hired a talented line producer, Kris Eber, and began the process of staffing up a crew and getting everything as perfect as we could for our pilot shoot.

Auditioning actors made me happy. Our *Sunnyside* characters were all immigrants, and each was grounded in a solid backstory independent of their appearance. This allowed Allison to cast an especially wide net to find the strongest, funniest talent regardless of specific background—we let her know that we'd lock in those character traits (ethnicity, country of origin, culture) based on whoever we cast, not the other way around, as was traditionally the case.

Comedian Moses Storm was our first hire, delivering a flawless performance of his character Brady, a closeted-about-his-undocumented-status all-American frat boy loosely based on an acquaintance in Detroit (the undocumented guy thrown in ICE detention while teaching English). Matt Murray modeled Samba Schutte's taxi-driving Ethiopian doctor Hakim after an Italian car salesman he knew. After Diana-Maria Riva booked the role of Griselda (based on Matt's crossing guard), Kiran Deol, Tudor Petrut, and Ana Villafañe rounded out the next few hires. There were only two roles remaining: wealthy Asian American siblings who were heirs to their father's fortune.

Our top choices were Chinese American actor Poppy Liu (whose vapid take on the character won her increasing points during each audition round) and Korean American comedian Joel Kim Booster. Joel took a character that was written more like a self-absorbed finance bro and added so many layers of quirky, flamboyant detail to him that Allison remarked, "Obviously you're hiring Joel Kim Booster . . . you don't just let an actor like that walk away from you. Somebody else will scoop him up." At this point, most producers would a) pick either Joel *or* Poppy and find a second-choice Chinese American or Korean American actor to play opposite them or b) say something like, "Cast Joel and Poppy, who cares if the brother is Korean American and the sister is Chinese American . . . blah blah blah . . . *all look the same anyway*."

We thought both approaches would have been misguided. Of course, we were going to cast them both! We loved that it offered an opportunity to accentuate the bizarre comedy we were pursuing in the first place. Matt re-tweaked the backstory: Poppy's and Joel's characters were now very strange half siblings who shared the same father but different mothers entirely, a by-product of an estranged billionaire oligarch dad who technically lives in international waters.

After the network table read of the pilot with our almost impossibly diverse and talented cast, the electricity in the room was palpable. Once the executives trickled out, Allison leaned in and said, "I haven't seen chemistry like this since *NewsRadio*. I just don't see how they don't pick this up."

"Holy shit, Allison! I'm not sure what to say," I mumbled through thankful laughter. "You're comparing us to Andy Dick, Joe Rogan, and Dave Foley? *NewsRadio* ran for five seasons! Today felt so great . . . but I don't want to jinx it!"

With our director Oz Rodriguez (*SNL*, *A.P. Bio*) on board, the rest of the week was full of production meetings and rehearsals in which the characters really sprung to life—it made us even more confident in (and thankful for) the great team we had formed. On Wednesday of that week, the NBC legal department called a meeting with the cast to talk about ethical standards and social media. "We want to make sure that you don't ever post photos that might give away any of the plot points or intellectual property of the show. If you ever have questions about whether it's okay to post something, ask your executive producers." Everyone looked at me. Oh right, I am indeed one of the EPs! "We also," they continued, "want to make sure you don't tweet anything that's racial or sexual in nature, or really anything considered inappropriate." Three-quarters of our cast happened to be stand-up comics. They all raised their hands.

"I have a question," Joel spoke up. "My brand is literally talking about sexual things, that's what I do. My stand-up comedy is about cum in butts. Are you saying I can't tweet about cum in butts?"

The now-shocked-and-amused lawyer assured all the performers that these things were really just issues of context—NBC had no intention of getting in the way of anyone's brand, as long as performers avoided mentioning the network by name in tweets that wouldn't pass their purist benchmarks. "You can do stand-up comedy and tweet as you normally would, as long as you don't mention or tag NBC."

The next day, when *Deadline* gave accolades to our talented, funny cast with a flattering article titled "NBC Assembles Cast of Mostly Immigrant Actors for Kal Penn Pilot 'Sunnyside,'" Joel retweeted the link with his own hot take:

Joel Kim Booster ✓
@ihatejoelkim

     ...

Yesterday I asked the NBC lawyer if I could still "tweet about cum in butts" and she looked me in my eyes and said "depends on the context." Anyway, love everyone involved in this. Very excited! deadline.com/2019/03 /nbc-as...

NBC Assembles Cast Of Mostly Immigrant Actors For Kal Penn Pilot 'Sunnyside'

EXCLUSIVE: NBC's comedy pilot *Sunnyside* (formerly Untitled Kal Penn/Matt Murray) has cast the seven co-leads opposite Kal Penn. Kiran Deol, Moses Storm, Diana Maria Riva, Samba Schutte, Poppy Liu, Joel Kim Booster and Tudor Petrut will co-star in the single-camera comedy executive produced by Penn, writer-producer Matt Murray, *The Good Place* creator/executive

Despite his clear violation of their rules, the network was very cool about it and nobody asked me to tell Joel to take it down.[2]

The pilot shoot was some of the most fun I've had in television. We edited and turned it in, the studio and network focus-group tested it, and a couple of months ticked by as we waited.

I'm at home in New York City, pacing in my apartment, on hold with the executives at NBC and Universal for a phone call I have dreamed about my entire career. "We just wanted to let you know," they say, "how excited we are to be picking up *Sunnyside* for a ten-episode season this fall!" I belt out a "woohoo" at the top of my lungs. "You probably won't see news about our other comedy pickups for a few days," the executive encourages. "We want to make sure you can grab great writers before they get staffed on other shows."

Across the apartment Josh smiles.

I quickly call my parents to share the good news.

I get back on the phone with Matt because it's time to hire a writing staff and I've never done that before! As the showrunner, he takes the lead on the time-consuming process, and brings together the funniest of the applicants. He composes a team made up entirely of immigrants and immediate family members thereof. As I read their bios and writing samples I can't quite tell if the ray of light I'm feeling is bursting out of my heart and onto these pages, or the other way around. We already assembled the most diverse cast in the history of network television, and I guess I'm the first Indian American leading man. Now I know we have the most diverse writers' room too. I'm very proud.

---

2   Maybe they called Joel directly, I don't know!

In fact, among the entire creative team, I realize most people are either first-generation, BIPOC, LGBTQ, or many hyphenates on top of that. What makes this so special to me is that it's icing on the cake: That our *Sunnyside* family reflects the real America is an important bonus that comes out of our desire—Matt's and mine—for both representation and diversity of comedic viewpoints, something my cocreator has been especially thoughtful in executing. And in his true humble Matt Murray fashion, when I ask him about it all, he downplays his own hard work, hinting at a changing system in the industry we both love, telling me, "There are plenty of great writers out there from all sorts of cool backgrounds. If other shows don't reflect that, it kinda seems like it's a choice."

I think to myself about the absurdity of the casting director who once told me she wouldn't hire me because I'm not "even" Latino; the trust fund boss who barked that Joseph Gordon-Levitt was unemployable because he's "fucking Asian." Our show is a real point of pride for those of us who've had experiences like that on our paths toward this big network television moment. "Wow," I say to our team, feeling thankful for it all, "we're really doing it!"

Sunnyside had a lot going for it: NBC put us in prime real estate: nine thirty on Thursday nights. In decades past, that was the same time slot occupied by *Seinfeld* and *Friends*—two iconic, hilarious New York shows (albeit each with a take on the city that looked more like Omaha than Manhattan). I was excited and anxious to be occupying that same real estate, being the new, not-from-around-here neighbors; the people of color who moved in next door, bringing our reflective, heterogeneous, modern-day NYC to the masses.

The NBC Thursday Night Comedy Block, as it was called, was formidable.

The first prime-time slot of the evening was for long-running *Superstore* (8 p.m.), followed by the series premiere of a musical comedy about a small-town church choir called *Perfect Harmony* (8:30 p.m.) starring the very funny Bradley Whitford. Our lead-in was Mike Schur's hit *The Good Place* (9 p.m.), with Ted Danson and Kristen Bell. And then our baby, *Sunnyside* (9:30 p.m.). After that, Dick Wolf's *Law & Order*, followed by your local nightly news.

Free television! No fancy streaming, no expensive paywall. Hopefully, that meant success in the ratings, but at a minimum, it meant that whoever wanted to watch the show could actually watch it. For a lot of the people in the cast—who grew up, like me, watching their parents pinch pennies—that meant something too. It's easy to look at the monthly subscription fees for various streaming services and treat them as an afterthought, but for a lot of people, they aren't. I was proud that anyone with a TV could join in the fun with us.

The chemistry among the cast and crew grew each day as we got into production. In between shooting scenes on our soundstage at Universal Studios, I'd head up two flights to our writers' room to check in with the team there, weigh in on an edit with Matt and the post-production people, offer script notes. Everything felt right. Everything felt—in a word—comfortable. Here's an example of what I mean when I say that. When I checked in with our writers one afternoon, they were sharing stories about home remedies for a potential joke runner. Two of our writers, Bosnian American brothers Dario and Damir Konjicija, recounted how whenever they got sick as children, their mother would chop mounds of potatoes, soak them in vinegar, and stuff them in their socks to ward off the sickness. "You'd just wake up feeling miserable from an awful fever, and nauseous from the smell of the vinegar, which made being sick that much worse. Our mom would insist the 'potato socks' were the reason our fever eventually went away, and not the Tylenol we also took!" Telling this story in a typical writers' room might get you some laughs at your expense. Telling it with the *Sunnyside* team meant you got hearty laughs with nods around the room. Since every person had an immigrant background, everyone could relate from experience on some level, and chime in with their own wholesome version of potato socks.

During this period, NBC began the marketing rollout for its Thursday-night lineup. This was the world's introduction to our show. The first interviews and write-ups about our existence started to run. We participated in long promo and press days with NBC's personable marketing and publicity team. There were profiles in earned media like the *New York Times* and entertainment magazines, and appearances on Seth Meyers and Lilly Singh.

I am not an expert in the rapidly changing business of television, but I do know the fate of any broadcast show depends on its live ratings. And whether people watch is a complex mix of everything from time slot to audience saturation to marketing (you can't watch a show you don't know exists). So when I thought I was seeing far less paid media—billboards and commercials—for *Sunnyside* compared to the other shows in the Thursday Night Comedy Block, I shrugged it off and chalked it up to me being paranoid and overly proud and just looking for something to freak out about.

Besides, I had something *else* to freak out about. Let's talk about the Mets game. The initial phone call from my publicist went something like this: "Hey Kal, there's an opportunity for you to throw out the first pitch at Citi Field to promote *Sunnyside*. Do you want to do it? It'll be fun!" I immediately thought about two things: 1) piling into a rented school bus and going to Mets games with my dad and Cub Scout troop at the old Shea Stadium *(Hell yeah, I'd love to throw out the first pitch. Nine-year-old me would love this!)* and 2) getting picked last in gym class throughout middle school *(Ha! You still can't throw a baseball, dummy! Do not say yes to throwing out a first pitch in front of thousands of people at a baseball game, it'll be embarrassing. You won't make it over the plate, and then people will not want to watch your show. Twelve-year-old you would not be excited, he'd be horrified, because he knows what gym class is like, except this could be much worse because your awful throw will make it onto SportsCenter and go viral. Remember Carly Rae Jepsen's terrible throw? 50 Cent's botched toss? That was more than five years ago and those two still get railed for having the worst first pitches ever. The ridicule from this will never go away. Definitely say no!).*

"Yes, definitely," I said to the publicist, "I would love that!"

I realize most people can't do what I did next, but it was critical that I not screw up this first pitch, so I texted a Major League Baseball player for advice. Chasen Shreve pitches for the Pittsburgh Pirates and had become a buddy through a promotional shoot I had done when he was with the Yankees a couple of years prior.

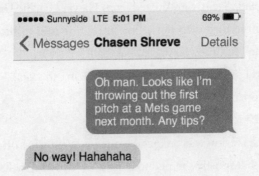

Was that a "you can't throw a baseball, I would have picked you last in gym class" no-way hahahaha or was it a "that's so cool worlds colliding" no-way hahahaha?

Practice, yes of course! It's the athlete's word for "rehearsal." I had Romen quickly scour the internet for pitching coaches in Los Angeles and we landed on a place called Baseball Central in Culver City. I had three weeks to learn how to throw.

My coach turned out to be a tall, handsome baseball player named Zach who had recently graduated from Hawai'i Pacific University.

"So, you're throwing out a first pitch," he said to break the ice. "When's the last time you played baseball?"

"I guess I probably last threw a baseball in . . . 1992?"

"I was born in '93."

"Great!"

Our first session was predictably messy. We started off with some warm-ups that mostly seemed to consist of throwing balls of various sizes against a net, then some groin stretching, and a lot of moving my arms in different ways while turning my body in directions it doesn't naturally move. "I don't think I have whatever muscles you're saying I should engage in order to turn this way," I told Coach Zach.

"You'll get there," he encouraged, "it'll just take a while."

"I have like three weeks."

"Oh. I can't teach you to pitch in three weeks."

What a thing for a coach to say! In booking these sessions, perhaps Romen neglected to state the obvious.

"So, here's the deal, Zach. I'm here because I need to look like I can throw a perfect pitch, once. I don't actually need to be able to build the muscles that will let me play baseball for a lifetime. Don't get me wrong, that would be really nice. I'd end up looking like you and getting lots of cool Marvel movie jobs, but really I just have to walk on that field like a boss, confidently nod to the catcher, do that cool thing where you stand on one leg like a flamingo, and then send that beautiful ball into the catcher's mitt."

"Good job knowing 'mitt.'"

"Thanks."

"The flamingo thing is called a wind-up."

"Right."

Coach Zach understood what I was getting at. "We're just going to start throwing, then, but don't worry about the wind-up. I want to make sure you're getting these five-and-a-half-ounce balls sixty feet, six inches over the plate!" He first led me through some sort of strenuous leg exercise that made me angry at myself because it was hard. "It's a first pitch," I mumbled to him, "not a first kick." In pitching, he explained, the power comes from your legs. That's what gets the ball over home plate. "Your legs drive the velocity of the ball. I'm warming you up, let's go."

I then spent half an hour throwing the ball from the mound

to the catcher. I was sweating profusely. Romen tried to discreetly hand me some water, whispering, "Why are you sweating? Are you okay?"

"I'm fine! It's harder than I thought. Why the hell is there a lunge involved?"

I woke up the next morning unable to move my right arm or my left butt cheek. (Thankfully I didn't really need my butt cheek, but the arm thing was real annoying.) Back in the writers' room, I shared some of the practice videos Romen took so that everyone could enjoy the absurdity of my situation.

Comments came quick.

"That's so cool!"

"Man, you're really sweating there. Is it hard?"

"Whoa, that's your coach?! He's so handsome! We should put him in the show!"[3]

A few days before I flew to New York, an inquiry came in from the Mets. I was going to be given a team jersey to wear when I threw out the first pitch. They wanted to know what name I wanted on the back, and if I had a lucky number.

"Penn or Modi?" my publicist asked.

"Modi, definitely. It's also my character's last name. And let's go with sixty-nine. If they'll let me." ;)

The following afternoon came the Mets' reply: "Yeah, you can't do sixty-nine. The team won't go with anything inappropriate."

"What if we say I'm a huge fan of the 1969 season?"

"Just pick a different number, Kal."

"Seven."

Game day. My parents joined me, along with Josh and some

---

3   Sorry we never made that happen, Zach.

friends, including Ronnie Cho (my good buddy from Obama world) and Jon Hurwitz (our *Harold & Kumar* cocreator, who flew up from Atlanta where he shoots his Netflix series, *Cobra Kai*).

Despite all the friends and family support, walking onto that field was nerve-racking. This was bucket-list stuff right here. I leaned into the positive—no matter what happens, it'll be fun. I had started to improve during my last two sessions with Coach Zach; instead of eight out of ten pitches going in any direction except the catcher's mitt, we were down to four out of ten. Would that be enough? The announcer's voice boomed, "Please welcome, the cocreator and star of NBC's *Sunnyside*, premiering this Thursday, September 26, at 9:30 p.m., actor Kal Penn!" I smiled. Strutted to the mound. Took Zach's advice and *didn't* do a wind-up. The ball left my hand and . . . made it over the plate! The crowd applauded. I smiled and waved cockily (come on, I earned this). "Dude!" Hurwitz shouted, "that was amazing!" And you know what? Depending on which camera angle you looked at, it really, really was.

Sunnyside debuted on September 26, 2019—and the first episode bombed. It was the worst-rated premiere in the history of big network television at the time. I felt that sting. The executives at NBC tried hard to soothe our anxieties by reminding us of our conversations during development of the pilot: "Don't be alarmed if you don't see good numbers at first. We're great at making comedy. Sometimes shows need multiple seasons to take off. *Seinfeld* didn't do well initially. *Sunnyside* just needs time to find its audience. We're one hundred percent committed to the show. It's hilarious, and we completely support you."

We were all more than a little worried, but these assurances came from every senior executive at the network, so we wanted to believe we'd be fine. Besides, in an unfortunate blow to NBC's entire lineup, their other new shows weren't faring much better—*Perfect Harmony*'s cast was far less diverse and rated only a tenth of a point higher than us. I was thankful for the network's promise of investing in the long-term goal of what most comedies need: time, space, and promotional support to find viewers.

Except I still wasn't seeing that promotional support firsthand. I barely noticed any *Sunnyside* ads, and certainly not with the same frequency of *Perfect Harmony* commercials. I tried not to think much of it since the majority of my days were spent on a creative high, making the actual show itself. But then I started to see that other Thursday night shows were getting a bevy of physical and television advertising in ways we indisputably weren't.

As I was cooking dinner one evening, I caught a thirty-second ad block for the Thursday lineup. It began with a narrator saying, "Thursday, it's a teenage takeover of *Superstore* . . ." followed by nine seconds of funny clips from their upcoming episode. Next up, nine seconds that began, "Then, *Perfect Harmony* is locked and loaded . . ." with some fun clips from their next show. After that, the narrator teased, "This Thursday, something bad is coming to *The Good Place* . . ." with another nine seconds of clips from their new episode. I intently watched with eager anticipation, full of the joy and pride I still carried in my heart from the day at work with my diverse, hilarious team. I was eager to record the clip and text them all. *What scenes did NBC use from our pilot? How would they tell the story of* Sunnyside *in our nine seconds?* As Ted Danson's smiling face faded out from *The Good Place*, my picture emerged on the screen holding an American flag next to the words *Sunnyside* and *Thursday*. The narrator quickly said, "FollowedbySunnyside" and the commercial ended. That was it.

If you blinked, you'd miss it. And even if you saw it, you'd learn nothing about the show, its characters, or its plot. While the other shows each got nine seconds of promo time with featured clips, ours got just one and a half seconds of a photo.

Ever since I was a kid, my parents instilled in me the reality that life itself isn't fair. I've been around long enough to know that in business too, there's no guarantee that something is going to be just. Still, as an artist, I have to admit the commercial left me a little heartbroken. Putting on my executive producer hat, I tempered my words, telling the network, "I am very disappointed with this" and asking, "Why isn't the network allocating commensurate resources to our show as they are to others?" I stopped short of vocalizing what else I wondered: *Was it just coincidence that the most diverse comedy was the one being excluded?* Their answers weren't great:

"You know, we're running different ads in different ways . . ."

"We have specific targets on what we think is effective . . ."

"We have a process here, Kal . . ."

"Don't worry about it, we have a lot of targeted ads coming soon . . ."

Absent any actual data, their reasoning sounded partially caught up in the fallacy I first learned about when I worked for Captain Moneybags (the archaic belief that mainstream audiences might refuse to watch compelling content unless the characters are white). I tried to let this go. And even though I also thought all their justification sounded an awful lot like code for "separate but equal," I cut myself off from going down the rabbit hole of racism, thinking, *This literally could have* nothing *to do with race or ethnicity, so stop making it about that, Kal. Stop letting old experiences cloud things. Maybe they really are investing in your show in ways that are commensurate but different given the tone of the comedy.*

I'd grown to really trust and enjoy working with our executives by this point, so I asked for hard data: specific advertising budgets, lists of our online and television ad placement, what resources were being spent where. It all fell on deaf peacock ears. While they were of course under no obligation to share any of this with me, their choice to ignore the requests themselves added to my sinking feeling that maybe something bigger was amiss.

For their part, our cast remained upbeat, and tried to have some fun with how the season was starting out. Joel tweeted:

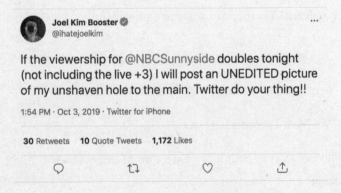

Joel Kim Booster ✔
@ihatejoelkim

If the viewership for @NBCSunnyside doubles tonight (not including the live +3) I will post an UNEDITED picture of my unshaven hole to the main. Twitter do your thing!!

1:54 PM · Oct 3, 2019 · Twitter for iPhone

30 Retweets **10** Quote Tweets **1,172** Likes

The next Thursday came around. *Sunnyside* aired again. And again, our ratings were awful, but again they were almost the same as that of charming *Perfect Harmony* and again, we were both up against *Thursday Night Football*, and again the network said, "Don't worry about it. We're completely committed to your show."

*   *   *

I'm standing in a lofty writers' room on the third floor of a modern glass building at the edge of the Universal Studios lot, and I am terrified. The AC is on full blast as usual, something that makes my thumbs numb and ears cold if I'm there for longer than thirty minutes. Usually, I don't mind icicle fingers because I like how they feel around the mug of fancy hot coffee that one of the writers makes in the communal kitchen.

Today, I just want water.

It's after 4 p.m. on Monday, October 14. We are shooting our ninth episode downstairs, our fourth one airs this Thursday, but we've paused production so that I can step into Matt Murray's office. The two of us are huddled around a landline on speakerphone, mindful that our writers can see us through the glass, mindful not to let our faces show too much of what we're hearing and feeling. The executives in charge of our show want to talk, immediately, for some reason that just can't wait until the next morning.

I have a deeply sinking feeling that goes from my throat to my stomach and wraps around my heart like the stubborn vines you trip on during a hike in the woods. I can sense that this won't be a nice call.

"Guys, as you know, unfortunately the numbers have not been great these first three weeks," one executive begins. "So we've made a decision that after the fourth episode airs this Thursday, we're going to be moving *Sunnyside* from linear to digital. We feel this gives us the greatest chance of success."

Moving from linear to digital, what does that mean?

"*Sunnyside* is going to air digitally from episode five onward. And we are going to shoot out the full ten-episode order. We're not canceling it. We're going to be moving it digitally."

No cancellation is easy for anyone. Certainly not for the artists who have poured heart and soul into the creative process, and also not easy—if I'm being fair—for the studio or network executives who have taken a business risk by investing in a show and now have to cut their losses. Still, whatever they are telling us about *Sunnyside* right now is very, very confusing. It's being taken off the air, but it's not being canceled?

"Just so I understand, you're pulling the show off the air and putting it where? Peacock?"

"We're very committed to this. The digital space is where this would lie. The Peacock streaming platform isn't launching until next year. We're going to direct the audience toward the NBC app and NBC.com. We're going to put resources behind it."

"Which resources would be behind this? Do people watch shows on NBC.com? We stream on Hulu the morning after we air on linear television. We were told our Hulu numbers were okay. Will we continue to stream there?"

"We don't know if you'll stream on Hulu, because the nature of our arrangement with them is that anything streaming with them has to air on the NBC network first."

"So, you're pulling us off the air, and you 'don't know' if we'll still be on Hulu, which is where most people who do stream the show are streaming it. And you're instead moving us entirely to the NBC website? We're now a web series?"

There is more back-and-forth, with executives injecting meaningless phrases like "we remain committed to the show" and "we are excited to pledge additional digital resources to market *Sunnyside*."

It's all too silly. We had had a conversation like this before, when I made the advertising data request that they ignored. They're repeating themselves without giving us answers. I am confused and the producer in me needs them to be direct.

"Let me ask you something," I say, remembering from my White House days that conversations like this work best if I eliminate passion and emotion from my voice to keep things professional. "You've spent the last four months telling us how committed you are to our show, how much you love the diversity, how much you love the jokes, how you know it takes many months for a comedy to find its audience. You've said since the start that you were supporting *Sunnyside*. We believed you, but clearly if you've made the decision to pull it off the air after only three episodes, none of that is true. You don't support us, and you weren't actually committed to the show finding its audience over time. Why should we believe—and how can we trust—that you'll be supporting us by putting the show on NBC.com and a phone app?"

Unable to remain professional, one executive explodes. "You know what? I can pull this show right now! I can pull it! I can end it! I can shut you down and pull it off the air right now if I wanted to, but I'm not!"

A good deal of life is knowing when and how far to push. I've stood up for myself, acquiesced, and negotiated in Hollywood and Washington enough times to know when I'm talking to someone who is not able to have a straightforward conversation. Maybe the executive is frustrated too. After having cared for the show from the beginning, maybe they're being told by one of their higher-ups that they need to "move us to digital" and are caught in the tricky middle. Or perhaps they're defensive because I questioned their intentions, and they know I'm right. I don't know which it is. But I do know that in speaking this way to me—the only person of color on our call—the subtext of their rant (gaslighting, withholding information, changing the subject) feels familiar: *I hold all the cards, brown man. You have none of them. Don't question my authority. If I want to, I can end you and your employees and not blink an eye.*

I don't want my writers, who are trying not to stare through the window, to lose their jobs; the two hundred people that make up the cast and crew—and who have labored so hard to make something so good—to lose their jobs. I don't think our exec actually wants to shut us down either. They've just lost the ability to have a civil conversation. I swallow this bitter pill, accept the "move to digital" (whatever that actually means), and get back to finishing out the season, which I remain very, very fortunate and thankful to still be able to do.

Television is indeed magic. They're not canceling us. They're just making us disappear.

———————

The network went public with news of our cancellation the very next day, with an announcement that season three of the *Will & Grace* reboot would replace us in the time slot. Given that show's status as a relic of an older, bygone television era, Joel Kim Booster expressed how we all felt:

Joel Kim Booster ✔
@ihatejoelkim   ...

To find out our show is getting pulled and replaced with an all-white cast ON Columbus Day? You can't write this stuff folks. Our time slot literally got colonized!!

> 🌐 **Gary Levin** ✔ @GaryMLevin · Oct 15, 2019
> Exclusive: TV season's first casualty is NBC's #Sunnyside, but comedy will continue online usatoday.com/story/entertai... via @usatoday

9:35 PM · Oct 15, 2019 · Twitter for iPhone

390 Retweets   **39** Quote Tweets   **5,405** Likes

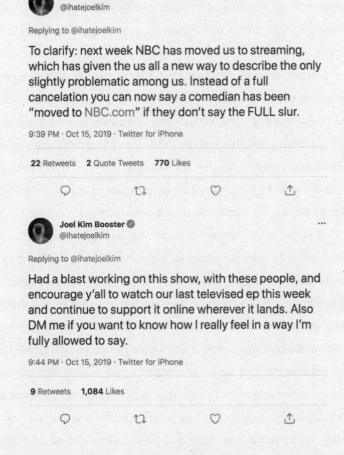

Joel Kim Booster ✓
@ihatejoelkim

Replying to @ihatejoelkim

To clarify: next week NBC has moved us to streaming, which has given the us all a new way to describe the only slightly problematic among us. Instead of a full cancelation you can now say a comedian has been "moved to NBC.com" if they don't say the FULL slur.

9:39 PM · Oct 15, 2019 · Twitter for iPhone

22 Retweets   2 Quote Tweets   770 Likes

Joel Kim Booster ✓
@ihatejoelkim

Replying to @ihatejoelkim

Had a blast working on this show, with these people, and encourage y'all to watch our last televised ep this week and continue to support it online wherever it lands. Also DM me if you want to know how I really feel in a way I'm fully allowed to say.

9:44 PM · Oct 15, 2019 · Twitter for iPhone

9 Retweets   1,084 Likes

With those tweets, the network was finally unhappy with Joel's posts. I got a panicked call from an NBC publicist.

"Kal, can you please talk to Joel? Can you have him delete the tweets he posted about the cancellation?"

"Happy to speak to him. What's the issue?"

"He said the *Sunnyside* time slot got colonized because we're putting an all-white cast, *Will & Grace*, in its place."

"Right." (There was a long, long pause.) "Sorry, what's the issue?"

"We don't like the message it sends. Saying that we pulled a diverse show off the air and replaced it with an all-white show might discourage other actors and writers from working with NBC in the future."

I politely told the publicist that I wasn't going to police Joel's Twitter account, especially since he was posting the truth. Still, I kind of felt bad for them. What they acknowledged had unlocked NBC's primary motivation for the we're-not-canceling-you-but-we're-canceling-you routine—it's not that they thought *Sunnyside* would do well digitally, they just didn't want to signal to others in Hollywood that they could be such a fickle partner.[4]

The reality is that networks don't really straight-up cancel shows anymore. They relocate them to digital platforms where they at least have the small potential to make some money while protecting a larger brand. That's an important part of the changing nature of broadcast television. As audiences move to streaming platforms, the big networks continue to lose a lot of their power and advertising revenue. It turns out that what I had hoped to do—unify live audiences gathered around their televisions at a specific time; change hearts and minds through comedy—isn't as possible in the traditional network format anymore because most people consume streaming content through premium platforms. Americans don't even have cable television like they used to—US cable companies lost 4.9 million subscribers in 2019.[5]

---

4   Kris Eber is such a great line producer, he had saved so much of our budget from the earlier part of the season that we had enough money left over to shoot an entire additional eleventh episode. Miraculously, for much the same optics reasons, the network didn't fight us on this.

5   https://www.techdirt.com/articles/20200305/10532244040.

*   *   *

On Thursday, October 17, the day NBC would air our fourth episode before moving us to their website, our wonderful makeup artist
Michelle gently asked me, "How are you doing today? I figured things
might be especially rough because of the *Ad Age* article . . ."

"What *Ad Age* article?"

"Oh, you haven't seen it?"

"No."

"I'm sorry . . . ," she said as she handed me her phone.

The advertising industry magazine *Ad Age* had published a
piece about NBC's marketing budget for the two new shows in its
Thursday Night Comedy Block: our historically diverse *Sunnyside*,
and *Perfect Harmony*, which had a talented but more-traditional cast
dynamic. The article rightfully acknowledged that advertisers want
higher ratings numbers than *Sunnyside* was delivering. Even though
other shows also had historically low ratings that were only marginally better than ours, the business is a competitive marketplace. We
were the lowest by a tenth of a point, so we had to go. That was all
reasonable and logical.

But it was the final paragraph that seemed to sadly confirm what
I had long hoped was merely my own paranoid suspicion—that the
network had been undermining us all along.

"NBC," *Ad Age* wrote about *Sunnyside*, "didn't seem to be tremendously enthused about the project from the get-go." In promoting *Sunnyside* on other networks, NBC spent $250,000; in promoting
Perfect Harmony that number *increased by 580 percent* to $1.7 million. In
promoting *Sunnyside* on its own stations NBC ran forty-three promotional spots; in promoting *Perfect Harmony*, 1,368 spots—an increase
of 3,081 percent.

1,368 ads for *Perfect Harmony*. Forty-three for *Sunnyside*.

I'm passionate about what I do, so the truth can be tough to digest. The business of television is complicated, with numerous factors at play in determining benchmarks of success and viability, but there's no parsing reality in this case. When someone chooses to provide 3,081 percent more resources to a project with a white protagonist than they do to a project with a protagonist of color . . . while measuring the *success* of both projects with the same scale . . . it is an example of systemic racism—the more diverse project has been set up to fail from the start.

After taking over our timeslot, *Will & Grace* aired to lukewarm numbers before repeatedly dipping to or under a 0.43 rating—lower than *Sunnyside*'s premiere.

Will & Grace was not pulled off the air.

Though things weren't ending the way I had hoped, I was extremely grateful. I share my story not to shame anyone or place punitive pressure, but because of my genuine hope that the system in the industry I love so deeply can continue to improve. And looking around at the panoply of people who made my dream of *Sunnyside* happen felt powerful and remarkable. Even if just briefly, we were doing creative work the way we had hoped it could be done. Through our characters, we brought our communities to life. We created a vibrant professional creative space in which we didn't have to explain ourselves. The opportunity NBC gave us and the skills I learned would make me a stronger artist and producer next time around. In any job, in any passion, things don't always work in your immediate favor. As a creative, you have to take your experiences and figure out how to evolve; this opportunity allowed me that growth and gave me the strength of knowing what's behind the curtain. The people who helped create *Sunnyside*—including those who allowed us to develop it at the network and physically produce the episodes—were some of the finest I've ever worked with in this business. It brought me a lot of happiness and artistic fulfillment. Most people don't get to say that in their jobs! If you're interested in seeing it, you'll find a link at kalpenn.com.

CHAPTER TWENTY-THREE

YOU CAN'T BE SERIOUS

"You always exaggerate things, Kalpen." That was my mom's response when I recently checked in with my parents about my tumultuous teenage years, when it seemed like everyone was trying to dissuade me from pursuing the arts.

"I'm not exaggerating, I really want to know. After you and Dad worked so hard to build a life in America," I asked, "how embarrassed were you when I'd tell everyone at those family gatherings that I wanted to be an actor?"

"*Embarrassed.* I don't know how you get these ideas into your brain. If we were ever embarrassed by anything, it was your horrible haircut. Thank God you shaved your head after your Yale rejection."

"I do admit the way I dealt with that was a little dramatic."

"But we were never embarrassed by your interest in acting. We just didn't know it was a real career somebody could have. We sacrificed so much to be in America, and we weren't sure what the future was going to hold for you. We were *scared.*"

Fear, of course. Until that moment, I had never considered the extent to which fear must have played a role in their reaction to what I wanted to do with my life. The pressure they felt was surely tremendous, especially starting a family in a new country. "At the same time," Mom continued, "even though we were scared, we respected your wishes and tried to encourage your interests."

That was true. While some adults in my life said things like, "You can't have your cake and eat it too," and "Are you not smart enough to go to medical school?" my parents *did* encourage me as much as they knew how—sending me to that Summer Arts Institute, letting me attend the performing arts magnet program, teaching me about why it was important to have a diverse range of interests. And they didn't lock me up for pretending to be pregnant with a math baby. Dad drove me to that UCLA audition in a snowstorm.

If Mom was right about my tendency to exaggerate, might I have somehow embellished aspects of my parents' incredible story? "I hope I'm recalling this correctly," I said to my father. "The entire family got all dressed up and came to the airport in India to see you off, right? And when you landed in America, you had only twelve dollars in your pocket?" Sitting in the living room with a wall of family photos behind him, of camping trips and graduations, college visits and movie premieres, and photos with the First Family, my dad looked at me with some amusement and said, "Unfortunately, you *are* exaggerating." He smiled. "When I landed in America, I had only eight dollars."

ACKNOWLEDGMENTS

This book has consumed the last five years of my life and wouldn't have been possible without continued support from family, friends, and a dedicated team of people who I've worked with on various stages of developing this baby. A deep, heartfelt thank-you to everyone.

Mom and Dad, who happily answered endless questions and without whom none of this book or story would have been possible.

Josh, who offered incredible insight and feedback and who had to deal with me essentially being absent and locked in the office for months and months on end, in my pajamas, at a desk, popping out every so often to ask, "Is this funny?"

Dan Spilo, my manager and friend, who for years encouraged me to tell my story and write a book in the first place (and without whom I probably never would have).

Bob Barnett, who is the <u>best</u> at what he does and offered irreplaceable guidance and insight through the entire process. Thank you!

The talented Aimée Bell and the team at Gallery Books: Max Meltzer, Jennifer Bergstrom, Jennifer Long, Sally Marvin, Sydney Morris, Abby Zidle, Elisa Rivlin, Michael Kwan, Ray Chokov, Caroline Pallotta, John Paul Jones, Jaime Putorti, and Jonathan Karp, and the audio team: Travis Tonn, Claire Tadokoro, David Turk, Katherine Cook, Don Hoffman, and David Weissman—thank you for helping me bring this to life!

Thank you to Jimmy Soni, Romen Borsellino, Doug Moe, Nick Campanelli, Chester Tam, and Kevin Ramlal.

The brilliant mind of my lawyer Michael Fuller, who I've worked with for nearly two decades, I appreciate you, Blake Zurbuchen, and the whole team.

Pulin, Christina, and Kripa, thanks for offering early feedback (especially Pulin, who told me it wasn't funny *at all*).

Gary Lee, DLC, Stevie Numbers, Ronnie Cho, Miti Sathe, Sarah Friedman, and Peter Friedman, thank you for all the thorough notes, feedback, and conversations over the years. (Gary Lee, in addition to the above, thanks also for letting me bug you with chapters and jokes and sentence fragments via text and email at all hours of the day and night.)

Thanks to my friend Beulah Pollock (Garrick), who turned one hundred years old this year—what incredible friendship and advice. Thank you to Ernest Filart, Marc Milstein, Dennis Ebuen, Sang Kim, Zohran Mamdani, Sam Walker, lots of childhood friends, parents' friends, Surekha Auntie, Ela Auntie, and frankly way too many incredible aunties and uncles to list.

From Obama world: So many people were kind enough to give me opportunities and encouragement, let me pick their brains on memories over the years, and offer anecdotes from the campaign and White House that made it into this book. President Obama, Mrs. Obama, Valerie Jarrett, Tina Tchen, Jon Carson, Ben Rhodes, Cody Keenan, Tommy Vietor, Jon Favreau, Pete Souza, Stephanie Valencia, Jenny Yeager Kaplan, Greg Nelson, Samantha Power, Secretary Clinton, President Clinton, Ryan Lynch, Rohan Patel, Liz Jarvis-Shean, Ben LaBolt, Michael O'Neil, James Schuelke, Courtney Hight, Matt Tranchin, Stephen Brokaw, Gary Lee again, Mitch Emerson, and Sadena Thevarajah.

My creative friends and coworkers in the entertainment industry who generously shared their stories with me over the years and let me fact-check memories: Matt Murray, John Cho, Jon Hurwitz, Hayden Schlossberg, Sara Hess, Peter Jacobson, Olivia Wilde, David Shore, Barbara Fiorentino, Sonia Nikore, Lauren Grey, Barbara Cameron, Alexander Hall, Dan Harris, Dario Konjicija, Damir Konjicija, Allison Jones, David Alan White, Jenna von Oÿ, Chasten Buttigieg. My team at UTA: Jason Heyman and Nancy Gates, Neil Bajaj, Geoff Suddleson, Andrew Lear, Peter Goldberg, Greg Iserson, Brett Duchon.

My speaking agent, Peter Jacobs, and his team at CAA.

All of the assistants and interns of anyone I've thanked here—we perhaps never met but you were probably on calls, Zooms, and emails, and likely worked tirelessly without accolades. I appreciate you and hope to meet in person to say thanks.

Our family and family friends—aunties, uncles, kids I grew up with—for unconditional love over the years, and always speaking your mind. That has made me a better person.

I have that feeling—like when you leave for a trip—that I forgot something. In this case, it's to thank a few key people who were likely left off this list. You probably know exactly who you are. THANK YOU.

And of course thank you to Piggy, who cannot read but still kept me company daily, snoring loudly while I wrote.

PHOTOGRAPHY CREDITS